"Straight edge culture is very diverse, and parts of it had always a strong emphasis on emancipation and equality, also with regard to gender and sexuality. It's good to have a book acknowledging this."
—Jenni Ramme, Emancypunx Records

"Forget the cliches, straight edge isn't just about buff white dudes—Kuhn's book shows that it's a multifaceted social movement rooted in the intersection of DIY culture and political resistance."
—Lori Black Bear, Sprout Distro

"Sobriety has historically played an important—and often overlooked—role in many social movements. As usual, Gabriel Kuhn tackles his topic with breadth and finesse. He manages to simultaneously address internal issues in straight edge circles as well as demonstrate the relevance of sobriety and straight edge outside of the relatively narrow confines of punk and hardcore scenes. Highly recommended and a great way to take necessary conversations about addiction and struggle for social justice to the next level."
—Anthony T. Fiscella, author of *Varieties of Islamic Anarchism*

"Kuhn once again brings a razor-sharp eye to straight edge, powerfully illuminating the gamut of liberatory possibility in the choice to not only reduce harm to oneself and this world but, crucially, experiment with caring, consensual social relations and spaces too."
—Cindy Milstein, editor of *Rebellious Mourning: The Collective Work of Grief*

STRAIGHT EDGE AND RADICAL SOBRIETY

Edited by Gabriel Kuhn

X: Straight Edge and Radical Sobriety
Edited by Gabriel Kuhn
© 2019 the respective authors
This edition © 2019 PM Press.

We have made every effort to identify and properly credit the images used in this book, but it is
possible that errors and omissions may inadvertently remain. Notice of such should be sent to the
publisher so that the necessary corrections may be made in any future editions.

ISBN: 978–1–62963–716–7
Library of Congress Control Number: 2019945458

Cover by John Yates / www.stealworks.com
Interior design by briandesign

10 9 8 7 6 5 4 3 2 1

PM Press
PO Box 23912
Oakland, CA 94623
www.pmpress.org

Printed in the USA.

CONTENTS

COLLECTIVES

RECOVERY

INTRODUCTION

Gabriel Kuhn

Ten years ago, I was working on the book *Sober Living for the Revolution: Hardcore Punk, Straight Edge, and Radical Politics*. It was published by PM Press in 2010. I had always wanted to do a book on straight edge and radical politics, as I felt passionate about both but had to acknowledge that they weren't necessarily connected. Straight edge is politically undefined and open to all sorts of interpretations. Besides, there have always been strong streaks of machismo and self-righteousness within the culture. My intention was to strengthen the culture's progressive currents and provide a platform for often overlooked and marginalized voices within it.

My passions haven't changed. The need for radical politics most certainly remains, and straight edge is today more diverse and colorful than ever. Under the term "radical sobriety," questions of substance use and recovery have also become widely discussed in radical circles. Out of this came the idea to put together a sequel to *Sober Living*.

X: Straight Edge and Radical Sobriety essentially follows the same premise: exploring the overlaps between straight edge and radical politics, but *Sober Living* is not required reading for appreciating its contents. The books supplement one another but stand on their own. *X* differs from *Sober Living* in three main ways:

1. There is an even stronger focus on the grassroots and the international scope of straight edge culture.

2. The boundaries are a bit softer. While the vast majority of contributors are and identify as straight edge, this does not apply to everyone. The term "radical sobriety" is also used by people who have very little (or nothing) to do with straight edge. But since many of them have things to say that are highly relevant for radical straight edge folks, their voices are included here. It is important to note, however, that this is still, first and foremost, a book about straight edge. A book about radical sobriety or radical advocates of drug-free living would look very different. It would have to account for a wide range of radicals, from Andalusian anarchist teetotalers to the MOVE organization to indigenous activists advocating sobriety. This is beyond the scope of what I've been able to cover.

3. *X* contains a chapter on harm reduction and recovery. Some readers of *Sober Living* pointed out that they missed contributions by people with a history of substance use and a discussion about what straight edge has to offer to them—if anything. The last chapter of this book is dedicated to this very question, looking at addiction, recovery, and support for people intending to change consumption habits.

HANGOUTS AND BEER TENTS: PERSONAL COMMENTS

There is yet another difference to *Sober Living*, although it's primarily a formal one. I'm going to try my luck with a more personal introduction. This has two reasons. First, a *Sober Living* review in *Classic Rock* magazine stated that "it's not a promising start; the preface reads like an Open University textbook." Point taken. More importantly, however, I thought—probably naively—that I as a person was of no relevance for the book. I saw myself as little more than the fellow who collected material and interviewed people. Yet some of the criticism of *Sober Living* focused exclusively on who I was— or, at least, on who people thought I was. In a review by a respected and long-standing punk rock zine, the author wrote: "My first question was whether the editor was qualified to compile this book and conduct these interviews, given his experience with hardcore or lack thereof. . . . Given some of the other books he's worked on, his background seems to be more in sociology and radical politics, and I am always weary of anyone with a cultural studies background attempting to document punk."

Well. Allow me to try clarify a few things. To begin with (since it often seems silently assumed), I do not work in academia and never have. There is no professional gain in putting together a book like this. The reason I do it is very much tied to my experiences with hardcore. I'll start from the very beginning.

I grew up in a small village in the Austrian Alps, a long way from CBGB's or Gilman. The only rebel music I knew of until I was sixteen was heavy metal. I embraced it and had long hair and the outfit to match. Yet I was always repelled by one aspect of the culture that was very pronounced where I grew up, namely the drinking. I didn't like the taste of alcohol, I didn't like how people behaved when they were drunk, I was appalled by the violence that often came with it, and I refused to accept getting wasted as some kind of coming-of-age ritual. The same was true for experiments with marijuana, amphetamines, and other substances in the town where I went to high school. For several years, I hung with crowds in which I was the only one not drinking or getting high.

Then, in the late 1980s, I was introduced to punk bands whose music appealed to some of my older metal friends, such as the Dead Kennedys. It opened up a new world for me, especially since I had gotten interested in radical politics as well. One thing led to another, and via the Rollins Band I discovered Black Flag and, eventually, Minor Threat. While discovering political punk had been an eye-opener to me, discovering straight edge turned my world upside down. I had always considered it normal that everyone around me drank, and while I didn't like it, there was nothing I could do but accept that I was the odd one out. But no more! Straight edge made it not only clear that there were other rebellious and sober kids out there, but that there existed a whole movement around hardcore punk and sobriety! It was one of the most exhilarating realizations of my life.

My everyday reality, however, remained the same. I was still living in a small village in the Austrian Alps. The closest city, Munich, across the border in Germany, had no straight edge scene to speak of. Neither did Innsbruck, the Austrian town I moved to after finishing high school. So, for the first few years of my identifying as straight edge, the "scene" remained very abstract. There was no internet at the time, and partaking "virtually" was not an option. My involvement was reduced to writing hundreds of letters, ordering all the tapes and zines I heard of, and making an occasional long trip to a relevant show.

I only got in closer contact with other straight edge folks when I moved to the US in 1994. Mind you, I moved to Phoenix, Arizona, which wasn't exactly a straight edge hotbed at the time. But bands were coming through, and communication with other straight edge folks was easier. However, this was a time when Hardline had made strong inroads into straight edge culture, especially its political currents. Homophobic comments and antiabortion stances were widespread. This was very alien to the politics I was used to and,

SOBER LIVING FOR THE REVOLUTION

HARDCORE PUNK, STRAIGHT EDGE & RADICAL POLITICS

Gabriel Kuhn will talk about his book 'Sober Living for the revolution' about the cossroads of straight edge and radical politics. A very inspiring read with in-depth interviews, manifestos and essays about the movements political history, critical reflections on straight edge and lifestyle politics, personal stories and ideas about punk, straight edge and radical politics.

WEDNESDAY 19 MAY INFOCAFE BOLLOX 8u

eerste schinkelstraat 14 - 16 (op het binnenplein) AMSTERDAM frankly, quite a shock. The excitement about straight edge, and my being part of it, quickly wore off. Disappear entirely, however, it did not. Straight edge meant too much to me, and I found comfort in bands and people who shared what I considered more compassionate and grounded politics.

Since then—that is, for the past twenty-five years—my relationship to straight edge has been characterized by a love for the ideas and by many precious friendships, but also by caution regarding a scene I often perceived as too conformist and uniform. I have published zines, helped organize shows, and tabled at many more. I have watched straight edge bands play in US community centers, Australian record stores, Israeli squats, and Swedish basements. I have visited and stayed with straight edge folks around the world, some of whom are featured in *Sober Living* and the book you are holding. When I go to a show today, I am one of the few forty-plus fellows in the audience, with most others young enough to be my children. Yet I have never been a "scenester" who knew all the right people (for the reason alone that I never lived in the right places), and I've always had interests outside of hardcore punk culture.

Now, if people want to hold this against me as an editor of books about straight edge, there is little I can do. The answers I have can be divided into a macho one and a less-macho one. The macho one goes something like this: If you think you're more straight edge because you think you're tuned into the right scene, then try to be straight edge where the only places to hang out are beer tents. The less-macho one is more sensible: Straight edge isn't defined by any particular scene and its codes and norms. Straight edge's beauty lies in its diversity and all the different geographical, cultural, and political adaptations it has undergone. It is this diversity—in particular its politically progressive and radical dimensions—that I try to convey with my books. And while there is no guarantee for a good result, both my motivation and the way I go about it are very much based on my personal story.

WHAT IS STRAIGHT EDGE?

Most simply, the term "straight edge" stands for a drug-free current within hardcore punk culture, with alcohol and nicotine being considered drugs as well. The band Minor Threat released a song of the same name in 1981. Ian MacKaye, who wrote the song, has said innumerable times that he did not want to start a movement. However, you're not always in control of what you set into motion. It only took a few years for straight edge to take on the form

Poster for a presentation of *Sober Living for the Revolution* in Amsterdam, 2010. Art by Sanne.

of a movement, with all that entails: collective self-identification, criteria for inclusion and exclusion, cultural markers, and so on.

A very short overview of straight edge history can be divided into four periods:

1. The early days of Washington, DC, hardcore punk when Ian MacKaye made straight edge a prominent part of a fledgling and visionary underground scene—roughly 1980 to 1983.
2. The first wave of self-identified straight edge bands across North America, often referred to as the "youth crew movement"—roughly 1984 to 1990.
3. The "new-school" straight edge bands of the 1990s, strongly characterized by the increasing significance of animal rights, hence often known as the "vegan straight edge movement"—roughly 1991 to 1999.
4. A diverse global straight edge movement, including old school revivals as much as vegan straight edge, straight edge acoustic acts as much as straight edge power violence bands, and anticonsumerist principles as much as a lucrative straight edge merchandise industry—roughly 2000 to present.

In the past twenty years, straight edge has also entered the mainstream in various ways. Metallica's James Hetfield, who completed a rehab program for alcohol addiction in 2002, sports a straight edge tattoo. The Straight Edge Society was a popular feature in World Wrestling Entertainment, with its leader CM Punk building his entire career on a straight edge identity. The former Major League Baseball pitcher C.J. Wilson introduced straight edge to the world of professional sports, while the movies *Ten Thousand Saints* (2015) and *Crown and Anchor* (2018) brought it to the big screen. Websites such as straightedgeworldwide.com ensure a slick online presence of the culture. And bands such as Carpathia, Maroon, and Throwdown have brought straight edge to big venues and festival stages. The developments that keep the culture alive and vibrant, however, still happen underneath the radar of mainstream culture and media. Straight edge might have got some mainstream recognition, but it firmly remains an underground phenomenon.

While the basic tenets of straight edge are uncontroversial (no consumption of drugs, alcohol and nicotine included), some of the finer points have been fiercely debated for a long time. To begin with, the Minor Threat song "Out of Step" includes the line: "Don't drink, don't smoke, don't fuck, at least I can fucking think." The third declaration has been interpreted in conservative (marital monogamy) as well as moderate ways (responsible, nonabusive sex) or ignored altogether. In the 1990s, the vegan straight edge movement made veganism an integral part of straight edge for many, while others consider animal rights unrelated to living straight edge. And then there is the perpetual discussion about what constitutes a "drug," with people throwing caffeine, sugar, and pharmaceuticals into the mix. None of these questions are explored in depth in this book, even though individual contributions may touch upon them. I was primarily interested in progressive and radical interpretations of straight edge's basic tenets, regardless of the individual contributors' respective concepts of a straight edge life.

ABOUT THE BOOK

The way the contributors to this volume were selected was largely based on a personal network of friends and acquaintances. Some people I did not know personally beforehand but sought them out specifically because I knew of their work. I made an effort to reflect the diversity of straight edge culture, but I claim to present neither its "most important" nor its "most representative" voices. Many readers will feel that a particular individual, band, project, or scene that should have been included is missing. This is inevitable, as innumerable people would have been worth including. I can only encourage everyone to highlight their voices in other forums. I am also always happy to receive feedback and commentary. The same is true for the contributors to the book. The folks at PM Press are pros at forwarding messages!

As far as the contributors' politics are concerned, I followed the same criteria I used for *Sober Living*. Readers will find a range of opinions within these pages. I don't agree with all of them, and some, in fact, contradict each other. Yet I consider them all based on anticapitalist, left-wing and/or anarchist, antiracist, and feminist convictions. I decided not to include views that I consider overtly macho or homophobic, no matter the language they are couched in. I also didn't include views whose political implications are unclear to me. Finally, I didn't include views based on dogmatic belief systems, among which I count most religions.

I understand that none of these boundaries can ever be clear-cut and objective. Based on the very criteria I just outlined, some readers would have included voices that I have left out. And, of course, the criteria themselves can be questioned. At the end of the day, I am solely responsible for the selection made. But I try to be open and transparent about how I reasoned.

The single biggest editorial challenge with a volume like this is to avoid excessive repetition. With close to fifty contributions, some of it is inevitable (let's be honest: how many sound political reasons for being straight edge are there?), but I believe that each contribution adds a particular perspective to our discussions about straight edge, sobriety, and radical politics. Needless to say, there are great texts out there that were not included, simply because they covered essentially the same ground as other contributions. It was not a value judgment.

US spellings have been used for interviews and original contributions. In reprints, the original spellings remain unaltered.

A common abbreviation for "straight edge" is "sXe" (or, capitalized, "SXE"). Some authors also prefer to capitalize the term ("Straight Edge") or write it as one word ("straightedge"). We have sought coherence only within individual articles, not throughout the book. "xVx" (also "xvx" or "XVX") is a common abbreviation for "vegan straight edge." "HC" (or "hc") is sometimes used to abbreviate "hardcore."

Straight edge bands often use X's to frame their names. In this book, they are only used for bands that have included them in their logos and have used them consistently (for example, xTrue Naturex or xFirstWorldProblemx).

I am responsible for all translations from non-English sources. I thank Clifton Ross for his help in the translation of the interview with July Salazar from Spanish.

All original interviews were conducted in the summer and fall of 2018, either in person, on the phone, or by email.

I owe an enormous debt of gratitude to all of the contributors to the book (text and art), and to the armada of people who have helped with advice and information! The sole reason for not providing a list of names is that I'm terrified of forgetting one. You know who you are, and I hope I've made my appreciation clear on a personal level!

GLOSSARY

For those not versed in hardcore punk and straight edge culture and its vocabulary, the following very general definitions may serve as guidelines.

punk: an antiestablishment counterculture, most notably expressed by provocative (anti)fashion and an aggressive minimalist ("three-chord") musical style, most iconically embodied by the British Sex Pistols in 1977.

hardcore: first used as a US-American synonym of "punk," developing into its own genre (often named *hardcore punk*) in the early to mid-1980s by favoring low-key visual aesthetics over extravagance and breaking with original punk rock song patterns.

DIY: a principle of independence and of retaining control over one's work, DIY (abbreviating *Do It Yourself*) defines original hardcore punk ethics and, to many, remains the decisive criterion for "true" hardcore punk; the most tangible aspects of hardcore punk's DIY culture are self-run record labels, self-organized shows, self-made zines, and noncommercial social networks.

zine (also fanzine): a DIY publication that is primarily distributed within a particular (sub)culture and often has a characteristic, "nonglossy," appearance; the term derives from "magazine."

to X up: the phrase refers to the most common straight edge symbol, the X painted on the back of one's hand. The symbol's origins lie in minors being marked that way at shows, so they could not drink. When the mark was turned into a self-affirming indication for drug-free living, it became a positive reference point for sober hardcore punk kids. It appears in countless variations in straight edge culture.

vegan straight edge: a blend of straight edge principles and veganism, mostly associated with a wave of early 1990s straight edge bands, with Earth Crisis being the best known; musically, often associated with metalcore.

Hardline: a radical political movement espousing vegan straight edge and, according to its manifesto, advocating "an ideology that is pure and righteous, without contradictions or inconsistencies." Hardline was influential in straight edge culture throughout the 1990s and is strongly associated with the band Vegan Reich.

crew: commonly used in hardcore culture as a reference to a group of hardcore peers; particularly popular within straight edge during the "youth crew" period of the late 1980s.

metalcore: mainly a musical category, it indicates a blend of hardcore and metal elements; popularized in the 1990s vegan straight edge scene, particularly by bands from the Victory and New Age labels.

emo (or emocore): an attempt to go beyond the hardcore "tough-guy" image, musically, lyrically, and image-wise.

screamo: a variation on emo, considered more experimental and intense musically.

riot grrrl: a feminist punk hardcore movement that emerged in the early 1990s.

queercore: a fusion of hardcore and queer identity/culture/politics.

TIMELINE

This timeline is meant to serve as a reference for the readers of this book, paying particular attention to aspects of straight edge history that relate to its contents. While it also aims to include "objectively" important periods, bands, and events, it does not claim to offer a complete overview of straight edge history.

1980–1985

✗ Dischord Records founded (1980)
✗ Minor Threat releases the song "Straight Edge" (1981)
✗ first wave of straight edge bands: SSD, DYS, 7 Seconds
✗ Lärm from the Netherlands pioneers straight edge in Europe
✗ first Positive Force punk collectives founded, strongly inspired by straight edge

1986–1989

✗ second wave of straight edge bands ("youth crew," later also referred to as "old school"): Youth of Today, Gorilla Biscuits, Bold, Judge, Uniform Choice, Chain of Strength
✗ Revelation Records founded (1987)

1990–1995

✘ left-wing ("commie") straight edge develops in Europe: ManLiftingBanner, Nations on Fire

✘ emo straight edge becomes influential: Frail, Blindfold

✘ the Hardline movement forms, tightly connected to the band Vegan Reich

✘ Earth Crisis is the flagship for the vegan straight edge movement

✘ New Age Records and Victory Records become the most influential straight edge labels, defining "metalcore" and the "new school": Earth Crisis, Strife, Snapcase, Outspoken, Unbroken

✘ "Krishnacore" develops around Equal Vision Records in New York: Shelter, 108

✘ Partnership for a Drug-Free America produces never-aired straight edge commercials

✘ straight edge bands form in several Asian and Latin American cities, often with left-leaning politics

✘ in Europe and Israel, political straight edge bands become influential: Cymeon X, X-Acto, Nekhei Naatza

✘ a particularly strong vegan straight edge movement emerges in Umeå, Sweden: Refused, Abhinanda, Doughnuts

✘ Refuse Records founded (1993)

✘ Ebullition Records releases the compilation *XXX: some ideas are poisonous* (1995)

1996–2000

✘ first Verdurada festival in São Paulo (1996), fusing radical politics and straight edge hardcore

✘ Point of No Return becomes the flagship of vegan straight edge in Latin America

✘ militant straight edge groups in Salt Lake City, Utah, draw a lot of attention

✘ xsisterhoodx.com launched (1997)

✘ Emancypunx Records founded (1997)

✘ Beth Lahicky's book *All Ages: Reflections on Straight Edge* released, a compilation of interviews with people involved in the straight edge scene (1997)

✘ bands such as Trial and Good Clean Fun stand for the "posi," nonmilitant wing of straight edge culture
✘ Limp Wrist, influential straight edge queercore band, formed (1998)
✘ Edge Day celebrated for the first time on October 17, 1999

2001–2005

✘ Catalyst Records develops into the most important political straight edge label in the US: Birthright, Risen, 7 Generations, Gather, Point of No Return
✘ Total Liberation Tour, blending music and politics, in 2004
✘ online journal DIY Conspiracy (diyconspiracy.net) founded (2005)

2006–2010

✘ bands such as Have Heart, Carpathian, Throwdown bring straight edge to big rock venues
✘ several "old-school" straight edge bands embark on reunion tours: Bold, Youth of Today, Gorilla Biscuits
✘ Ross Haenfler's study *Straight Edge: Clean-Living Youth, Hardcore Punk, and Social Change* released (2006)
✘ Robert T. Wood's study *Straightedge Youth: Complexity and Contradictions of a Subculture* released (2006)
✘ Raymond McCrea Jones's photo book *Faces of Straight Edge* released (2007)
✘ National Geographic documentary *Inside Straight Edge* aired (2008)
✘ Brian Peterson's interview-based book *Burning Fight: The Nineties Hardcore Revolution in Ethics, Politics, Spirits, and Sound* released (2009)
✘ Marc Hanou and Jean-Paul Frijns's book *The Past the Present 1982–2007: A History of 25 Years of European Straight Edge* released (2009)
✘ documentary film *Edge: Perspectives on Drug Free Culture* released (2009)
✘ Gabriel Kuhn's book *Sober Living for the Revolution: Hardcore Punk, Straight Edge, and Radical Politics* released (2010)
✘ the Straight Edge Society, under the leadership of CM Punk, is featured in World Wrestling Entertainment (2009–2010)

2011–2019

✖ straight edge becomes musically very diverse, including acoustic and hip hop acts

✖ straightedgeworldwide.com launched (2011)

✖ *XGRRRLX* zine founded (2013)

✖ Warzone Distro founded (2013)

✖ Swedish straight edge documentary film *Trogen till döden* (True till Death) released (2014)

✖ the feature films *Ten Thousand Saints* (2015) and *Crown and Anchor* (2018) introduce straight edge characters to mass audiences

✖ Tony Rettman's oral history book *Straight Edge: A Clear-Headed Hardcore Punk History* released (2017)

✖ documentary film *UxÅ: A Journey to the Heart of the Umeå Hardcore Scene* released (2018)

ARTISTS

"WE ARE EVERYWHERE"

Interview with Martin Sorrondeguy

Martin Sorrondeguy is a legendary figure in the US hardcore scene, best known as the singer for the bands Los Crudos and Limp Wrist. He runs the record label Lengua Armada Discos and directed the film *Beyond the Screams: A US Latino Hardcore Punk Documentary* (1999). For his photography visit martinsorrondeguy.com. The following interview was published on August 21, 2010, by DIY Conspiracy (diyconspiracy.net).

Let's start with an introduction to you. Who are you? How old are you? You were born in Uruguay, but located to the USA in an early age. How did you grown up as a latino-kid and what brought you to hardcore/punk?

My name is Martin Sorrondeguy. I am 42 years old. I was born in Uruguay and was raised in the US. I came into hardcore punk when I was a teenager. I wanted something different than what was existing in my area at the time. We have many gang and violence problems there and I did not want to be a part of that. I needed something different, and punk was new and interesting for me and it provided options for an alternative life.

How did you come up to form the band Los Crudos and become involved in the DIY scene?

DIY ethics came to me before I was in Los Crudos. I had learned through DIY that there were always ways to having things happen that were outside the limits of what mainstream culture presented to me. Los Crudos was able to really make out impact due to a strengthened DIY belief system and methodology.

What brought you to the radical politics expressed by the band?
Our lives that we were living, our history as immigrants into the US and the circumstances we were faced with, led us to take a radically political stance. It was more of a necessity in order to survive and keep our sanity.

Can you give us a brief history of Los Crudos and the other activities and projects that you were involved in during the band's existence?
Crudos began in 1991 on the Southside of Chicago. We sang all our songs in Spanish as a means to communicate with other Latino immigrants about our frustrations with the way Immigrant populations were being treated in the US. We took our message and involved ourselves with punk as well as non-punk people, artists, activists and social workers within our community. We had built alliances with many people and we did benefit gigs, records, and involved ourselves in meetings as well as actions to make change.

It seems the main purpose of Los Crudos was to unify the Latino/Chicano punk community and expose the message of anarchism, immigrant rights and anti-racism to these poor Latino neighbourhoods in Spanish language. What was the reason to broke up with Los Crudos and are you satisfied with what you have achieved with the band during all those years together?
We really spread our message to many types of communities not just poor Latino communities. The impact that Crudos made went noticed because we spread ourselves out to even wealthier white communities as well. If we had stayed only in poor Latino communities Crudos and our activities would most likely not have been known. We stopped because it became too much about the band and music. It seemed that we were being pressured to play gig after gig and tour again and again, and it seemed that we were being cornered in a way that if we committed ourselves to gigging only we would lose our impact message wise, so we decided to stop the band.

After Los Crudos you started the band Limp Wrist and exposed your sexuality. Why did you become involved in the gay rights issues so late? Why not talking about being gay when you were in Crudos? And what's the story behind starting Limp Wrist, was this a serious project in the beginning?

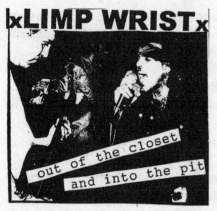

Covers for the first self-released Limp Wrist tapes, *Out of the Closet and Into the Pit* (1999) and *Don't Knock It Till You Try It* (2000). The Out of the Closet cover is taken from terminalescape.blogspot.com, where it is described as "an impromptu cover of sorts."

Actually, I was talking about being gay when Los Crudos were playing, it was when I first "came out" due to the conservativism within the many communities I felt it was important to talk about these issues. So I did. There were two songs on the Crudos LP that address the issues of love and sexuality.

Limp Wrist was always serious but we chose to take a humorous angle to make our point instead of an angry approach which was successful in the US.

I guess there were a lot of troubles when you have started Limp Wrist, because the lyrics and live shows of the band can be easily seen as extremely provocative with all that nudeness, homoeroticism and making fun of all the gay clichés. What was harder for you, to spark the social awareness and talk about political ideas with Los Crudos or to threaten homophobia and be an all-gay hardcore band with Limp Wrist?
All of the above were challenges, and as an artist and activist one has to create strategies to making your voice and point heard. Both bands were vehicles to express many things and we wanted to be smart about what we did and steering away from just being confrontational. That is what is usually expected from people we have lived with confrontation and are accustomed to it, so doing something that does not engage aggressiveness is strategizing.

What's the difference between the Queercore scene and the political DIY scene? Is the queer scene open to the different social ideas and things like supporting the immigrants and minorities, being involved in social

movements, animal rights etc., or it's mainly single-issue oriented on identity politics and only few people are aware of other things except being gay?
It is very difficult if we begin to speak in terms of whole groups of people. So with any group of people you have a lot of overlap into differences because we are not flat human beings we all have differences. So when speaking about a gay person who then is also an immigrant or from a Third World nation or if you are a gay person that is poor as opposed to the stereotype of having money. Or if you are transgendered it gets more complicated/ interesting. There are folks who juggle all of these dimensions of their lives so in punk queercore is an identity and it comes with expectations and a consciousness/ awareness. So you cannot identify as queercore and not have a greater scope of the world around you, in fact, being queercore or a gay/ lesbian/queer/trans punk has opened up expanded dialogue and actions to make real equitable change in the scene and in the world.

Some people recognize gays only as middle or upper class privileged people, who spend all of their free time in gay bars and clubs. What is it like to be immigrant, gay, working class and living in a poor Latino neighborhood?
This is what I was getting at above, you do have the mainstream gay world which can be what you described above and it is what gets media attention. Gay is not an umbrella group that we all fit under it is impossible to flatly define, so when people can embrace that being gay transcends the economic and social boundaries that we are used to see, we can begin to understand that the possibility of having someone who is gay living next door to us or within our own families is very real and it is happening, this goes for any community Latino/White/African-American/Asian etc., etc.

As it seems gay bars and clubs are the most recognized places where gay people could meet other gay people and socialize. But these are also places where they spend a lot of money on alcohol and drugs. What's your opinion on this as Straight Edge person? Do you think alcohol, drugs and AIDS are a big problem in the mainstream gay communities and is there a way to stop this? What was your reason to become Straight Edge?
I no longer want to call myself Straight Edge as of two years ago. I was calling myself Straight Edge though when I first went to gay bars 15 years ago and I was comfortable with being Straight Edge it was part of who I was and I did not feel I had to surrender that in order to gain acceptance from gays who frequented bars. Gay bars in most cities are places where we can be social and meet one another but there are other places to meet as well, now there is

the internet and one no longer has to go to a bar to meet other gay folks. The issues of gays and money is a very mainstream look at the gay world, there are many gays who do not have a lot of money so if you have I suppose you spend if you don't have money spending is not an option.

You told me about your work as a high-school teacher. What do you think of the educational system in the USA and don't you have troubles with the school-board or angry parents, who don't want the teacher of their children to be gay? Are you talking with your students about LGBT rights, homophobia or historical events like the Stonewall riots?
I am an art/photo teacher so this is my focus of teaching at times current events and social issues come up in discussions during class, I think my job is to make sure the discussion is healthy and a true dialogue not one that comes from anger and intimidation, most students are able to have these discussions in this manner. I do not walk into a class room and say "Hi, I am Martin and I am gay", I have never heard of a teacher doing this. There are students that are gay or lesbian and sometimes they can tell when a teacher is gay or lesbian but it depends on the context if that issue comes up and how it is dealt with. I once taught in an alternative high school where I was asked to teach a queer history class and it was great. This was an alternative school that was small about 40 students and a place where students were tired of being lied to and as a teacher I could be honest and prepare these students for real world experiences not hide things from them in hopes of them never having to be exposed to anything. Sort of strange but that is how fear of the unknown begins and many conservative approaches do this.

What's some other stuff that people should know about the history of gay rights movement except Stonewall?
There is so much, I think having an awareness of many great works and activities created by gay/lesbian/bi/trans people is important. Queers did not just riot, we are in medicine/arts/politics etc. We are everywhere!

I guess here in Bulgaria no one is familiar with the history of the queer punk scene. So can you give us some information about the first and about the most important bands with gay members or people unframing the issue in the hardcore/punk scene? In the song "The Ode" you're singing about people like Gary Floyd and Randy Turner, who are they? Which are the most important gay bands today and which queer bands do you recommend to hear?

Martin Sorrondeguy at the University of Pennsylvania, 2015. Photo by David Ensminger.

The earliest of US punk in particular had many many queer people involved and active in the scene. The more known people were Darby Crash of the Germs, Tomata Du Plenty of the Screamers, Bob Mould from Hüsker Dü, Gary Floyd is the singer of the Dicks, Randy Turner is the singer of the Big Boys. There were also many many old punks who experimented with sexuality but may not have identified as gay. Some even prostituted themselves to men like Dee Dee Ramone. So whatever the reason sexuality was pretty fluid.

What about the Latino hardcore/punk scene? You made the movie "Beyond The Screams: A Latino/Chicano Hardcore/Punk Documentary", but it seems there's a big difference since the time you did the movie? Bands like Los Crudos, Huasipungo, Youth Against are not active for years. What's happening now?
In the Latino Punk scene there are tons of great bands and a strong scene of it, some of the bands are Ilegal from Montreal, Canada, Sin Orden is still happening, Tuberculosis, La Voz, Rayos X, Polizkitzo, Outraged, Ultratumbados, Venganza, Mugre, NN, Peligro Social, Ruleta Russa, and tons more there is some great stuff happening.

Tell us more about your bands and musical projects besides Los Crudos and Limp Wrist.
I have newer bands, one is a Spanish/Latino punk band called NN. I also have a total hardcore band called Needles, I am also still running Lengua Armada Records and releasing many great bands that I think need support.

Bands like Bad Brains or . . . Vegan Reich . . . are well known for their negative views on homosexuality. What's your opinion on these bands?
Everyone has had their opinions and they are entitled to them. As a kid I grew up listening to Bad Brains, and I loved their Positive Mental Attitude and that spoke to me and I lived it, it is a shame that H.R. did not.

Is there anything you want to add? Something important that you would like to impart, but I forgot to ask you about?
No, not really, I think there are truly great discussions that need to happen, I am willing to partake in these discussions whenever I can. I hope the folks in your scene can read this and have a newer understanding of what we have been doing. Thank you for the time and curiosity.

TOTAL LIBERATION

Eva "Genie" Hall is the former vocalist of Gather (2004–2007). From 2012 to 2018 she sang in Rats in the Wall. Today she is in a new straight edge band with some members of Gather. She lives in California, where she spends her free time volunteering at a wildlife rehabilitation center, doing art, reading, and drinking tea. You can follow her on Instagram at xevageniex.

I always saw Gather and 7 Generations as two bands that brought together the dedication and militancy of 1990s vegan straight edge with a broader understanding of social injustice. They were able to build bridges to activists who perceived the bands from the 1990s as too macho and narrow-minded. Is this just a fancy theory I made up or do you think there is truth to it?

I'd say you nailed it, at least with Gather! Our love for punk and hardcore had everything to do with the progressive ideas and radical politics that appealed to us when we were first introduced to those genres. To us, those ideals were one and the same with the music. During the time right before Gather formed, the straight edge hardcore scene in the Bay Area where we were all living felt very apolitical, had a grossly misogynist "jock" vibe, very few women were in bands, and so we just didn't feel much connection to the music scene, despite being straight edge and into hardcore music ourselves. We talked about how we wanted to bring the anarcho-punk ethics we all believed in into this "macho" hardcore scene that we loved musically. Why not start a band that sings about radical feminism and anarchism, but still has mosh parts and breakdowns? We were angry, and that kind of music felt most fitting for us to express that!

One reason why many radicals in Europe eyed vegan straight edge suspiciously was because the focus on animal rights and environmental issues seemed to override social causes. Were you ever confronted with this while playing and touring with Gather?

For the most part, we did not really experience that. Instead, it truly felt like anarcho-punk kids (who may have previously been skeptical of straight edge hardcore) did also see the value in being sober, and they felt like their ideals were still represented in this kind of music that typically didn't address them. We were playing anarcho-punk fests with bands like Resist and Exist, and it felt as natural as can be. It really felt like there was unity between punks and hardcore kids who might have otherwise been part of different scenes. Crusty kids were wearing X's on their hands, and camo-clad hardcore kids were wearing circle-A patches! Activists who were yelling into bullhorns at demos the day before were also singing along up front at shows about things they were passionate about.

There was only one show that I can recall where we felt like we did not fit in because of our politics, despite being vegan and straight edge, and it was surprisingly at a show with other prominent vegan straight edge bands, but who tended to have a more conservative following. One vegan straight edge band that was Christian and had members that were extremely patriotic and, I think, in the military played after us and they started making a hateful speech about how women actually don't belong in hardcore and shouldn't go to shows. It created a weird tension, and some of their friends ended up attacking our drummer, who is my brother, and our merch girl. Both ended up having to go to the hospital, and our merch girl had to stay overnight, got some teeth replaced, and had a lot of emotional trauma when recalling the whole ordeal. It was a sad reminder to us that just because someone is vegan and straight edge does *not* mean they care about social issues. They do *not* care about equality and compassion for all, and in fact, we have nothing in common with them fundamentally. I sometimes would forget that not everyone got into hardcore through punk ethics. It was horrible, but it reminded us that even if our bands sounded similar musically, without the ideals it meant nothing to us, and there was no sense of community at all.

"Total Liberation" was not only the title song of your first EP but a theme that Gather as a band seemed based on. Can you explain what the concept meant to you? Do you still hold the same convictions?

In 2003, there was an event in Pennsylvania called Total Liberation Fest. It had hardcore bands like Undying playing one day, and the next day had different speakers who talked about animal, earth, and human libera-

tion struggles. Dustin, Allan, and I were all friends and rode a train all the way out to that fest, and it is what inspired us to start Gather. (Randy was in a band that was actually playing the fest.) We knew we weren't alone in our longing to bring these issues back into hardcore on the west coast. Earth Crisis had that iconic "Animal Liberation" shirt, and the very first shirt Gather ever made was a mock version of that with the same font, but it said "Total Liberation." We simply wanted to be clear that we weren't a single-issue band and that we believed in animal, earth, and human liberation. For us, that meant anarcha-feminism and the end of patriarchy; it meant acknowledging that a "vegan revolution" doesn't challenge the problems with modern totalitarian agriculture; it meant that we were aware that consumerist choices about our diets wouldn't lead to a magical downfall of oppressive capitalist systems; and it meant acknowledging the horrible costs of imperialism/globalization and industrial civilization. "Total liberation" was our way of talking about "intersectionality," I suppose. And yes, I certainly do still hold those same convictions!

"I Hate Ayn Rand" is one of my favorite song titles ever. Do you think that the hyper-individualism propagated by Rand has left traces in hardcore and DIY culture as well?

Thank you! I think since it is so ingrained in all of American culture, and most of the industrialized world, many people even in the hardcore scene probably don't question that philosophy. The weird thing is that I think a lot of people are drawn to hardcore because it's a community, a "family," and that's the opposite of individualism. I would hope no one would confuse "individualism" in the Ayn Rand sense of the word (that everyone is on their own, we shouldn't look out for each other, community is bad, etc.) with the struggle to not rely on corporations, and the desire to keep hardcore from being an "industry," that is, to defend DIY hardcore.

What are the political issues you consider most important today?
Wow, everything is so fucked, where to even begin? With climate change, the depletion of topsoil, the killing of ocean life, and the displacement of indigenous people and the destruction of their land, I'd say the greatest issues are the ways in which capitalism, and all of industrialized civilization, is devastating this planet and everything on it. Our society as we know it could not exist without deforestation, strip mining, industrial agriculture, and the exploitation of the poor. Corporations, which have gained their power through extreme wealth, are running this world and destroying everything for the sake of profit. Taking them down is nearly impossible, it seems. Even though there's incredible class inequality, the poor don't seem to have much solidarity with each other and tend to continue to blame each other and identify with billionaires who don't give a fuck about us. As long as we continue to see each other as the enemies while worshiping the rich, things will never change.

How does straight edge play into this? In the song "Escalate," one of the 2000s most important declarations of straight edge, the first line says: "Straight Edge cannot be considered the final goal / but in order to achieve the things that count the most, we must use it as a tool." Do you still feel that way?
I recognize that there are as many reasons to be straight edge as there are straight edge kids, and that each reason is valid. With that lyric, I was trying to say that being straight edge does not make someone superior to someone else, especially if they just embrace the same negative aspects of mainstream culture and aren't trying to make this world—or at least this scene—a better, more inclusive place for everyone. So, I do not think that one has to be an "activist" or something if they're straight edge. But I was referring to an unjustified sense of self-righteousness amongst straight edge kids who were otherwise assholes who just happened to be drug-free.

How about the song's last line? "If you think that we have things in common just because we both wear X's on our hands, you're wrong! / We both may abstain from substances, but that is not enough to make a bond." Who are the people you didn't—or still don't—want to bond with?

Drawing by Eva "Genie" Hall, 2018. Lyrics from the song "Force of Change" by Strife.

I think the point I was trying to make with that song was specific to the local scene at that specific period of time. . . . I'm pretty sure it was the first song we ever wrote, and I didn't really think anyone but my close friends would ever hear it, haha. Where we were living, there were a lot of straight edge kids and bands, but they were pretty apolitical, embraced conventions that felt oppressive to us, and, for the most part, didn't seem any more progressive than a frat boy at a college or something. That's a huge generalization of course, but it did feel like no one cared about anything, and they just used "straight edge" as a way to feel superior to others. It wasn't uncommon to hear homophobic jokes, and some people even threw around shit like "Women can't be straight edge," etc. Hardly anyone was saying anything on stage about their beliefs or passions. They were all very "safe." Shows felt soulless and empty to me, and I did not feel like I had any real connection to the people there, even if we were all X'd up. So, like in my previous answer, my point was that simply being straight edge does not make you better than anyone else, especially if you embrace and perpetuate a lot of the fucked-up aspects of mainstream culture.

"Escalate" (2004)

Straight Edge cannot be considered the final goal / but in order to achieve the things that count the most, we must use it as a tool. / There is more to it than simply being drug free. / It's the clarity of mind to act most effectively against this system we're fighting. / It's the first step, it's the key to unlock you from your apathy / but if you stop at that, you're just a waste to me. / You've broken your addiction, but now you just sit / as stagnant as a passed out frat-boy—you're no threat! / I know plenty of Christians who don't drink / Do they deserve praise for being revolutionary? NO! / Do you really believe that Straight Edge alone is going to do shit? / If drugs are the reason everyone's so passive, use your sobriety to act! / Do you think it's just about health? / Then how does it affect anyone but you? / Now that you're liberated, what are you going to do? / Merely Straight Edge—not enough! / Merely Straight Edge—step it up! / If you think that we have things in common just because we both wear X's on our hands, you're wrong! / We both may abstain from substances, but that is not enough to make a bond.

In the 2010 documentary *Edge: Perspectives on Drug-Free Culture*, you speak about how women in the hardcore scene were "discredited," "judged harder," and made to "feel uncomfortable." Have things changed since then?
Oh yes, they certainly have! Compared to ten to fifteen years ago, when it was rare to see women in hardcore bands, today there are *so many* more women in bands. It's staggering how much more inclusive it feels (even though it's still not perfect of course), and how we have carved a space for ourselves in a scene that once was such a "boys' club." It kind of feels like there was a revival of riot grrrl aspects, but this time, instead of being separate from the hardcore scene, they were incorporated into it. It's clear that a lot of the women in current hardcore bands reject the idea that they need any male approval, and they're here to be themselves and have fun, and "fuck you" if you don't like it. They're singing to each other, they're addressing things *they* care about, they're contributing their voices, and it's awesome. Of course not everyone is suddenly super progressive or identifies as a feminist, but there's no question that it's much more common to see women up on stage now, or moshing, and just taking up space, and it's much more accepted, which makes me *so* fucking happy.

How did you yourself cope in the environment you started out in?
To be honest, when we first discussed the idea of having me sing in Gather, I was a bit nervous, because the scene *was* so male-dominated and I had heard so much misogynist bullshit that I was afraid to put myself out there. However, we were all such good friends, I knew that we would have fun, and I felt it was important to go for it since it made me sad that women were so underrepresented. The majority of the response we got was positive, and I felt a lot of support from other women in hardcore. In this "boys' club," I wanted to have a song that represented the experiences of other women in the scene, so I interviewed some of the women I saw at shows all the time. The song "Who Belongs?" is a bunch of different quotes and ideas that I took from those interviews. There were only a couple times in the three years of playing shows that we experienced overt sexism, but the vast majority of my time in Gather was very positive and I connected with so many other like-minded people.

In a more recent interview on the blog *Conversations with Bianca*, you said, "Another struggle I've been having has to do with getting older and still being involved in punk/hardcore and holding on to all my ideals from my youth. . . . I'm happy that I still care about these things, but it certainly is more alienating the older you get—you're more of a weirdo to others around you who are the same age, but who 'grew out of it.'" I think most of us who are beyond thirty feel in similar ways. What do you think makes the difference? Like, why do you think that, as you said in the interview, you're "doomed to be a weirdo forever"?
Obviously, the older you get, the more friends break edge and just generally become "normal" and live conventional lifestyles. I get that they're just over "the struggle," they don't want to always live against the grain, and they just want to enjoy a simple life of not overthinking everything. While I know that embracing that way of living might be easier in many ways, it still seems so bland to me, and I'm just not interested. I've heard people who stopped being straight edge say that it is just a "youth movement," which seems like a cop-out to me. The pressure to participate in drinking culture only seems to grow the older we get and it is completely normalized. People assume you're either super Christian or a recovering addict if you don't drink—they can't fathom that someone just isn't interested in intoxicating themselves for fun! Even aside from straight edge, I've seen other friends who used to take a stand against oppressive systems, like capitalism and classism, simply buy in completely because they themselves were born into class privilege and want

to continue benefiting from that without giving it a second thought. There are so many examples, but what it comes down to is that I've always felt like an outcast in many ways, even amongst other outcasts, and I don't think that will ever change. My circle of friends becomes smaller as I've gotten more picky about who I give my time to, so that can be seen as alienating. But it's more alienating to me to be surrounded by vapid people who don't question the roles and paradigms they were born into. Thankfully I love being alone!

After Gather you were in Rats in the Wall. What were the main differences between the bands?

Aside from being completely different musically, the biggest difference for me was that no one else in Rats in the Wall really shared my ideals or convictions about anything. I also didn't really know any of them until I joined the band, so we were sort of just thrown together and had to make it work! It didn't feel as natural as it did in Gather. I felt limited in the sense that I didn't want to sing about things that I didn't think the other members could represent, but I also didn't want to censor myself. For the most part, the others in Rats were pretty apolitical. The first few years were great, but later on, their goal for playing in a band was simply to get "maximum exposure," and I got extremely disappointed when there would be talk about how "image is all that matters" and it's important to "sell ourselves" and be a "professional band." It wasn't that way in the beginning, but it was clear that's what they were trying to go for eventually.

On top of that, some things were said that lead me to believe that a particular member sort of just saw some "market" for "women in bands" and was trying to fulfill it. I felt like I was being used as a gimmick, and my actual beliefs didn't mean shit—I just happened to be a woman and therefore "fit the bill." When I had differing opinions about the band, that member would tell me I was "disposable," and "*just* the singer." Those concepts were absolutely repulsive to me in a punk/hardcore band, and that's when I felt like it was time for me to quit. It became pretty toxic, stressful, and it was emotionally exhausting.

Lastly, I was the only person who was straight edge—or, for that matter, cared about punctuality—so that was frustrating to deal with. I tried to stay in the band as long as I could and make it work but ended up quitting abruptly after an unnecessary argument with that member, and I couldn't deal with the dysfunctional dynamic anymore.

On the other hand, everyone in Gather was more or less on the same page as far as our ideals went, and all we could hope for was to build community based around those ideals. We were all good friends, and even family, before the band, and that's why we started the band with each other. The members were *not* disposable in Gather—we chose to start that band with each other for a reason. We all had so much passion and cared about the message. If people liked us, cool! If they didn't, so what? We weren't going to compromise ourselves for approval. It was genuine and sincere. We ended up breaking up because one member wanted to dedicate all his time to become a teacher, and even though we were sad, we understood. So we planned a last string of shows and had a blast.

You also draw and have worked as a tattoo artist. Do you want to focus on a particular creative outlet in the future or do you need the variety of visual arts, music, and writing?
Sadly, one thing I've learned about myself is that anytime I take something I like and make it a job, I quickly start to hate it. I didn't like tattooing at a shop, but I do enjoy it as another medium. And I would never want to try to be in a "professional" band with whatever the hell that entails. So I guess I like being able to turn to different creative outlets depending on my moods and circumstances. I think I'll always be involved in punk/hardcore bands in some way, and as someone who is extremely introverted, I know I'll always create art as well since it's something I can do by myself.

Feel free to speculate: where is straight edge heading?
I honestly haven't given much thought to where I see straight edge heading. I just assume it will continue the cycle of being cool, then not being cool, over and over again with tons of people selling out with each wave, but a handful of people enduring and remaining true throughout.

"IT MEANS REVOLUTION"

Interview with July Salazar

July Salazar is the founder and lead singer of the Peruvian hardcore band ¡Tomar Control!. She was born and raised in Lima. She is a straight edge and vegan activist, and a huge lover of music, dance, gig, movies, sports, travel, animals, friends, and family.

¡Tomar Control!, Lima, 2015. Photo by Samuel Girón.

Can you tell us about the history of ¡Tomar Control!?

Take Control is a hardcore punk band founded by women in early 2014. Our intention was to provide a female presence in a space normally occupied by men and to address social and personal issues, including veganism, Positive Mental Attitude, feminism, and straight edge. We reject any type of discrimination and wanted to sound out a clear and direct message.

We released an album in 2015, a split 7" with the American band Spirits, and we are included in a world compilation of emerging hardcore bands that was also released on 7" vinyl.

We have played in every corner of our city, sharing the stage with various bands from the local and the wider South American scene. We also did a tour in October 2016, playing twelve shows in Chile and Argentina.

At present, we are in the process of putting together and preproducing our second album—which should be out by the time this book appears!

Can you provide a little background about hardcore and straight edge in Peru in general?

Hardcore in Peru was born in the 1980s in response to the country's social and political situation. The youth responded as best as they could through music and art. The first hardcore band was G3, founded in 1985. It was followed by bands such as Kaos General, Situación hostile, and Desarme. In the 1990s, Futuro Incierto, SNA, PDI, Metamorphosis, Asmereir, Dios Hastío, Anfo, and Maestro Canibal appeared. Starting in 2000, things got more interesting with the birth of our present hardcore scene and access to more information. More and more often, you would see people being X'd up at shows. From my personal perspective, the show of Fuerza de Voluntad, a band from Chile, marked an important breaking point. People became more interested in straight edge and what it meant. A couple of small labels were founded (Renacer, Fair), and there were bands with straight edge members like Alhambre, Seko (which, unfortunately, only lasted a year), Paroximia, and Esto Está Mal, and also bands that were entirely straight edge like Axion and Trascender, a band that was born out of a fanzine.

From 2005 to 2009, there weren't really any shows or labels that were straight edge, but straight edge people were active in several bands, particularly in the north of the country: in Defensa Absoluta, 3prm, Por una vida mejor, and Nueva Dirección. In the south, a straight edge community formed around the guys from Opción Positiva. They managed to bring international bands to the country and made bigger labels interested in what was going on in Peru—that was something we never thought would be possible.

In 2011, the straight edge band Coraje was born, and straight edge people continued to play in bands such as Regret, Estructuras, P1Yo, Pérdida—and ¡Tomar Control!. You can't really say that there is a proper straight edge movement in Peru, but, in 2017, xLa Malezax was created by anarchists. xLa Malezax is an autonomous space with a library. It hosts talks and film screenings on topics such as straight edge, antispecism, feminism, and antiauthoritarian practices.

In a 2015 interview with *Noisey*, you said: "We see many more girls at shows. Before they were seen only as girlfriends of band members, but now they're going on their own. They're believing in the bands' messages, they're doing fanzines, making information desks, doing shows, selling food free of animal exploitation—they're taking part in a thousand ways. It fills me with joy." Is this continuing?

Currently, there aren't many hardcore punk shows, but when there are, we see girls enjoying them. We are still few but we are here. At the moment, neither women nor men do much more than being out in the public. We are going through a "dead cycle." I hope that things will pick up again in 2019, with the existing bands playing frequently and with new people arriving, bringing new ideas.

Do you and other Peruvian bands have strong contacts to bands in other Latin American countries? Is there much mutual influence?

Yes, we have contact with many bands in Latin America we feel close to. They have always been a great influence on us, especially the bands from Argentina and Chile. Not only musically, but ideologically—with their political positions and principles—as well.

What does straight edge mean to you?

For me it means revolution. It helps you to escape the paradigm that in order to create or strengthen social relationships you need to consume toxic substances altering who you are, when there is absolutely nothing wrong with being the way you are, as a unique person. When I discovered straight edge, I questioned my relationship to alcohol, which, up to that moment, I had never reflected on, and I became aware of the negative consequences it had brought into my life. I thought about the reasons why I was drinking, and I

¡Tomar Control! performing in Lima, 2017. Photo by Junior Dávila Córdoba.

realized that it was because I did not accept myself and I did not like who I was. I felt like a boring person, and I thought that alcohol would help me to become a person who was more fun. I realized that this didn't make sense and that it didn't contribute anything positive to my life. So I decided to quit, I got into hardcore punk, and from then on, it all seemed like a natural process; I didn't even realize how fast the time passed after I had become sober, and I no longer needed alcohol.

After some time, I understood that while straight edge was a personal decision, it is more than just personal implications. Society is made up of individuals, and if these individuals are dependent people who only wait for the weekend to spend all of their money to get drunk and forget their sadness, it has negative consequences for society. It affects their families, and they can be abusive in various ways. People who become dependent on more expensive drugs can kill you for a watch or a cell phone just to get their daily dose—and every one of their victims leaves children, mothers, and fathers in despair. The world of drugs is full of disastrous chain reaction. I believe that straight edge is a powerful weapon with which to engage in struggle.

In Europe and North America, people mainly talk about the negative effects of drug use. In Latin American countries, not least in Peru, you are also

35

dealing with the effects of people being involved in—and sometimes economically dependent on—producing drugs for consumers in the Global North. Can you talk a little about this?

The production of coca leaves in poor rural communities is increasing, but that would not be a problem if it wasn't that 90 percent of the production was for drug trafficking. The coca leaf itself is not a drug. It is a food native to the Andes and has fed the population for centuries. It contains protein, vitamins, and minerals, and is an effective natural medicine against a wide range of diseases. But the producers are in need of dealing with drug traffickers in order to survive. The government and NGOs have taken measures to train these producers in the cultivation of other crops, such as cocoa, but the presence of drug traffickers remains strong. Recently, the demand has even increased due to increased cocaine consumption in the US, Europe, and Asia.

Are there overlaps between straight edge in Peru—and perhaps in other Latin American countries—with broader social movements?

The xLa Malezax, which I mentioned before, is a good example. The collective is involved in many solidarity projects and does workshops on self-management and DIY distribution, which are free for everyone to attend. There are people from the hardcore punk scene (straight edge and non–straight edge) who play benefit shows for homeless shelters and poor people in rural areas. In Argentina, Colombia, and Chile, there are many benefit shows for causes reaching from supporting animal sanctuaries to raising money for friends in need.

What potential does straight edge have in Peru? Do you feel you are able to influence society? Does your message reach people outside the hardcore scene?

I think we need to have a stable hardcore punk scene before we can even discuss straight edge's potential. I don't know if I can influence society, but while I'm onstage I'll talk about straight edge and why it is important to me. And there might be someone among the audience to whom my words make sense and who will look for more information and form their own opinion.

Ideally, where will straight edge be in ten years from now? And, for that matter, in Peru?

Well, the straight edge in myself will last! I have it internalized, and it seems impossible that I change my mind because I am so sure about the decision I made. Now, straight edge as a movement? I think it will continue in Latin

America because, sadly, I believe that drugs will still be a big problem ten years from now. The bands will have to continue talking. In the case of Peru, I think it is difficult. There will still be straight edge people, but whether they will do much to spread it is another question. Within the next two to three years, we would need young people who are interested in it and motivated to build something that lasts over time.

¡Tomar Control!'s second album, Nunca más callar, *was released in February 2019.*

ACOUSTIC VEGAN STRAIGHT EDGE

Interview with Keegan Kuhn

Since 2008, Keegan Kuhn has been recording and touring with the acoustic vegan straight edge act xTrue Naturex. He codirected the acclaimed documentary films *Cowspiracy: The Sustainability Secret* (2014) and *What the Health* (2017) and runs the video production company First Spark Media.

Tell us about xTrue Naturex! Why did you decide to play acoustic music?
xTrue Naturex is an acoustic hardcore music project I created with the mission of promoting radical ideas of ecology, society, and ethics. Hardcore punk music has had, and continues to have, a tremendous impact on my life. The messages and ideas I found in hardcore have shaped the way I live my life and view of the world. I became straight edge and vegan because of hardcore bands like Earth Crisis, but I realized that unless people liked aggressive music they weren't going to listen and get these messages. Because of that I started messing around doing acoustic covers of some of my favorite vegan straight edge hardcore bands. I would take their lyrics and rewrite the melody to make it easier for people to listen.

I recorded a few of these covers and released them on MySpace back in the day, and it got a bunch of attention thanks to the band Gather, whose song "Total Liberation" I covered. It really took off from there, and I was able to tour internationally with the project for years.

I choose to do the project acoustic because I lived without consistent access to electricity most of the year back then and I liked the aesthetic of not needing "power" to make music. I was (still am) interested in ideas of radical ecology, and I like that we could play a show in a club as easily as we could in a forest.

When xTrue Naturex and other acoustic straight edge acts such as Mike XVX appeared, there was a general buzz around the so-called folk punk movement. Do you see a relation there, or was this purely coincidence?
The folk punk scene was alive and well when I started xTrue Naturex, but it wasn't really my scene. I loved the music, but so much of folk punk was about drinking and smoking and being a shitbag. Coming from hardcore, I wanted more of the hardcore scene in acoustic music and so I started to refer to xTrue Naturex as "acoustic hardcore." The acoustic music scene influenced by punk/hardcore is still going strong. There are super talented artists like Gab De La Vega who are creating amazingly beautiful music that carries the same sort of messages of hardcore but in a genre that most can enjoy. There are a ton of hardcore/punk musicians who have transitioned to doing acoustic music, and I love that!

What venues did you play at, and who was your major audience? Have you been able to reach beyond hardcore circles?
We would tour about six months out of the year and would play every single kind of venue out there. We played a lot of social centers, clubs, underground bars, squats, cafés, parks, festivals, houses—you name it, and we played it. I always loved playing shows in liberated spaces like squats because it was a way of illustrating that another way is possible.

Most of the people who came to our shows were vegan/straight edge kids. It started first just being hardcore kids, but slowly became more non-hardcore kids who were involved in activism of some kind. I was frustrated, though, that we didn't reach more people outside of activism circles.

You were known to tell stories at your shows and engage the audience in discussion. How would you sum up those experiences? I imagine they must have been very different depending on the venue and the audience.
I always wanted to use the music as a tool to speak about issues I felt are important. There is only so much information you can cram into a three-minute song, and so I always wanted to speak more between songs. The messages between songs at hardcore shows were/are always my favorite part

of a show. It was how you knew what a band was really about and how much thought they put into their lyrics.

With xTrue Naturex shows, I always wanted to create discussions. I or another member would speak and then try and get the audience to engage in a discussion. I wanted to get people comfortable with speaking up, so I would say super radical ideas to get a reaction from people. Sometimes it would work and we'd have amazing conversations all together and debates; other times it would be just a few people who would speak up. But I liked that people started to think about speaking up when something was being said that they didn't agree with. My favorite shows were when people really pushed backed and challenged me on my lyrics or ideas. It always made for a more entertaining show and made me grow as a person. If all we ever hear are people agreeing with us, where do we grow?

Doing these sort of shows gets really tough when you need a translator, but we still did it and had great responses. It was my favorite part of playing for sure.

I remember dropping a few bucks into a donation box at one of your shows almost a decade ago. I don't exactly remember what it was for, but I like to think it was for you working on the film *Cowspiracy*, which got much attention when it was released in 2014. Three years later, another film about the connections between our eating habits and natural devastation was released, *What the Health*. Tell us about these projects and what you are working on at the moment.

The donation box would have been for a nonprofit I started years ago called RESCUED. It was a farmed animal advocacy and open rescue organization with dreams of having a sanctuary. Sadly, RESCUED is no more. I was struggling to keep it going on my own and ended up working for other sanctuaries and rescue groups instead.

Part of RESCUED was doing undercover investigations where I wanted to raise the quality of investigation footage. I wanted to use higher-end gear and have cleaner images. I figured it was hard enough to get people to watch investigation footage, so we might as well make it visually easier to watch. I realize now this is the same logic behind xTrue Naturex: I want to take away all the excuses why someone won't listen or watch or learn about exploitation.

Through filming I realized that activist films really needed to step up their game. We have lots of well-intentioned activists with amazing hearts that want to make films but they don't take the time to learn how to use the

xTrue Naturex performing in Prague, Czech Republic, 2012. Photo by Hlava Derava.

tools of the trade, and so we end up with videos and films that just won't reach mainstream audiences. I really wanted to change that.

After doing my first feature-length documentary film called *Turlock*, about a small group of activists who saved over 4,400 animals in three days, I teamed up with a fellow activist/aspiring filmmaker, Kip Andersen, and we made the documentary *Cowspiracy: The Sustainability Secret*. *Cowspiracy* looked at the environmental impact of raising animals for food on the planet and why leading environmental organizations weren't talking about it. Amazingly, the film did really well! It has international distribution through Netflix and is translated into over twenty languages.

After the success of *Cowspiracy*, Kip and I made a film called *What the Health*, a documentary about the health implications of eating an animal-based diet and the benefits of eating a plant-based diet. That film also has had a tremendous response promoting veganism through Netflix.

After making these films I kept hearing people say that they couldn't be vegan because of some sport they do, which always frustrated me, so I made a film called *Running for Good* about three-time world record marathon runner Fiona Oakes, who is vegan. The film follows Fiona as she runs 250 kilometers through the Sahara Desert in six days in what has been called "the toughest foot race on earth."

I'm always working on something new.

Why did you decide to focus on filmmaking? Will we see more of xTrue Naturex one day?

I decided to put my attention into filmmaking because I felt like I wasn't able to reach as many people with xTrue Naturex. Music and film have influenced my life choices and so I have tried to use those mediums to do the same. I would play shows to between twenty and two hundred people each night, but with films I could reach so many more people so much quicker.

I've kept xTrue Naturex alive by doing the scores to my films and playing a few shows here and there. I have plans of doing a new xTrue Naturex record at some point, but it is a little tough to find the time these days.

Final question: What do you think the future for straight edge hardcore will look like? And what would you want it to look like?

I think the future of straight edge hardcore will go back to what it looked like in the early days. I think things are cyclical and that kids will become disillusioned with the fakeness of social media SXE. They will start to get more radical with their ideas again. I think SXE HC will circle back around to messages as it was in the early '90s, and I'm hoping to see that. I love bands that have a political message and are sober enough to articulate it. A strong idea in a sober mind is a powerful weapon.

"MORE THAN JUST WHITE-MALE-PRIVILEGED STRAIGHT EDGE HARDCORE PUNK"

xFirstWorldProblemx played as a band from 2012 to 2014. It consisted of Anna Vo (guitar and vocals), Sarah (guitar), and Andrea (drums).

On your Bandcamp page, the description reads: "xFWPx is a DIY feminist anarchist xVx all-lady social worker band from Vietnam/Aotearoa and Germany." This might very well be the most intriguing description of a straight edge band I've seen. Can you lay out the details for us?

Anna Vo: We all worked as social workers, and I think we all still do. This frames our perspective and work as people who are serving people and working for communities, instead of artists serving just ourselves. I think that is an important distinction to make, when much of hardcore, punk, or music in general can be just self-promotional. The rest means that Sarah and Andrea are from Germany, and Anna Vo was born in Aotearoa and is from Vietnam. Lastly, we have heard about so much abuse and assault coming from famous male hardcore vocalists and musicians, and to identify as femmes or ladies obviously speaks to an experience that might understand what it feels like to be objectified by or pushed out of the scene because of gender—and in my case, because of race and stereotypes around being an Asian immigrant.

Andrea: It was important for me to show that there is more than just white-male-privileged straight edge hardcore punk. There always were different

xFirstWorldProblemx performing in Berlin, 2013. Source: annavo.wordpress.com.

people and opinions and always will be. With these labels it's really easy to make these things visible. Political issues and community accountability are really important for me and frame my understanding of straight edge and hardcore punk more than just going to shows, "bro-ing up your life," or feeling better than other people because of being drug-free. I am always happy when I look at a lineup and there is a band with two or three adjectives that speak to me or that I can identify with—not least because it happens very rarely.

Can you explain the band's name?

Anna Vo: Andrea and I had noticed a lot of dude bands singing songs and lyrics complaining about specific problems—like someone saying something negative on the internet, or their ex-girlfriend not wanting to be friends anymore—and putting on a performance of anger and rage. We noticed that the anger and rage about "scene politics" and such didn't seem to be on the same scale as the anger and rage about genocide, fascism, systemic oppression, etc. So we wanted a name that referred to being in a band, playing music, and touring as a very "first world problem." This is in reference to a common saying that exists about problems that are not really problems when looking at a larger context. We wrote songs about feminism, independence from patriarchy, and the systemic racism that I was experiencing as an immigrant in Germany.

Andrea: I agree with Anna Vo. It feels kind of silly listening to people singing about being outsiders in this world and dealing with exclusion and apparent discrimination and oppression, when they are white hetero males in their twenties and obviously privileged. You can also see this in several hardcore punk movies and books, and it makes me angry and frustrated.

For me, the name also symbolizes the possibility to look outside the box in an intersectional way instead of just focusing on your own needs and feelings. This is what I would like to see in a perfect straight edge hardcore punk community, but it rarely exists. The expression "first world problem" should remind people of the diverse and complex problems people deal with.

xFirstWorldProblemx was fairly short-lived. What were your experiences playing in the band and touring? Did you feel any affiliation with the wider hardcore/straight edge scene?

Anna Vo: I think our shows were not attended as well as dude-band shows, we were not taken as seriously, and we were always put as the opener, even if other bands were newer or we were touring in another country. We received positive support from the Berlin straight edge scene, but they realized quickly that our music was a little less tough-guy and more doomy, which musically falls out of an official "straight edge hardcore" scene.

It always surprises and disappoints me when people are one-dimensional or attached to particular categories—as humans, we all transcend categories, with the understanding that many people can be many things at many times in their lives; especially in a subculture that proposes to be reflective or political, I would really hope that people think beyond what identities and subcultures they consume, and are more intentional about what they create and can change in the world, especially aspects that they see as unjust.

When we played the US, the shows were very well attended and we were appreciated, which to me shows a less classified and strict idea of genres, identity, and aesthetically driven punk subcultural rules. Lastly, my experience of living in Berlin and Germany as a whole was that conformity was valued and rewarded, but things that did not fit into categories easily were not easily consumed. Lyrics about racism and sexism were also not readily consumed by the majority of the hardcore scene—or the patriarchal crust, squat, doom, or D-beat scene—but the queer and feminist scene loved and appreciated what we were about.

Drawing by Anna Vo.

Andrea: I have to say that I have also had bad experiences within the straight edge scene. Simply being straight edge doesn't mean you are super cool. Some people are abusive and sexist. Some are rapists. I have been involved in the hardcore punk scene for ten years, most of them living drug-free, and I have never felt really safe or welcome, never felt that I belonged. That was true for when we played with xFirstWorldProblemx as well.

Sometimes it seemed we were accepted as a straight edge band but not because of our music, our lyrics, and the topics we stood for. But xFirstWorldProblemx was about so much more than just straight edge. In the end, I felt more respected and empowered in the feminist and queer (music) scene.

One poster described us as "all-girl Pussy Riot straight edge." What does that mean? That, if you are an active political woman in a band, you are like Pussy Riot? Both our music and content are so far away from that.

Sarah: Like Anna Vo, I always felt that we didn't really fit into any scene musically in Germany. And I felt the same way about the US shows.

The label straight edge was really important for me when I was younger. It helped me to not feel all alone in the small village I grew up in, with the only people I knew who didn't drink living 600 km away.

When we started xFirstWorldProblemx, the label was no longer that important to me. Maybe because at that point I knew more people who didn't drink. I still don't drink or do drugs, but that's just how it is. The queer-feminist scene was also more important to me than the straight edge scene.

Where do you see hardcore's and straight edge's strongest potentials?

Anna Vo: Using that tribal mentality to advocate for human, animal, and civil rights, and doing direct action work. Using that mob mentality, and the platform of being in bands, to fight misogyny and rape culture.

Andrea: Like Anna Vo said, I think it is good to find people who care about similar issues. Straight edge itself always talks (or preaches) about being active and wanting to change things. So let's start this ourselves and open our minds to fighting discrimination and oppression, because we are all part of it: as victims, perpetrators, or people who can open their mouth to speak. It's about organizing ourselves, and if people feel confident in a sober peer group, it can be the basis for becoming more active. I don't think it is crucial to be straight edge in order to be active, but it can give you more self-confidence. Furthermore, straight edge can help people with a tendency to be abusive when drunk or high to control their behavior.

Anna Vo, for many years you edited *Fix My Head*, **which I saw you describe as a "far-far-left DIY non-profit punk zine" and a "people-of-color focused publication." It might have been the most important zine coming out of hardcore in the last decade. You said that issue 10, released in 2017, was the final one. What did the zine mean for you and why did you decide to stop bringing it out?**

Anna Vo: It started with conversations about "DIY vs. capitalism" and "sexism in hardcore" seven or eight years ago, and then it moved to being an anarchist punks of color-centered zine for the last six to seven years, when very little existed around that conversation. Now, almost a decade later, those conversations are way more common due to the internet, evolution of feminism, and increased awareness of racism and privilege. I ended the zine because I feel like there are many political sources of the viewpoints of people of color currently. And I like even numbers: ten issues!

What have you all been doing musically since xFirstWorldProblemx?

Anna Vo: I run an antifa record label called An Out Recordings. And I have a solo project, playing lots of shows and fests locally. I am also in a few bands and have been performing poetry and stand-up comedy. I work as a trainer and radical educator about transformative justice, mental health, antiracism, and trauma. I am also in several activist groups. One related to hardcore is No! To Rape Culture PDX, which came out of a conversation around feminism and consent in hardcore.

Sarah: I played in two bands after xFirstWorldProblemx: guitar in Tall as Trees (Andrea was also in the band), and drums in Kaywinnet. Now I am taking a baby break. Let's see what happens after that.

Andrea: I played bass and screamed for years in the feminist grrrl band Respect My Fist. In Tall as Trees, an emo/screamo band, I played drums. Now I have a new band called Let's Start With A Forest Level. I also play drums in the queer feminist vegan straight edge band Eat My Fear, which, at the moment, is the most active. Some more stuff will come along in due time! Music is my life. It's the best way to express myself and to meet awesome people around the world. Let's hope for many more years to come!

2–0 TO THE ARSENAL

Interview with Kaila Stone

Kaila Stone is a lifelong Londoner and has played in innumerable hardcore, punk, and post-punk bands over the past decade. She can be found studying at Goldsmiths Library during the week and screaming at Arsenal through the television on the weekends.

Kaila (on bass) performing with Nekra at the Static Shock Weekend in London, 2017. Photo by David Garcerán.

In 2012, you did an interview for the zine *Fix My Head*. You had just turned twenty and said that you now had to "start building a life." How has that been going?

I was experiencing that weird late teenage feeling that you get where you feel like you should be really well-rounded and self-assured by the time you reach twenty. I was depressed, anxious, and really stressed out about being nowhere near feeling settled in my brain, or anywhere, and desperately wanted to just be a chill person. But, like a poetic racist once said, "these things take time," and all you can do is take it day by day. In the six years since, I've done a lot of cool things and feel really good about myself and my life. I'm halfway through a degree I'm really enjoying at Goldsmiths University, have plenty of spare time to spend with friends and loved ones, have fun playing in bands, and Arsenal have a striker worthy of wearing the number 14 shirt for the first time in a decade.

> From 1999 to 2007, Arsenal's number 14 was worn by the French striker Thierry Henry, one of the most popular Arsenal players of the Premier League era (from 1992). Since February 2018, the number 14 shirt is worn by the French-Gabonese striker Pierre-Emerick Aubameyang.

You also said you couldn't imagine living in London for the rest of your life. When will you be leaving? And where will you go?

My girlfriend has lived in London for the past couple of years but is originally from Stockholm and wants to go back home eventually. If I don't scare her off, I would love to go there with her and really challenge myself by living somewhere new. It's a really uncertain and particularly scary time in the UK, and it feels like it could be a good moment to push myself to seek change, which I am so averse to. It's bittersweet because great new veggie/vegan restaurants open up every couple of hours in London, and it seems silly to run away from them, but it's also an opportunity to try a different type of life.

You've been playing in numerous bands, Self Defense Family only being the one that's probably best known. Can you give us a rundown of all the musical projects you've been involved with?

Can't Relate was my first-ever band, which started in 2008, I believe. We all loved Minor Threat, Negative Approach, and Siege, and tried to rip them off as much as possible. Nick who played guitar in Can't Relate went on to play in one of the best UK straight edge bands for me, Violent Reaction. From 2010, I played in Ten Speed Bicycle with Tommy, who had also been in Can't

Relate, and Jimmy Wizard, who sings in Higher Power now. We were around during a big resurgence of '90s-emo-sounding bands in the UK, which was really cool. A lot of the bands overlapped and I was in a couple at the same time. Alongside Ten Speed Bicycle I played in a punk band called Tortura with some incredible women. I was already playing in Self Defense Family/ End of a Year at this point. After Tortura broke up, I started a new band called Dregs. Bryony who played guitar in Tortura (and one of UK's best bands, Good Throb) sang in that. One of our last gigs was with Negative Approach in 2015 (imagine how excited fifteen-year-old me was after ripping them off in my first band!), but we called it a day when Bryony moved to Australia not long after. I think that's it for past bands! At the moment, I play in Nekra and Child's Pose, who are both pretty new. Child's Pose is influenced by post-punk bands of old like Vain Aims and Kleenex. Nekra is a hardcore band!

What about xPelliarmusx, which you have described as a "Hogsmeade Straight Edge" band? Is that a very exclusive thing or can those of us who know nothing about Harry Potter still listen to it?

xPelliarmusx is an idea that came about in 2009 with my friend DBC (Breaking Point, Abolition, a bunch more). I started a "record label" called Kai's Mum Records and put out the Can't Relate tape and the Waste Away (pre-Abolition) demo. For the logo on different releases I used Edward from Twilight and Harry Potter from . . . yeah. So, we were talking about that and joking that we should start a jokey straight edge Harry Potter–themed band. "Butterbeer—no way! Hogsmeade Straight Edge here to stay." Then my friend Max Kuhn gifted me a drawing of Dobby with "Hogsmeade Straight Edge," which I posted online and now people who weren't around at that time think it is a real thing. It's probably a good thing that it isn't!

When I approached you about doing an interview for this book, you were hesitant because, and I quote, "not wanting to add my voice to an already bubbling pot of opinions." Can you tell us why?

Yeah, for the most part I just don't know what to say, haha. Like, if I'm at a pub watching the football with people I don't know very well, and they clock onto the fact that I'm just ordering lemonade or lime and sodas, people will usually jump on me and demand to know why. What traumatic alcohol or drug-related experience did I have that tragically forced me to avoid it altogether? Then I become the center of attention and people's attitudes towards me completely change. It sounds bizarre and over-the-top, but it does happen. I remember when my friends and I first claimed straight edge as teenagers at like thirteen or fourteen, older people would be like, "It's easy as a kid—when you're an adult the real test (nightmare) begins." It hasn't been a test as such, but it's just annoying to have the same conversation over and over again. When someone finds out that you abstain from something so prevalent in society, there's an intrigue and a need to question or even challenge it, which I just can't be bothered to deal with most of the time.

I'm also pretty wary of being seen, by default, as judgmental of people who aren't straight edge. Somewhat understandably, if people know you don't do something that they do, then they assume you look down on them for it. It comes up more within vegan/vegetarian circles in real life and online—that utter self-righteousness and lack of empathy for people who don't adhere to the same certain habits as you, with no room for understanding. I think it's a really awful way to be, and my aim in life is not to change the way anyone else lives, so I have little reason to shout from the rooftops about my own sobriety and dietary choices, you know?

So, if you had to give the least self-righteous explanation for being straight edge possible, what would it be?
I had one brief week of binge-drinking when I was twelve, and it just confirmed that that life wasn't for me. I tried it because my best friend had found this new group of kids who were a bit older than us and into house parties and stuff, and I was terrified of losing him because I wasn't doing that. I tried it, and it sucked for me. I think I got drunk once, and the rest of the time I was faking just to fit in with everyone else. I grew up around family members who had quite unhealthy relationships with drugs and alcohol, which definitely affected my own principles. I could see the joy it brought them, but also the pain, and very early on in my life I realized that I had no desire to partake. Even though I knew it didn't have to be as extreme/destructive an experience as I had witnessed, and I knew plenty of casual/dinner drinkers or whatever. But I just didn't care for it in any capacity. I felt scared about that because I wondered how I would ever make friends or fit into a world that seemed preoccupied with substances. Especially in London at that time for teenagers and adolescents it was such a rite of passage to get drunk, it was like a personality trait. But by the time I had claimed straight edge at thirteen years old, I had already decided that drinking wasn't for me. Finding the straight edge scene was a bonus! Bonding with other awkward weirdos who also didn't want to do that stuff and discovering an incredible global hardcore scene to obsess over and history to retrace.

As corny as it is, bands like One King Down, Earth Crisis, Chokehold, and Undertow really helped me get through my teenage years and reflect on myself and my politics and attitude in a way I personally wouldn't have been prompted to had I not fallen into that scene. The squat scene in London was really integral to that as well and my introduction to radical politics in general, but in terms of my sobriety it was really important for me to find that space as a depressed teenager and have a bunch of friends who I could be myself around without having to fake wanting to get drunk in Trafalgar Square.

As I've grown older that need for a network of other straight edge friends has dwindled. My friends don't make a big deal out of my sobriety and know that I'll gladly go to the pub for a soft drink to hang out, especially if there's a football game on. It feels less combative as it did when I was younger. And while I'll happily head bang to the riffs of some of the more militant straight edge bands, I don't share sentiments like "Kill your local drug dealer," and the shaming/condescension towards people with drug and alcohol addictions—or even casual drinkers/users of substances. I think that's a really ugly part of the subculture's elitism and really simplifies what is a complex and personal matter. Could talk about that for days but in short: I worry about myself and wish everyone else well, however they chose to live.

The UK seems to be at the forefront of pretty much any Western subcultural phenomenon, but it has never taken center stage when it comes to straight edge. Belgium seems to have better-known straight edge bands than England. Why is that? Can you enlighten us about the straight edge scene in the UK?

Yeah, UK straight edge has had its ups and downs since I've been going to shows, but I think there have been some really incredible periods. It's been great to see bands like Abolition and Violent Reaction push on and get recognition outside of their local scenes and across the pond. My earliest memories are of a band called OurxCause, which had Nick and Charlie from Violent Reaction, Arms Race, etc. in it, as well as Harry who sung in my first band Can't Relate. Can't Relate shared members with Abolition and that was like a core group of 16–19-year-old mates in the mid–late 2000s who were all straight edge, so there was a lot of enthusiasm.

I think Abolition deserve a lot of credit for igniting the flame and running with it. They were a really important band for a lot of people, old and new to hardcore/straight edge, especially as they were influenced by the metalcore of the '90s which was a reference that wasn't widely drawn from in the scene at the time. We mainly looked to the United States and Europe for bands to get into. I didn't learn about older UK straight edge bands like xCanaanx, The Break In, Harmony as One, and others till a while after from talking to people like Bod, who is a straight edge guy who has been going to punk shows in England since the '70s.

In the early 2010s, we had a few Edge Days, which were really well attended, and it was cool because the bands were all so varied, even if they shared members. My band Ten Speed Bicycle played one year and we were like an emo/pop band whose members all happened to be straight edge. Jimmy played guitar in that band but bass in Abolition. It wasn't a big deal what the sound was. It was a really exciting scene to be a part of and we really felt like we were involved in and contributing to something important after years of being new jacks and posers in the eyes of some of the gatekeepers of the scene whose words and stares stung us as teenagers!

Kaila's incomplete list of UK straight edge bands (with a lot of input from Ola, Quality Control HQ): Harmony as One, Hello Bastards, OurxCause, Waste Away, Abolition, The Legacy, xPelliarmusx, Guidance, Regiment, Break it Up, McDonalds, Inherit, In the Clear, Breaking Point, Never Again, Stab, xCanaanx, Obstruct, Age of Kali, The Break In, Regiment, Iron Curtain, Survival, Can't Relate, Shrapnel, Rated X, Reflect, Ten Speed Bicycle, xRepentencex, xCurraheex, Violent Reaction, True Vision, Sectarian Violence, Day of Rights, Shrapnel, Unjust, Speak Up, Insist, Standpoint, Payday, Firm Standing Law.

We must talk football before we end. You're an avid Arsenal fan. Fair enough. But what's really impressive is that you've played for the club as a teen. What was the experience like? And why did you stop?

Yeah, so I played for the Arsenal Ladies' under eleven and twelve teams, and it was incredible. I was one of a handful of girls at my primary school who played football, and one day when my mum came to pick me up from after-school club, a worker called Dwayne told her I was really good and I should trial for Arsenal. So my mum looked into it and drove me to Hertfordshire, outside of London, where a lot of Arsenal stuff is based, to attend the first trial. I think there were three in total, and hundreds of girls turned up until they whittled it down to the final squad for each year. It was a massive commitment from my mum, and I owe it all to her for making it possible. We lived on the Islington/Hackney border, so it was an hour and a half drive each way to get to training, matches, meetings, etc. I asked her to go through her e-mails to check the age I was playing, and she found this e-mail to her friend from November 9, 2004: "Well once more I'm in my usual hurry as got footy training with Kai soon. Literally as soon as she gets in (which will be quite soon) we merely have time to eat get ready and go. Training is in Stevenage, so you can imagine me through the rush hour traffic as training starts at 6."

The experience really changed my life. I was a very shy kid and the thing that brought me the most joy in life was football, playing it, watching it, talking about it, anything. So you can imagine how incredible it was to play for the team I supported and be exposed to this whole new world of other girls who loved football and weren't made fun of at school because of that. I gained a lot of confidence during those years. I played for a few other teams in Hertfordshire (Stevenage and Hatfield) for a couple of years after, but my mum's car broke down, she couldn't afford to repair it, and the dream ended. At that time there wasn't as many options for girls to play football even in London. It was quite concentrated in Hertfordshire.

Do you see any relation between your passions for football and straight edge? I've come up with plenty of fancy explanations myself—citing the 1920s workers' movement, in which both sports and sobriety played an important role, has been among the less obscure. But, in all honesty, it's probably just coincidence in my case. What would you say?
It's funny to think about the fact that my love for football means I spend a huge chunk of time in spaces where people don't expect sober people to be! I find myself in a pub or sports bar almost every week to watch Arsenal games cause a lime and soda or two a week is much cheaper than a full sports TV package. But a friend of mine recently started drinking after years of being straight edge and was taken aback at how many invitations he got to go to the pub for a drink within days of his first post-edge beer! He was like, "Why couldn't they have invited me when I didn't drink? That kinda sucks." And there's been so many instances where my friends have got really insecure around me in those settings and expressed that they were embarrassed to be drunk around me if we're in the pub a few hours after the football has finished and they've been caning it. But unless the vibe is really bad, annoying, or aggressive—I don't care! I love the pub, its history and atmosphere. It's one of the few places where you can properly connect with people in your community, and honestly the stories you hear in there are incredible. So I'm very grateful that my being straight edge isn't in conflict with spending time in those spaces and football is very much to thank for that. I know

a lot of straight edge people who can't stand the pub, but I'm happy I'm not one of them!

We have a contribution in this book by St. Pauli Straight Edge, a supporter group of the famed Hamburg club. How about Arsenal Straight Edge?
Tony Adams is sober, right? If he claims, we'll be two people strong! 2–0 to the Arsenal.

Tony Adams spent his entire career (1983–2002) at Arsenal, playing over five hundred games for the club. For many years, he was the team's captain. He also captained the English national team. After a long struggle with alcoholism, Adams became sober and, in the year 2000, founded the Sporting Chance Clinic for athletes recovering from addiction.

PINOY STRAIGHT EDGE

Interview with Tweety

Tweety is best known as the guitarist of the Philippine hardcore punk band Choke Cocoi. Occasionally, she plays with the straight edge hardcore band Staid. She has been part of the hardcore punk community Far South Resistance in Quezon Province since the 1990s. Today, she resides in Metro Manila and, like most people who inhabit the city, is busy working and juggling the demands of raising a child with her husband Butch.

The term "pinoy punk" is thrown around regularly when people discuss punk rock bands from the Philippines. What do you think of the term?
Pinoy punk music has its own identity and sound. It is full of anger and expresses huge disappointments. Most pinoy punk bands have lyrics about politics, government, corruption, etc. because of the great injustice we experience in our society. Each one of us has something to say and complain about because of all that is wrong with our government.

While punk rock culture in the Philippines has received a fair amount of international recognition, little is known about the straight edge scene on the islands. Can you provide us with a little history?
Straight edge in the Philippines took off in the late 1990s. The band Feud and the Takefour collective were very important for the scene. Takefour

Records was the first record label run by straight edge kids. They also did the zine *Conspiracy*.

Thanks to the efforts of the Takefour collective, straight edge remained strong until about 2010. They also managed to bring touring bands to the Philippines such as Vitamin X, Second Combat, and Have Heart.

Feud formed in 1997 and was always strongly political. As the first Filipino straight edge band, they were featured on the *More Than X on Our Hands* sampler, released by Commitment Records in 2000. Feud is still around, but not all members today are straight edge.

Tweety (right) performing with Staid, Manila, 2009. Photo by Dha Vereña.

When Feud lay low in 2008, their singer Raymond, Led from The Weapon, and I formed Staid. Other important straight edge bands included One Against All from Batangas Province, Mihara from Laguna Province, and Unforce and Bonded by Conviction from Quezon Province. Riot Kids was an important zine at the time.

Today, there are fewer straight edge bands, but several bands have straight edge members, such as Value Lasts, Prayer of Endurance, Veils, Indifference, Barred, and Clean Slate. Straight edge bands that regularly play shows at this point are Fortress and Move from Batangas Province, and Define from Laguna. A new and upcoming straight edge band is Collect whose members are based in Manila.

In 2003, the online platform Straightedge Pilipinas was founded. One of the founding members, Tin, organized the first Climate Action Festival in 2009 in Quezon City. It featured an exhibit on wastefulness and disposable lifestyle, vegetarian and vegan food was served, and ended with a hardcore show featuring bands like Staid, NFS, Mihara, and Crucial. Tin went on to win academic awards, and she is currently working on her research project about critical genealogy and institutional ethnography at the Metro Manila Flood Management Master Plan and Informal Settler Families (ISF) Housing Program.

Straight edge people have also made an impact in other ways, especially in the animal rights movement. They were behind the first animal rights march in the Philippines in August and run a clothing brand called Declaration of Purity.

Tweety (front) performing with Choke Cocoi, Quezon City, 2016. Photo by Keith Dador.

Most straight edge bands here in the Philippines are short-lived—not least because, like many Filipinos and Filipinas, many straight edge kids move abroad.

You are probably best known for playing in Choke Cocoi, and you've already mentioned Staid. What other bands have you played in? Which have been straight edge bands?

I have been in different bands since 1995, but most of them were short-lived. The first band I played with was UOM, a three-piece all-female punk band. Then I played guitar in the grindcore band Catalepsis and bass in the punk rock band Panchito's Way. Staid is the only straight edge band I have ever played in. We toured in different parts of the Philippines and in Malaysia.

In 2012, I stopped playing and focused on work and family. But in 2016, when Choke Cocoi decided to reunite, I agreed to be part of it.

We have common friends among Philippine anarchists. How political is the straight edge scene in the country?

The lives of Filipinos are fucked up. Most of us are poor, so boycotting big alcohol and tobacco companies by not consuming their products makes a difference. Not having vices in the Philippines is a matter of survival. People need their money to buy food. But pinoy straight edgers don't shove their beliefs down people's throats. I personally respect everyone's choices, and I hope they do the same. The only way that straight edge in the Philippines delivers its message is through music.

The Philippines' current president, Rodrigo Duterte, has made a name for himself by coming down hard on drug dealers and users. How do straight edge punks view his policies?

In my opinion, the present administration's approach is violent and inhumane. One afternoon, I was riding a jeepney and saw a parked jeep with the driver's seat covered in blood. The lady passenger said that the driver was killed by two men riding a motorcycle. No one knows why. People aren't even shocked anymore, and no one seems to care. It is apparently assumed that if gunmen kill someone, that person was a drug user or pusher. It seems that killing has become very easy in the Philippines. Who are these grim reapers taking away the lives of Filipinos? I don't want my kid to see this kind of horror.

You don't beat drug dealers and users by killing them. The president should focus more on programs that will keep the Filipinos away from drugs. Eliminating drugs starts with educating young individuals to stay away from them. Addiction should be cured, but the Philippines don't have enough facilities and rehabilitation centers, especially for the poor.

Children and poor Filipinos are being killed while the drug lords are still alive—where is the justice there? This country is so poor that some people engage in drug pushing just to have money for their family. People with money living in exclusive subdivisions can bribe the cops, go to a private rehab center, or travel abroad.

Unemployment, hunger, corruption, and population growth are big problems in the Philippines—drug use is only a small part of it. I don't understand why the "war on drugs" is such a priority. The president talks about it in every speech he delivers. He should focus on the causes instead!

Poor countries are the target of drug cartels because they can easily export drugs or set up a meth lab there due to corrupt officials. For example, who knows where all the confiscated drugs go? Nobody . . . There is a lot of work to be done. About the only good things that have come from the current government are the bans on street drinking and strict no-smoking policies.

What are your personal reasons for being straight edge? And do you think it has political significance? You have already hinted at that . . .

There was a point in my life when I stopped fooling myself. I understood that drinking alcohol and smoking did not have to be a part of my life. But I didn't become straight edge overnight, it was a process. Here in the Philippines, being straight edge is a bold move. I commend the people who remain straight edge in spite of pressure from family, friends, colleagues, and society. One of the largest beer companies in Asia-Pacific is here in the Philippines, and drinking is part of the Filipino Culture. It takes guts to break this norm. The big alcohol companies are protecting their businesses by establishing strong ties to politicians or by having managers run for office themselves. It's a vicious cycle. Poor Filipinos work in their factories and consume their products.

Based on your experiences from touring and having many international friends, what have your impressions of straight edge scenes outside of the Philippines been like?

I've had conversations with friends living in First World countries, sharing almost the same views, but I will never forget the conversations I've had with Ein of Second Combat. I met him in 2008, and I'm so amazed how far he's come with his straight edge principles. He started the Drug Free Youth project in Kuala Lumpur and is gaining positive responses and support from schools, NGOs, even government institutions. I wish the Filipinos would engage in programs that will keep them off using drugs! But our government doesn't have any good programs for the youth. It hadn't even recognized skateboarding as a sport before a young Filipina from Cebu won gold in the recent Asia Games!

I hope more Filipinos will realize that having no vices is a good choice in a poor country. You'll have fewer friends, for sure, but it doesn't mean your world will stop. There are better and more productive things to do in life.

What does the future hold for straight edge?

I hope that there will be more room for straight edge in the Philippines. Ten years ago, veganism was almost unheard of. Now it is widely embraced. This gives me hope for straight edge, too.

DRUG FREE YOUTH MALAYSIA

Interview with Khai Aziz

Khai Aziz, better known as Ein, is the singer of the Malaysian band Second Combat, founded in 1996 and a flagship of the straight edge movement in South East Asia. Ein has authored a straight edge punk autobiography (*Aku Anak Punk*, 2017) and founded the Drug Free Youth Malaysia project, a registered NGO since 2010. He regularly tours as a motivational speaker. The following interview—with the included introduction—appeared on April 20, 2015, on Unite Asia: Punk/Hardcore/Metal News from around Asia, a website run by Riz Farooqi, singer of the Hong Kong hardcore giants King Ly Chee (uniteasia.org).

2004 was the first time my band traveled to Kuala Lumpur to play. It was a life changing experience for myself and especially my band at the time. We arrived at a venue called Blue Planet and one of the first bands we saw destroy the venue with love and positivity—not mosh parts and breakdowns—was a band called Second x Combat: a straight edge youth-crew inspired hardcore band from Malaysia. What I was seeing in front of my very own eyes was the Malaysian/Muslim version of a hardcore scene. I will never forget that image—Ein the singer was completely surrounded by all sorts of Malaysian kids (punk, metal, hardcore) but especially Malaysian Muslim females wearing hijabs finger-pointing the lyrics he was spouting out. The equipment at that show wasn't loud enough to hear everything but the kids in attendance were screaming the words so loud that all I could hear and feel was immense passion for this thing called hardcore from everyone in attendance who whole heartedly believed in it.

Fast forward to 2015 and I consider Ein one of Asia's greatest hardcore representatives because of the path that he has found for himself. Not only that, but because he took the ideals of hardcore out of sweaty club shows and onto the actual streets trying to make a difference.

He started up an organization called Drug Free Youth Malaysia trying to impact and change the lives of hundreds of hundreds of people . . .

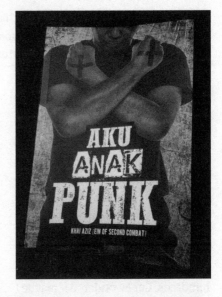

It is my immense honor to introduce Ein and his phenomenal work through this website . . .

Give us a background to yourself before you became the face of Drug Free Malaysia?

I'm 36 years old now. I got involved in punk in 1993 through skateboarding. I was introduced to hardcore in 1994 and that's when I started my first hardcore punk band called the Pistons. We played a few shows in our hometown and disbanded in 1996. Our favourite bands were Bad Religion, Black Flag and NOFX—that type of stuff. After that I started the band Second Combat which means one more fight. At the time we were certainly not a straight edge band because a few of the band members smoked weed and cigarettes including myself. The band was not very serious about music at the time either. That era had a *lot* of bands that sounded like us. So we decided to try something different and become a little more serious. We really got into bands like Minor Threat once we started listening to Dischord Records. We immediately changed and tried to mimic Minor Threat but of course we could never be like them. Eventually, we accidently created our own sound. In 2000 we became straight edge band when most of the band members decided to accept this lifestyle. We, as people in the band, were already facing a lot of drug issues within our own families so the whole idea of straight edge really made a lot of sense to us. We then decided to take this opportunity that we were given as musicians with access to a stage to inform other kids about the dangers of drugs and the many poisons of the world.

Currently I'm an active volunteer in a few NGOs like Untoxicated, MFADA, MAHA, MCTC and MASAC.

How did you go about starting Drug Free Malaysia and what was your inspiration to do this?

I was really inspired by the Straight Edge movement. I think it's something an important philosophy that needs to be promoted. It's been about 17 years that I've been talking to kids in the scene and in this time I have managed to inspire hundreds. But I wondered if maybe I could try a different way to promote the message. I've seen Toby Morse and how he promotes the drug free message through his One Life, One Chance organization and I thought to myself "Hey, I could do this!" It all really started for me in 2009 when I

Poster for Edge Day 2015 in Shah Alam, Malaysia.

was working at a college as a consultant. My job was to get students to enrol at the college where I worked. The college's main focus was to aid poorer children. Within my job requirements it was also part of my work to find sponsors to financially support students. So I had to find two things: students and sponsors. So I started thinking about trying to get these students through a similar format that Toby used by doing school talks. So that's what I did. At first, I was a bit messy and pretty nervous. I showed videos about drugs and about straight edge and started explaining it all to kids. After the talks I did a little survey by posing a simple question to the kids: what were you more interested in, baking bread or studying electricity? Through these surveys I managed to start getting students. But then I still had to figure out how to get the sponsors to sponsor these poor kids. The way I did that is a long story and I'll maybe explain that some other day.

After a while I had to quit this job and I started my own work. I studied how to open an organization and tried to figure it all out. That's where I started the Drug Free Youth Association with the intention to help educate kids with drug problems, alcohol/smoking addiction, and especially work with families from poorer backgrounds. Through the years the organization has gotten even more serious now with our focus shifting to prevention. Up until this date we have about 200 bands part of the organization and 5000 kids who have joined us!

Besides giving presentations, what else does your organization do?

We used to do charity programs but we've run out of two important resources: time and manpower. So we decided that to make this really work we have to combine forces with another organization which is what we did by working together with The Traveller Group to continue our commitment to charity work. We realized there were other problems on the streets that needed our help like homelessness, drug addiction, alcohol addiction, depression, poverty and so many others. Poverty was what brought them to the streets and begin their lives as drug addicts. The Traveller Group is run by my wife. She is more focused on problems such as homelessness, refugees, human rights, shelter and all kinds of things related to humanitarian issues. So as to not confuse all our volunteers we had to clearly divide the programs so that our assistance to different initiatives were clear especially to our volunteers who are putting in the time and effort. Now we are teaching school kids in our programs to help their communities. One of the programs that we are focusing on right now for the Traveller Group is building schools for the Somalian and Rohingya people. The great news is that the Somalian school is already up and running and is sustaining itself. We are currently working on building a Rohingya school but it has been a slow process because we are short of manpower.

Have you gotten support from Malaysia's hardcore scene?

One of my main objectives is to get the hardcore kids to come along. Most of them are older now and busy with other activities. I want to show them that this is what we should do because this is what we sing about in our songs! The way I see hardcore is that it is more than just music. It's about social change and a highly creative intelligent weapon that can cure problems. The bigger world outside our underground scene would certainly steal from us if they only knew the values that we fight for and hold dear. We have the best communities in the world that can't be broken by the mainstream. The hardcore I listened to was totally about change and empowering communities. Bands like New Winds, Morning Again, Catharsis, Larm, Man Lifting Banner, Seein Red were really inspiring because they turned music into revolution. They were the 90's hardcore. It's totally different from what bands are singing about nowadays. I'm a believer. I easily believe in things and if it's something that I fully understand then I will continue down that path and apply what I've learned. I believe in hardcore and its power to change the world. It has educated me and many others about worldwide problems. It also has the power to converge communities. It has connected me to the whole world. I can't believe somewhere in France and Mexico there are people who think like me. That's an element of hardcore that people can't put a price on especially when comparing to the world of the mainstream that teaches us to be materialistic and shallow.

I've gotten support from various underground scenes. People from hip hop, punk rock, indie, post rock, metalcore have all volunteered for my programs. For me it's good enough because I need trustworthy people in every scene to make this change. I actually need to clone myself a hundred times to help benefit this world.

Was there any backlash from people? If so, why?
Some people still don't understand the connection between music and the drug-free culture. They don't know the subcultures of this world such as punk rock, skinheads, straight edge, drug-free, vegetarianism, veganism, and so on. Drugs are not the popular issues that people want to talk about. The general public still thinks that we are a bunch of junkies in Malaysia because of the way we dress and look. To them we would be better off if we looked like Korean popstar idols.

It is a dangerous job and I think a lot of people feel threatened by us. At a few places we get a lot of hate from kids and sometimes we get threatened by communities where drugs are heavily used. At one place where we were holding an event our van was smashed by drug dealers. Sometimes our van tires get slashed by broken bottles. The most common thing that happens is our windows get smashed.

Then we also have the issue that some schools don't like the way we look. Some of our volunteers have colored hair, mohawks and/or long hair. Some of these schools don't allow our volunteers to enter their vicinity because of their hair. Basically, the Malaysian people are still living in the 80's. They basically want us to dress up like salesmen speaking to kids in a suit and tie to show them how "successful" we are.

But, all of these experiences have really thickened our skin and allowed us to build some strength and confidence especially when dealing with communities who do not welcome our assistance or presence.

Ein educating the youth. Private collection.

What is your main goal for Drug Free Malaysia and how can people help?
Our main goal is to get kids well informed and educated about tobacco, alcohol and drug abuse at schools. We keep trying to approach more schools but the resources are very limited. Only few schools have the means to stay informed. We want to go into rural areas where drugs like meth, marijuana, ketamin, karthong are very popular. Our ultimate plan one day is to have our own youth center where the youth can partake in positive activities like skateboarding, music, art and other sorts of educational experiences.

I highly recommend bands volunteer. By using their status to teach kids about the drug free lifestyle and activities, they can inspire so many more kids to go down this path. People can also donate money to us in order for us to have the means to go to schools and do workshops training kids to help their schools in solving community problems.

What's next for you and Drug Free Malaysia?
We plan to expand to Indonesia and the Philippines. We want to teach bands in Indonesia and Philippines to do the same thing as what we have done here. We want hardcore to be the catalyst to change lives not just by lyrics but by action.

I know this story is mainly about Drug Free Malaysia—but how can I not ask for a brief update about one of my favorite Asian hardcore bands! Give us a brief update of what's going on with Second Combat?
Haha, good one Riz! We're currently writing new songs for our last album next year. We plan to release a book and a discography for our 20th anniversary. Hopefully it all goes well.

Inshallah my friend!

FROM BELOW

xMontagx was one of the guitarists of the influential Colombian straight edge band Res Gestae (2001–2015).

Straight Edge in Colombia—stereotypes abound: drug cartels and the like. Enlighten us about daily life and how it impacts straight edge culture.
Well, we were all born in the 1980s, so our childhood was marked by the violence between the Medellín and Cali drug cartels. Some of us have stories of heavy drug consumption when we were young. Hardcore helped us to live through that, and straight edge offered us a new way of life. Some of us embraced straight edge culture at a young age to escape from a society that was terribly penetrated with drugs on different levels: in the streets, in social relationships, in habits, and in life aspirations.

Res Gestae was the first political straight edge band in Colombia. Please tell us about the band's history and its politics.
Res Gestae started around 2001. All of us came from the Bogotá DIY hardcore scene, but some members were additionally involved with anarchist organizations in the state universities of Bogotá, mainly with the *Coordinadora Libertaria Banderas Negras*. We played some shows with local punk and hardcore bands and released our first demo in 2002. We later recorded various albums and some songs for compilations and released a split with

La Vendetta (Colombia) and Yacopsae (Germany). From 2002 to 2013, we toured Colombia on various occasions, and in 2005 we played a number of shows in Brazil with our friends from Reacción Propia.

Our lyrics were centered on anticapitalist struggles, the denunciation of paramilitarism and police repression in Colombia, and the criticism of bourgeois society. We also did a lot of work as a band to defend LGBTI rights inside the punk/hc scene. We played fast and heavy hardcore punk and we used to label the band as "vegetarian anticapitalist straight edge."

All band members were straight edge, but we conceived it as a personal choice, a way of life that was really useful for left activism. We didn't care much about the "straight edge movement" and were seriously against all those people who used straight edge as a form of discrimination.

Res Gestae played a lot of shows to support local causes, like raising funds for political prisoners and anticapitalist organizations. Some band members participated in a collective called *Contracultura*, which organized an annual festival called "Odradek," mixing concerts with political activities related to anarchism, animal rights, and LGBTI rights. For some years, the whole band was also involved in a collective that organized film screenings and public debates in a barrio in Bogotá.

Can you give us a wider perspective on left-wing politics in Colombia, also to situate Res Gestae? The ELN and, particularly, the FARC are well-known among international radicals.

Left-wing politics in Colombia has been notoriously dominated by the Marxist-Leninist-Maoist tradition since the 1960s. Around 1964–65, two guerrillas were formed: FARC and ELN. A few years later, the EPL emerged, and in the 1970s, another guerrilla, called M-19, began their armed struggle. The country has suffered armed conflict for more than fifty years. During this time, paramilitary forces were formed and state terrorism was established. In this context of violence, which involved communist, anti-imperialist, and Maoist ideologies, little space was left for anarchist ideas and actions. However, when we played with Res Gestae, we managed to reach a lot of kids that were interested in anarchism, although we always labeled ourselves simply as "anticapitalist." We were never only involved with anarchist organizations. We wanted to work with different people involved in

Res Gestae's final show, Bogotá, February 2015.

broader left, popular, and grassroots organizing. Most important for us that their political work was *desde abajo*, "from below."

Can you say something about the guerrilla organizations' relation to the drug trade?

That is a really complicated subject, especially because the information is less than precise. We hope we can know more about it when FARC members begin to speak about it in the transitional justice process that will take place in the following years.

Let's turn to hardcore in Colombia. Can you give us a short history of it and describe the scene? How political is it?

The history of hardcore in Colombia is very odd, to say the least. It started in the late 1980s with a band that had openly right-wing lyrics, supported the military forces, and spoke about "social cleansing" in the streets of Bogotá. This band was strongly influenced by NYHC and very present for more than a decade. However, in 1996, new bands emerged and a hardcore scene with regular shows, different bands, and labels was founded. Santa Fe de Bogotá Hardcore (SBHC), as we called it, was still strongly influenced by NYHC, but also by the Victory and Revelation bands of the 1990s, and it was no longer associated with right-wing ideologies or practices.

By 1998, there were plenty of shows, some fanzines, a couple of labels, and thriving DIY scenes outside of Colombia. In the year 2001, some SBHC people got heavily involved with alterglobalization protests after visiting the hardcore scene in São Paulo, Brazil, and getting in touch with Catharsis and CrimethInc. They organized themselves with anarchists in one of Colombia's major public universities, and soon began to establish a new DIY hardcore punk scene that merged with the existing anarcho-punk scene in Bogotá. This caused new bands to appear, lyrics began to change, new fanzines were made, there were more DIY shows, and anticapitalist and animal liberation activism became really strong. The Colombian situation (social injustice, violence, repression, etc.) was increasingly addressed by the hardcore punk scene.

Why did Res Gestae end? Have any bands followed in your footsteps?
Our bass player, who was a founder of the band, left the country, and the rest of us decided that it was time to call it quits. Most of us were involved in other activities—political as well as personal stuff—and it felt natural to end the band. We did one last show in 2015, playing songs from our last album. It was really exciting. Anticapitalist straight edge is alive in Colombia!

BLACK X

Interview with MArk X Miller

MArk X Miller is a straight edge hardcore veteran living in Buffalo, New York. He currently plays in the band Black X, runs the *HMNI Fanzine Podcast*, and is well known for his photography of hardcore shows.

Mark, you have been involved in the straight edge scene for about twenty-five years. What changes have you observed? It seems to me that the scene has diversified a lot since about the year 2000. You don't have individual bands that define the entire scene, as it was pretty much the case in the 1980s and '90s. This goes for the music, the fashion, and the message. Straight edge today comes in many forms. Would you share this perception?
There seems to be a pretty diverse cross section of straight edge bands these days and there really isn't a sound or fashion that defines it all. One thing I've noticed today though is that many bands that are straight edge don't seem to wear it on their sleeves. Even Black X. I mean the name Black X might cause you to think we are a straight edge band, but we aren't one of those bands that X up and have a million different straight edge anthems and songs only about straight edge.

Why not?
Truthfully, I think it's because of inclusion, and also at forty, even though I'm straight edge for life, there are many more issues in the world today that I'd

72

MArk X Miller photographed by Jeff Barnes.

rather be writing about. Straight edge is a very personal choice that you either make or you don't. Social injustice affects all marginalized groups and we've got to do what we can to raise awareness of those issues. I'll fight crooked cops, but I don't need to fight to make people straight edge. It's not the goal.

In the 1990s, you did a zine called *Hi My Name Is*. In recent years, you revived it as a "fanzine podcast" under the acronym *HMNI*. Where did the idea come from, and how has it been going?
The podcast is called the *HMNI Fanzine Podcast*, named after the fanzine. I just kind of started it as a way to stay relevant and in touch. I've gotten to know some of the younger kids as a result of it. I love hardcore and I will do anything I can to help and promote it.

You also have a reputation as a terrific photographer of hardcore shows. Are you still taking pictures?
I do still take pictures wherever I get out to shows. Again, it's a good way for me to stay relevant. It makes it easier for me being the over-forty guy there when I'm actually contributing.

Thanks for the compliment and believing in my reputation! There may be some sort of publication of my photos in the works but it's in the very early stages of development.

Plagued with Rage, Buffalo, 1996. Photo by MArk X Miller.

You already mentioned your current band Black X. Tell us about it and explain the name!

Black X is a band that my old friends and I formed. We are a straight edge band and, more importantly, a band of friends. Chris and Eric were in a total Danzig-worship band called The Grail from here in Buffalo, and they've been in tons of bands before (Plagued with Rage, They Live, and Halfmast, among others). They wrote what became most of our demo after The Grail practices. They decided that I should sing over the tracks and I guess we were born. We asked our friend Bill and Jay to also be in it. Jay is from Buffalo but lives in Chicago. He did some time in Harm's Way and a few other bands as well as Plagued with Rage and Halfmast when he was in Buffalo. I had no idea how to write lyrics or anything, so Jay wrote the lyrics to four of our demo songs, but I've penned everything since. The name is kind of a joke. I'm black and we are a straight edge band. This the name Black X. All of our songs are either about Black or X!

The straight edge scene in North America has often been considered predominantly white, and I've heard you confirm this in interviews. Yet I've also heard you say that you found a "home" and a "community" there. Can you say more about this?

I guess a color doesn't make a community. Hardcore and straight edge are predominantly white but these are white folks that have my back. Many of my friends are antiracist and have come to blows with neo-Nazis and the like. Growing up, I never quite felt at home until I got into the hardcore scene. As soon as I fell in love with it, I haven't looked back. It's given me a voice and relevance that I don't think I personally could have gotten anywhere else.

In your opinion, what are the main barriers that have kept hardcore punk and straight edge predominantly white?

That's easy, because America at large is predominately white! That was a half joke, but I think it's because the artists and members of the scene are predominately white. Many people associate what something looks like with what they like and, apparently, if you are black you are only supposed to like black artists. I can't tell you the amount of times I've been looked at funny because of the choices I've made as far as the music that I like.

In a 2017 interview on *DIG: A History Podcast*, you said, and I quote, "I think it's a lot harder for someone from the inner city to adopt straight edge." I'm testing a thought here, but couldn't straight edge fit in with the politics of people organizing in inner cities? It seems that sobriety has been made an issue by several grassroots and community organizations both as a basis for struggle and in light of analyzing the drug industry as a means of oppression. Are there correlations here that might be worth exploring? Or is this a clueless European talking?

I didn't realize that you were European, haha. I think you are right about the ideology lining up, but I think the problem with straight edge and why so many people have dropped it is because it's an all or nothing thing. You either are or you aren't. That doesn't fit in with anyone's politics. Politics are—or at least used to be—about inclusion and compromise. There really isn't any room for compromise in straight edge. Many people see the issues addressed by straight edge, but they cherry-pick what they are for and against. I can't do that . . . In a recreational sense, for me all drugs and alcohol are bad.

On your Instagram account, there are a few pictures of you wearing an "I Can't Breathe" shirt, referencing the death of Eric Garner at the hands of New York City police officers. Do you feel that the Black Lives Matter movement had an impact on hardcore as well?

I think the BLM movement has touched everyone in America, the hardcore scene as well. The tough thing is that today not many bands are talking about things on stage. That is the one major thing the scene today is lacking.

There's no activism, generally speaking. I guess you could call straight edge activism in a way, but it's more of a personal thing.

What future do you see for hardcore punk and straight edge?

There's a lot of new bands spreading the message, so that's good. I'm assuming straight edge will be there right alongside its family members hardcore and punk and probably go the way that they go. It will always exist, and I'm glad I'm in a bit of a hotbed for it in Buffalo. The kids here are working hard to promote it and I couldn't be prouder. Hopefully, they keep it up—and the kids they inspire keep it up, too.

In an *HMNI* episode, you say that you still aspire to write the "ultimate straight edge anthem." What could a possible title be?

I haven't written it yet, so I don't know. It would be something kind of artistic. So it wouldn't be called "Straight Edge blah blah blah." It would probably be a little cryptic but have that great singalong hook. Hopefully!

ANARCHIST STRAIGHT EDGE HIP HOP

Interview with GAEA

GAEA is an anarchist straight edge hip hop act from Portugal. The protagonist is a longtime participant in the country's vegan straight edge scene and producer/distributor of political literature and vegan clothing. You can follow GAEA on Instagram at gaearreiro.

The first time I met you was at the London Anarchist Bookfair. I was excited to see someone selling straight-edge-related zines and badges. That was about ten years ago. Now you have just released your third hip hop CD. What has happened in between?

Yes, we met quite a long time ago and I remember your excitement when you saw that I was selling political Straight Edge zines, T-shirts, badges, patches, and stickers. I think that was the first year that I had a stall at the London Anarchist Bookfair. A few days later, I managed to go to V-Cross for a presentation of *Sober Living for the Revolution*, which I ended up selling through Brave Heart Distro.

Brave Heart Distro was founded in 1998 with just a few tapes and zines. Then it evolved into merch, accessories, books, magazines, patches, stickers, and more music. In 2007, I founded the label eco.nspiracy, which also released the GAEA CDs. I also screenprinted merch for the bands I've released, and in 2008 I decided to give a name to my screenprinting project, so Rise Clan was born as an Eco Vegan Straight Edge clothing brand. In

2012, I started an online vegan shop named Fair Fair and I released the first issue of my zine *Núcleo Duro*, which means "hardcore" in Portuguese. I got involved with an annual local vegan festival called Veganário Fest, booked shows with my friends from Nova Vaga Crew, played in two hardcore punk bands, xVenenox and AIM, and cooked and catered for events with my girlfriend in a project called The Revolution Starts in the Kitchen. In 2017, Rise Clan evolved from a vegan clothing brand into a vegan grocery shop—it also carries all the stuff I used to sell through Brave Heart Distro. At that point, I had to make serious decisions in my life because I was getting close to a burnout. I decided to focus on Rise Clan and GAEA and quit all my other projects. Now, I just want to print new designs, work at my shop, record new songs, release new albums, launch more video clips, tour the world, and travel as much as possible.

Why did you choose hip hop as a musical outlet?

I've always listened to rap, and in 2007 I decided to give it a try with a friend of mine. After a while we split up and ended up doing solo projects, but in 2012 I released my first EP. The second was released in 2015, and my first album was released in the summer of 2018.

I love boombap and I believe that rap is a more direct and effective way of communicating your thoughts, views, and feelings with other people. If we compare punk or hardcore to rap, the kids who have the first contact with it will understand the message and the lyrics more easily if they're not screamed at.

I grew up listening to punk, hardcore, rap, and metal. After so many years of playing in hardcore punk bands, I've decided to start rapping because I always followed the Hip Hop movement and really enjoyed writing lyrics. It took me 5 years to record a few songs but nowadays I'm taking this project more seriously.

What does GAEA stand for?

In Greek mythology, Gaea is the personification of the Earth and one of the primordial goddesses born from the void of chaos. Gaea is the ancestral mother of all life, the primal Mother Earth goddess. I'm not a religious person and I don't follow any religion, but I wanted to find a strong and meaningful name that represented radical ecology but wasn't obvious. I like mystic and mythological creatures and stories, so when GAEA came to mind, I knew it was the perfect name for this project.

At which venues do you play and who is your audience? Do you reach beyond regular hardcore circles?

Funnily enough, my first show was with other rappers at a vegan festival. Mostly, however, I play with punk and hardcore bands. I also play at vegan fairs, events, animal rights marches, and benefit shows. There are usually plenty of different bands. From time to time, I do hip hop gigs. I like all the experiences. I play indoors and outdoors, from squats to fancy venues.

In *Sober Living for the Revolution*, we had an interview with Bruno Teixeira from New Winds, one of Europe's most influential political straight edge bands of the early 2000s. What does the Portuguese straight edge scene look like today?

I grew up listening to X-Acto and New Winds and tons of other super cool bands. I ended up playing in New Winds at different periods of time. I never recorded anything with them, but I did the cool stuff: playing shows and touring.

In the mid-90s and early 2000s, straight edge was huge here in Portugal. I don't know what happened, but things changed. There's almost no new blood coming into the scene for sure. Fewer straight edge bands, fewer straight edge zines (unfortunately, there are hardly any zines published at this point), and therefore fewer straight edge kids. It's no longer common to see X'd-up kids at shows. I always rap with X's on my hands, and I really intend to keep on doing it.

To me, straight edge still makes as much sense as it did when I was a teenager. I try to keep contributing to the straight edge scene, both locally and worldwide. I do that with GAEA, with some of the designs I print for Rise Clan, and with my shop: its slogan reads "Choose Fire over Apathy," and underneath it says, "Dedicated to the Vegan Straight Edge."

You just released a video to the song "My Shoes," in which you talk about how much you love traveling. How has this shaped your view of the world and the role that straight edge plays in it?

I have always loved traveling. I dare say that traveling is what I love the most in life. I started traveling at a very young age because I went camping every summer with my parents and my sister. That was the highlight of the year. The first time I did a bigger trip I was twenty years old. I was invited to tour

GAEA on stage with Luís Luz, Lisbon, 2015. Photo by Luís Silvério.

with Time X, an old school straight edge hardcore band. After that trip, no one and nothing could stop me. I traveled to other countries and continents, with friends and by myself. I've hitchhiked, traveled by car, bus, train, and plane. I have also walked a lot. I lived in different places and my main goal always was to save enough money for my next adventure.

I learned a lot with every single trip and, like I say in my song: "My shoes have seen the world." They took me to a lot of different places, where I met a lot of different people, ate a lot of different food, and had a lot of different experiences. Traveling has opened my mind and taught me plenty every time.

I believe that I would be a different person if I hadn't traveled so much, and because of that I really want to keep traveling. Being straight edge and walking the Earth sober is great. I love to be aware all the time, to engage in every situation with a clear mind, and to live as simply as possible.

To hear about a place doesn't compare to the experience of actually visiting the place. During my trips, I have met a lot of other straight edge kids and it's always cool to hang out with like-minded people. But I've also been the only straight edge person in a group. There are many different dimensions to straight edge, but for me it's mainly about social security, simple living, and courage. I've seen people struggling with addiction pretty much everywhere I went. It's interesting to see what kind of substances they use and why, depending on the place. In my eyes, drugs will always have a negative impact on communities and societies because if we strip it down to its roots, it all comes down to violence.

Can you elaborate?

Human and animal exploitation are one of many consequences of drug dealing. Guns are some of the tools used for the protection of drug lords, king pins and street dealers. Prostitution and selling guns are two activities very often connected to the drug world. Drugs, legal or illegal, destroy entire families, kill their dreams, and are intentionally introduced in specific communities to numb their people one by one as it happened in most Native reserves in North America and also with Aboriginal communities in Australia, as a way to avoid the last line of defense to fight for their rights. Street fighting, night life ordeals, rape, domestic violence, road traffic accidents, and collisions are amplified by the consumption of drugs, all kinds of drugs. With this I'm not saying that violence doesn't exist without drugs, I'm just saying that drugs make the world more violent.

If you have to take a guess: What will straight edge look like in ten years from now?

In ten years from now, straight edge will be an app . . . No, seriously, I think a lot will change and maybe the essence might get dissolved along the way. The scene will change, the bands will change, the number of straight edge kids will change, but the meaning and the reasons for it will stay the same. I believe kids will keep on embracing straight edge if it makes sense to them.

Today, people listen to music in very different ways and at a very different pace. Kids are one click away from downloading pretty much all the songs from hardcore's history. There are almost no zines around, it's harder to find flyers at shows, hard to see X'd-up kids at street actions or protests—the scene is drastically changing. Maybe kids no longer have strong connections to the origins of straight edge anymore, but well, everything in life evolves. Straight edge will live on nonetheless. Certainly for me!

"FRIENDSHIP NEVER ENDS"

Interview with Eat My Fear

Eat My Fear came together as a band in Berlin in 2016. I interviewed the original members Andrzej (vocals and guitar), Adriessa (vocals and guitar), Dirk (bass), and Andrea (drums) in the fall of 2018. Dirk has since been replaced by Helena.

When I asked among my friends who to interview for this book, Eat My Fear was heavily recommended. What makes your band so important?

Adriessa: You need to ask your friends, but I guess there aren't many straight edge queercore bands. We are also all over thirty now, and our needs and perspectives might differ from younger people playing in hardcore bands.

How did Eat My Fear come together?

Andrzej: Andrea and I knew each other from playing shows and touring together. During one tour, when I was in Friend Crush, an all-trans emopunk band, and Andrea in xFirstWorldProblemx, we talked about how we would really love to be in a band that plays more classical hardcore.

Andrea: I definitely wanted to play an instrument in a hardcore band. Most importantly, however, I wanted to play regularly, which we couldn't do with FirstWorldProblem because Anna Vo, our guitarist, was in Germany only for short periods. Eat My Fear was the band I was looking for, and it is very important for me personally. Before we formed, the only bands I could identify with were bands like Beyond Pink, Pettybone, or Landverraad, who brought together the personal, the music, and the politics. But there weren't many such bands, and I didn't know any in Germany. All the concerts I went to, and all the concerts I organized, had almost exclusively white cis-guys on stage. This frustrated me a lot. Wasn't the hardcore straight edge scene supposed to be against sexism and racism? Why is it so hard to find bands who represent this and talk about it? And why did it take me years to find these amazing bands and people who I can share the same feelings and experiences with?

Adriessa: I arrived in Berlin just at the right time to join. I had left Brazil where I had been playing in Anti-Corpos for a long time. Anti-Corpos still exists since the other band members have also moved to Berlin.

Dirk: I knew Andrzej and Andrea from different bands. I heard that they were looking for a bass player and tried out. It worked.

Looking at your online presence, Eat My Fear is described as "vegan hardcore" and "queercore," but straight edge is missing. Why?

Adriessa: The straight edge bit is not so important for the band, even if it might be important personally. I stopped drinking when I came to Berlin. Alcohol and drug culture is very big in this city, and it seems easy to lose control if you don't stay away from it altogether. But it took a while for me to feel comfortable with the straight edge label. The straight edge scene in Brazil and all the "brotherhood" bullshit never spoke to me. I also identified as queer, which seemed to contradict being anything straight. But I appreciate the space that straight edge has created within the hardcore punk scene. It was fairly easy for me to stop drinking, because there was still so much cool stuff to do: go to shows, organize shows, play in bands, and so on. Other people who want to stop drinking might have to break with their social circles more radically. This can be very difficult.

Andrzej: The straight edge label always raises questions. I know quite a few people in the scene who don't want use it despite being sober. They don't want to be associated with the tough-guy nonsense. At the same time, our "Queer Edge" shirt is very popular. Queers come to us after our shows and tell us how hard it is for them to be part of the

queer scene because it's so much about hanging out in smoky bars, going to parties, and being expected to drink and take drugs.

I would love to see both the queer scene and the hardcore punk scene become more accessible for people who are now excluded because they can't or don't want to be in places where people smoke or get drunk or high. I hope to make a change by sending the message that being a queer punk can also mean living a drug-free life, and I hope to help other sober queer punks feel less alienated and alone.

Dirk: Straight edge for me is a personal choice. To be honest, I can't relate to a lot of things associated with straight edge. On the other hand, I do understand why people want to "reclaim" straight edge and try to connect it with emancipatory politics. I am always kind of in between.

Andrea: I realized the power that labels can have when we discussed how to present ourselves as a band. In some way, "hardcore punk band" seemed good enough, but then I remembered how excited I got every time I saw something like a "queer-feminist hardcore punk" band being announced. I always felt like: This is a band I really need to see! So, we do use some labels, but straight edge is not important enough for our politics to put it everywhere.

Andrzej: Besides, the advantages of labels only go so far. The message is the most important part. The first time that I heard a band tell people to stop dancing violently was a really important experience for me. This was in 2001—and the band was At the Drive-In.

The straight edge identity might not be so important for you as a band, but you have a song titled "It's Still Okay Not to Drink."
Adriessa: I wrote it because some people questioned my decision to no longer drink. What I wanted to say was:

"Look, I no longer drink, but I'm not subscribing to some exclusive ideology." Quite often people will ask: "If you don't drink, what are we going to do together?" My best friend asked me this when I decided to quit. But you can do anything!

Dirk: For me the song is also about doing things together rather than just going separate ways. Adriessa did a patch that says, "Friendship Never Ends," with one hand being X-ed up and another holding a beer. I really like that.

Who are the people you are addressing in "No Rescue Needed"? You speak, for example, of "assholes under the rainbow flag."

Andrea: We wrote that song after I had come back from Fluff Fest in the Czech Republic. I was really angry about all those guys I know who said sexist things and treated women badly but wore antisexist patches and sat under rainbow flags. What the fuck?

Andrzej: It's also a song against tokenizing. We experience that quite a lot. Promoters ask us to play at their shows because they want some people on stage who are not cis-men. Sometimes it might just look better for them, and sometimes the intentions might be really good, but it always feels weird.

I find it interesting that people can be very critical of the hardcore scene yet still remain committed to it. They look for "different kinds" of hardcore bands rather than something different altogether. What ties you to the scene?

Adriessa: I love the music. I've been listening to Sepultura since I was eight years old. Hardcore is a mixture of metal and punk. It also raises important issues such as anarchism and feminism, even if there are many contradictions and people can't live up to the ideals. When I go to a show where the only women I see sell patches, I don't feel I don't belong there; I want to change things.

Andrzej: In fact, I never wanted to be in a "different kind" of hardcore band. I have always just wanted to be myself. The mentality in hardcore can be very narrow-minded. I loved how emo changed the image of masculinity in the 1990s. We are all vulnerable, and we all need to find out who we are and what we feel comfortable with. Hardcore allows me to put my experiences into words and to express my feelings. All of the sexism, homophobia, trans-discrimination, and the rape culture we are confronted with, also within the scene, causes me a lot of pain and anger. But if I just screamed while walking the streets, people would look at me strange, judge me, and maybe call the police. In hardcore, I can scream as much as I want; it's an important emotional release. I can also say what I want between the songs we are playing. After every show, people come up to me and thank me for things I have said. It can make a difference for them. This is very beautiful and empowering. It's important not to feel alone in the shit we're experiencing. By sharing our experiences and by understanding how they are connected, we can try to make a change. This is much easier if we do it together rather than if we have everyone fighting for themselves.

Andrea: Hardcore was certainly empowering for me. I had a difficult time growing up. My youth was affected by rape, depression, eating disorders, and addiction. The DIY ethos of hardcore made me for the first time feel that I could do things, that I could be somebody. I had never felt like that before, and it changed my life profoundly. When I formed a feminist straight edge crew with two friends, it was mainly for fun, but we got a strong sense of being able to do whatever we wanted.

It is true that, at one point, I became very frustrated with the hardcore scene. The sexism and the talk about "brotherhood" brought back many painful experiences, and I no longer wanted to have anything to do with it. I went through a rough time again, but after some years I started to go back to shows, met new and really awesome people, and then xFirstWorldProblemx and Eat My Fear entered my life. Despite everything, I feel there is hope!

How strong are your ties to the straight edge scene?

Andrea: I don't know many people from the scene and never really felt welcome. I don't think we're even part of that. I think we've played one straight edge show.

Andrzej: It sometimes feels that we're not invited because we criticize the scene. Maybe people think we wouldn't want to play at their shows anyway.

Folks might feel threatened by you pointing out the contradictions and problems of the scene. Thinking that you wouldn't want to play at their shows is an easy way to avoid dealing with them.

Andrzej: Maybe. But it means that it's very hard for us to leave the queer-feminist bubble. That bubble is great, but I never wanted to be limited to it.

Adriessa: It might be ironic, but we tend to connect better with drunk punks. We get weird reactions when we play in front of typical hardcore crowds. I remember a show where Andrzej talked about rape culture within the scene, and when they were done, the entire room was silent. It felt like we were at a funeral. Afterwards, some guy came up to us and said that "it was okay" to talk about these things. What the fuck does that mean?

Andrzej, in *Sober Living for the Revolution*, Jenni of Emancypunx talked about your former band Störenfrieda, and we had a photo of you and your "Sisterhood" tattoo. It sometimes seems that people think transgender identities render the notion of sisterhood obsolete. This confuses me. Can you say something about that?

Andrzej: The tattoo is very meaningful to me. My sister has the same. For me, sisterhood means standing against misogyny; it is not detached from trans struggles, as long as you fight side by side with your sisters, not just your "cis-ters."

I heard that your next 7-inch will be co-released by Refuse and Emancypunx.

Andrzej: Yes, they haven't done many co-releases. I'm very excited! Emancypunx' X The Sisterhood X compilation was extremely important to me. It made me, for the very first time, feel visible as a non-cis-guy in the straight edge community. I played in Störenfrieda at the time, and Störenfrieda was a straight edge band. But we always felt quite lonely—at straight edge shows for being the only band with female and queer members and at feminist shows for being the only straight edge band.

I think this is an important reason for why I'm so excited about Emancypunx and Refuse collaborating to bring out our record. Emancypunx reaches the feminist community and Refuse the straight edge community. I hope that this will illustrate that feminism and straight edge can be connected.

The release also feels very special because I have always admired Jenni of Emancypunx for all the activism she's doing, and especially for having created a space for women and queers in the hardcore punk scene. I always hoped that one of my bands would be released by Emancypunx!

Any plans beyond that?
Adriessa: Playing as much as we can!
Dirk: Sadly, this is also the reason why I have to leave the band. I can't play that much since I'm trying to finish my dissertation on classism.
Andrzej: The new band member might not be straight edge. Some people already told us that we no longer will be a straight edge band then.

How tragic! But seriously: I guess the only real disadvantage with that is the question of representation. It can send an important message to people if they see you as a straight edge band.
Adriessa: Yes, it would be nice to find someone who is straight edge. But what's more important: to have a good and active person in the band or anyone just because they are straight edge?

"NOT GAY AS IN HAPPY BUT QUEER AS IN FUCK YOU"

Interview with Jara Pohjonen

Jara Pohjonen lives in Turku on the southwest coast of Finland. She has been active in the Finnish political hardcore punk scene since the mid-90s. In 2006, she cofounded the queer edge band Species Traitor, in which she played guitar and was the primary songwriter. After Species Traitor disbanded in 2016, she joined the queer edge band Raivoraittius (founded in 2011) as a drummer. Both bands have been influential in queering the Finnish hardcore scene and creating visibility for queer and gender-nonconforming punks. Today, when not dj'ing, hosting danceoke parties at DIY queer clubs, or playing queer punk and metal with friends, she spends her time organizing free all-ages gigs and other cultural and political events at a vegan queer feminist book café co-op in the center of her hometown.

Can you tell us about your bands Species Traitor and Raivoraittius? I understand there is some personal overlap, but they are separate bands. What are the main differences?

We all got to know each other through the local punk and anarchist scenes, as both bands were based in Turku. When one of our members was asked to leave Species Traitor, he went on to form Raivoraittius. However, in 2016 the other Raivoraittius members decided they didn't want to play with him either, due to his unpredictable and insensitive behavior. They asked if I'd like to join the band, and I did.

An obvious difference is that the lyrics of Species Traitor are all in English, whereas Raivoraittius sings mainly in Finnish. With Species Traitor, we discussed our lyrics collectively, but I was the one who mostly wrote them down. It's much easier for me to write in English, because in Finnish I sound very pretentious. Being so used to hearing lyrics in English gives you a sort of free pass to come up with sillier lines than you would in your native language. But more importantly, words and concepts that would sound very academic and difficult in Finnish are more or less common in English, such as "intersectionality"; even if you are not familiar with the concept's political and theoretical use, it still has conceivable everyday meaning as a word. It's very different in Finnish, where most contemporary concepts—including "queer"—are not translated at all.

There are slight musical differences, too. Species Traitor songs are a bit more complex and experimental. We were influenced by so many different subgenres of punk, metal, and hard rock that pretty much all of our songs ended up sounding very different. Raivoraittius plays more straightforward old-school hardcore, with some '90s vegan straight edge influence. It can be pretty chaotic, especially live.

Can you explain the names?

"Raivoraittius" is an old Finnish term for teetotalism. It combines the words "rage" and "sobriety." I always thought it was an amazingly fitting name for a straight edge punk band singing in Finnish, so when I was asked to join, one of my conditions was to keep the name. A few years before I joined, I filled in at a show together with their former bass player, who was no longer straight edge. That night, we called the band Kohtuukäyttö, which means "Moderate Use."

Cover for the Raivoraittius album *Hidas räjähdys* ("Slow Explosion"), 2015. Art by Raivoraittius singer Pääsky Piikkilä.

The name "Species Traitor" was inspired by critical race theory, in particular discussions around the New Abolitionist journal *Race Traitor* and the critique of white privilege. Identifying as an antihumanist vegan straight edge band, we liked the concept of species as our starting point, but, mainly, the name was about privilege and how to recognize and address it. This ambition is expressed in most of our lyrics as well.

Where would you place the bands in the Finnish underground music scene? They seem hard to categorize if we stick to a strict separation between genres.
Both bands have played at a wide variety of events and spaces, ranging from street demonstrations to art galleries. But both bands have also been strongly rooted in the DIY punk scene. Camille, guitarist and founding member of Raivoraittius, often talks about the importance of context, and considers things that can be clearly categorized rarely very interesting. I agree at least with the thing about context.

One major incentive for the formation of Species Traitor was that there didn't seem to be queer and femme folks playing the heavier "new school" music of the 1990s. At least we didn't know of any. We liked the music but hated the scene with all its cis-hetero macho posturing and toxicity, so playing "their music" while looking and living the way we did was our attempt to disrupt and confront the macho scene. A safer and more inclusive environment for doing heavy hardcore, not just for us but for others like us as well, was a major concern from the very beginning.

Have you found that environment?
I think we have. At first, among our own group of friends, but later within the broader radical queer community.

The formative years of Species Traitor were the years when queer anarchism burst into the Finnish political scene. In 2007, the Pink Black Bloc marched for the first time in protest against the commercialism and assimilationism of Helsinki Pride. The next year, radical queer activism got a lot of public visibility due to provocative Pink Black Bloc slogans such as "Death to hetero culture!" This caused quite a conflict with the consumerist and capitalist mainstream gay and lesbian community.

Queer feminist DIY clubs and festivals started popping up in Helsinki, Turku, and Tampere, and queer and trans issues made their way into anarchist workshops and gatherings. In 2013, Species Traitor members were asked to write a report on the Finnish queer punk scene for the queer issue (no. 368) of *Maximum Rocknroll*, and in 2014 we organized the first ever queer punk tour in Finland, together with Raivoraittius and some other friends. We named it "Queer Punx Night Out" and chose the motto "It's time to destroy cisheteropatriarchy!" I made a zine by the same name.

Turku queer edge crew representing at Kirjakahvila. Photo by Jara Pohjonen.

It has certainly become easier to be openly queer and trans in the scene, and nowadays I have much more confidence and courage to get on stage than I did throughout the 1990s and most of the 2000s.

Has sobriety played any role in all this?

Even though a lot of the people we've networked and collaborated with have been straight edge—or, at least, substance-free—I have little experience with specifically straight edge or sober spaces. I've kept my distance after the Finnish scene went macho in the late 1990s, and I've only ever played at one straight edge gig: with Raivoraittius at the 2017 Edge Day show in Stockholm, organized by Stockholm Straight Edge. Most of our gigs have been at queer feminist and other political events, where alcohol was consumed. So when I speak of a safer environment, it's mainly about organizers and workers at venues recognizing issues of accountability and not tolerating offensive behavior; it's about queer, feminist, and anarchist principles and politics of community.

For the last ten years, one extremely important space for Species Traitor, Raivoraittius, and the entire vegan, queer punk, and sober queer community in our hometown has been Kirjakahvila, a volunteer-run anticapitalist book café. Most of us have been active there for years. Established by anarchist and leftist university students and squatters in 1981, it went vegan in 2008, and gradually turned back to its anarchist roots. During the 2010s, it became increasingly queer. Even though Kirjakahvila is not alcohol-free, many of the volunteers are straight/queer edge or otherwise sober. There are even a few revolutionary pro–straight edge posters on the walls. Since 2013, all events have been free, and, in 2015, we implemented an all-ages policy. In fact, I've discussed your questions with friends there and received great input. The importance of radical, and radically sensitive, spaces like this—for sober and nonsober people alike—can't be emphasized enough. We are losing way too many of them!

Species Traitor was labeled queer edge, and in an interview Camille called Raivoraittius queer edge and transcore. Can you explain that?
Queer edge recognizes that drugs play a big role in queer party culture and that sober queers often feel excluded and alienated in queer spaces. But in Species Traitor, we understood queer edge as something more than just to be queer and substance-free, or to critique the cis-heteronormativity of straight edge. The idea of a lifelong commitment—a common feature in straight edge—implies a vow that must not be broken. And if it is, it proves that you never were really committed in the first place. The Species Traitor song "A Lifetime of Choices" tried to turn such rigid thinking around, saying that queer edge was about *choices* in the plural—not one choice ruling out all others. We were more interested in, as the lyrics suggest, "strange encounters in uncharted territories," and in decisions made based on the specific situation we'd find ourselves in. You can't reduce the complexity of human beings—of being human—to some fixed, binary, either-or categories. Ideals of purity and strength, strict rules, and demands for uniformity can quickly become borderline fascist.

I see queer edge as a critique of normativity, as the embracing of ambiguity and change. It's not an identity—queer theory doesn't understand queer as an identity either—and it's not about an individual betterment of the self. It is about transformation and creation, cooperation and collectivity, surprise and, not least, failure. My OCPD (obsessive-compulsive personality disorder) is trying to shut me down while writing this, but it's really okay to be wrong. You can embrace failure, even if there isn't much space for that in straight edge circles that deem themselves the straightest.

I asked the other Raivoraittius members how they would respond to this, and Camille said that she likes the terms "queer edge" and "transcore" because they both reclaim and invert concepts such as straight edge and hardcore: they challenge the masculinity that was originally implied but hold on to the aesthetic essence. We aren't your standard XtoughieX stuff, we are XsissiesX.

In a Species Traitor interview from 2014, you were talking about metal influences and called Judas Priest "more gay than queer." Is this about a generational change? How important was the influence of Judas Priest— and metal in general—on you?

I wouldn't say that it's generational per se, as there have been plenty of radicals within the gender and sexuality spectrum for decades. It's just that based on what Judas Priest singer Rob Halford has said in interviews and such, he comes across as a plain old assimilationist gay dude vouching for the normalcy of the homo. We are more of the "not-gay-as-in-happy-but-queer-as-in-fuck-you" school. As a curious side note, Halford has been sober and drug-free since 1986. He's not straight edge, though, just Christian.

I was listening to old-school heavy metal long before I found punk and hardcore. When I was growing up in the 1980s, I got into bands like Judas Priest and Black Sabbath and the so-called New Wave of British Heavy Metal. A working-class kid with working-class tastes, I guess, but I also looked up to my older sister, who introduced me to stuff like that. (Perhaps this is a good moment to reflect on just how middle-class Finnish hardcore, and especially straight edge, is. For a long time, I thought that all anarchists and hardcore punks shared my poor working-class background. Why else would they talk so much about class struggle and social hierarchies?) A decade later, I found old-school doom metal, again more of the working-class variety. I never really got to appreciate the so-called extreme metal styles that much— except black metal, which has serious problems—and I always hated the local metal scenes. But when it comes to my songwriting, there is certainly a lot of metal influence.

How important has the straight edge part been for Species Traitor and Raivoraittius?

I remember that back in the mid-90s, when I stopped doing intoxicants of any kind, I didn't want to call myself straight edge because I didn't want to reduce a political choice to an identity. I was even reluctant to call myself vegan, because I thought that it would direct the focus too much on myself instead of the oppressive speciesist system I wanted to struggle against. (The Species Traitor song "Fighting the Plague of Identitarian Veganism," with its pompous faux macho title and all, addresses this question in terms of consumerist identity vs. political action, and criticizes the idea of the activist hero.) Compared to veganism, I considered straight edge more of a personal choice, at least for myself: substance abuse doesn't necessarily affect anyone apart from yourself, while animal abuse always and automatically does.

When Species Traitor started, we spelled our name with X's, both to distance ourselves from the anarcho-primitivist journal of the same name (we didn't like anarcho-primitivism at all) and to make our stance as an edge band known. After all, we hardly looked like your regular straight edge crew. Since the whole point of Species Traitor was to be a different kind of straight edge band, we felt that it was important to make sure our sobriety was really visible, too. I don't think that it would have been acknowledged otherwise, with us looking the way we did and playing crusty punk and metal to mostly drunk audiences. We handed out lyric sheets at our shows and, when able to overcome our shyness and insecurity on stage, said a word or two between songs. We even started X-ing our hands, which felt super silly and very awkward, at least to me and our bass player Ninni, who always shared my dislike of scene identity markers. So, yes, being a straight edge band was important for Species Traitor, but most important was being a *feminist and queer straight edge* band.

I think it was pretty much the same with Raivoraittius. Camille says that it was important for her to challenge intoxication culture because it played such a big role in the lives of many of her friends. People were so passive, just drinking and doing nothing. But Raivoraittius has always had a broader political outlook as well, and straight edge alone has never defined the band.

How is straight related to your own politics?

Some say that a sober mind creates more accurate social analysis than an intoxicated one. There are also those who claim that alcohol just pacifies people and ruins revolutions. I don't know, there are many cases in which alcohol and drugs have played a major role in inciting people to revolutionary action and helping them overcome their fears, not to mention the more personal and social benefits of moderate use if you are shy and socially insecure. Authorities have historically tended to discredit unruly working-class uprisings as confused chaos brought upon by drunken lowlifes, so, to some extent, we're facing a class issue here as well.

However, the question of safety is an important one, both in terms of interpersonal relationships and security culture. People are more prone to mistakes and accidents when they are drunk—this reaches from outing people as queer to revealing too much to the cops to blowing themselves up. Maarit, one of the vocalists of Species Traitor, cites this as the reason why she went straight edge: she didn't feel safe going to demonstrations anymore because people were so drunk and behaved so erratically.

In certain situations, being wasted can indeed be a serious problem. I've seen queer feminists, who fight against toxic masculinity in their everyday lives, become oblivious to certain things when drinking or doing drugs—for example, when their big, tough-guy friends turn aggro after too many beers and start to throw around chairs in a so-called safer space, because they're at a punk gig and "need to blow off some steam." It then becomes really difficult to call out such behavior since people either don't remember or don't take it seriously or are in denial. Whenever that happens, I catch myself thinking: "Why can't everyone just be sober—it would make things so much easier!" But then I think of all the times when similar—or worse—things happen among sober people. So, being sober is not enough. It can make accountability easier, but it's far from guaranteed.

Quitting going to bars and spending money on cigarettes can free a lot of your time and resources, which can go into political action—or just survival, but survival is a political act as well. I don't know if I really like to think of political action in terms of efficiency and a capitalist work ethic, though. Personally, it hasn't helped me to overthrow any oppressive regimes, I just have more time to play board games and procrastinate.

I would say, however, that being part of a substance-free community can help you survive, which, in turn, can help extend that community and help yet more people survive. Building community based on solidarity and care is a bold political move in this individualistic capitalist society.

In a 2018 Raivoraittius interview with the London Bent Fest zine crew, Camille calls mental health issues your main concern as a band. Can you explain this?
We are often asked about the difficulties we face as queer and trans folks in predominantly straight and cis environments. We have, of course, been confronted with the occasional homo/transphobic slur, and misgendering can lead to devastating anxiety attacks in spaces we're not familiar with.

But gender and sexual discrimination hasn't actually been our biggest problem. With Raivoraittius (and to some extent with Species Traitor, too), our biggest problem has been the inability to handle everything that is expected of us within the punk community. We aren't always coping that well and can't be as accommodating as most punks. This is what Camille referred to in the interview.

Personally, I have been diagnosed with OCPD, which has effectively prevented me from finishing any personal projects for decades now—including the Species Traitor albums that we recorded in 2014! But both Species Traitor and Raivoraittius have had members suffering from severe depression and anxiety, too. The noise, the lack of proper food and rest, and especially the uncertainties that come with playing punk gigs and touring can be very intimidating and triggering to some of us. It's quite common that gig organizers are not entirely clear about details such as when and where to get food (if there even is food), and whether or not they have secured a place to sleep. You might think that's not a big deal for a punk band and that punks can sleep anywhere, but for sober people who have to cope with panic attacks it's a huge fucking deal. In fact, we have stopped doing extended tours. When Raivoraittius was invited to play at Bent Fest, we just went to the UK for that one show, even though it would have been economically and environmentally more sensible to play a few gigs along the way.

The same interview raises the question of how to best take care of yourself and others. Can straight edge help?
Sobriety is—or at least can be—mental health self-care, and it's easier to hold on to it when you are surrounded by others who are sober, too. So, straight edge can help as a culture that provides a framework for being substance-free; not just out of necessity (for example in the case of a prior addiction or medical condition), but of your own choosing. Also, sober people don't behave quite as erratically as people who are drunk, and even if mistakes are made, communication is easier. It just feels safer. But I don't think that straight edge helps if it becomes a doctrine; something you have to follow to be "pure." I think it actually becomes a problem then.

You mentioned the difficulties of touring, but you did tour quite a bit with both bands. What have your experiences been like?
All in all, our experiences have been mostly on the positive side. Or, let's say we prefer to emphasize the positive aspects of touring: all the nice people we met (and wouldn't have met otherwise), all the beautiful networks we have become part of. The sober queer punk niche is so tiny that you have to cover a lot of distance in order to meet like-minded people. For me, touring with a band also opens up possibilities to see a bit more of the world, because I can't afford to travel on my own.

Really important for us has been the largely sober Swedish queer and trans punk scene. When Species Traitor started out, there was no queer punk scene to speak of in Finland, certainly not a sober one. We pretty much felt out of place wherever we played. But a couple of years after putting out

the *Silence Equals Death* tape, we came across a Swedish punk zine with an autobiographical comic, in which the author falls back in love with hardcore listening to our tape. Around that same time, we came across a sticker featuring disco dancing queer punks, one of whom was wearing a Species Traitor shirt (one that, in reality, we didn't have). In both cases, the artist was Ane V. They later invited Raivoraittius to play at Umeå Punkfest.

We also made important connections in Malmö. In early 2014, after the first Species Traitor gig in Stockholm, we were contacted by the Malmö-based queer feminist hardcore and punk label Crush & Create Records, as they wanted to release our songs. Sanna and Sabina, the people behind the label, emphasized that they were both sober, that their release parties were totally sober, and that they worked in line with the xSAFTx manifesto. They were also part of the Malmö Transcore gig collective, and invited Raivoraittius to play in the city twice. In terms of hospitality and friendliness, these gigs stand out in the band's history.

I recall you saying that while touring with Species Traitor there were some venues where you didn't feel comfortable setting up your queer zine distro. Has that happened a lot?

Not really, it was probably only one time, eight years ago in Poland. I'm not sure if it was just my prejudice, but all those big, bald, old dudes waiting for the gig to start in a shady-looking, small-town bar made me feel uneasy. Everything went perfectly fine, though, and the big, bald, old dudes actually really liked us. I felt embarrassed for having been such a scaredy-cat.

In most cases, the zine distro I've been bringing to gigs since the late 1990s has actually helped me feel more at ease. It has served as my shield and, at the same time, provided me with a purpose and the courage to actually talk to people.

I'm a tad worried that my final question might annoy you, but I have to ask: What's your take on Sairaat Mielet?
I've never listened to them much, but Camille used to be a fan, so I asked her. She pointed out that Sairaat Mielet were sober at a time when the only people who didn't drink were religious senior citizens. This was the late 1980s, and sobriety wasn't considered compatible with Finnish culture. But the band had some disturbingly authoritarian lyrics, celebrating the police arresting drunks and the like. Politically, early straight edge history in Finland is not a proud one. There is another straight edge band from the late 1980s, Today's Waste, incidentally from Turku. Their bass player was proudly homophobic, became what I would call a Nazi in his later years, and deeply hated Species Traitor and Raivoraittius. "Freaks" is what he used to call us. He passed away last year. Within the scene, he is still regarded as a legend. It is common in Finland—and in Turku in particular—to tolerate old punks that have become right-wing racists. This says a lot about what we have to deal with here. Sairaat Mielet had at least some positive lyrics about gender equality and such. Musically, Camille finds them harshly beautiful.

HAILS FROM PARTS UNKNOWN

Interview with UltraMantis Black

UltraMantis Black is a professional wrestler from the first class of students trained in the Chikara Pro Dojo. He hails from Parts Unknown by way of Philadelphia. UltraMantis Black has played in numerous hardcore bands and now fronts an outfit of the same name.

You are not the only straight edge wrestler. CM Punk and his Straight Edge Society have introduced straight edge to popular culture and a mass audience. Do you have any fancy theories about the straight edge/wrestling overlap, or is this just coincidence?

I don't think there's any specific underlying reason that there are more straight edge/hardcore/punk folks involved either directly in the wrestling business or as wrestling fans. I think that there are probably more of "us" becoming wrestlers now than there were ten to fifteen years ago, partly because of greater accessibility, and partly just because, like with anything else, we are just another active segment of society. As for the crossover with wrestling fandom, I think the sport is just much less one-dimensional than it has long been perceived and has a broader appeal now, whether from an artistic standpoint or just because it's fun.

What's your take on the Straight Edge Society? Would you have wanted to be a member?

No. Besides never having had an interest in working for the WWE, I think the Straight Edge Society was created by writers more for the sake of character development than anything else. I'm not even sure all of the wrestlers in that stable were even straight edge. Straight edge has never really been a focal point of the character of UltraMantis Black.

For the uninitiated—like myself—can you explain the differences between various wrestling promotions? And what, in fact, is a wrestling promotion?
Promotions are simply companies or organizations running their own wrestling events, often with their own unique rosters, characters, storylines, titles, wrestling styles, etc. In the United States, in the days before the WWE had bought out or forced out its competition, many promotions tended to stick to their own "territories." Territories were simply select regions of the countries where usually only one organization would run wrestling shows. Today, there are many independent companies promoting wrestling in the US and all over the globe.

How do you choose the promotions you want to be active in?
That depends entirely on the individual. Some wrestlers will go wherever they are offered work in an effort to gain more exposure. Some never leave their local territory. There's other factors like pay, your coworkers (or "locker room"), the nature of the audience you are wrestling for, etc. For me personally, I stayed loyal for most of my career to the promotion where I got my start. It was where I trained and where I developed and grew my character. It was also a place that I really felt I helped to build. I had still had the opportunity to travel the world and work for other promotions far and wide, but I always had a home.

Are there big differences in style?
There are many styles of professional wrestling. Several of the predominant styles have distinct cultural origins. Lucha libre is a style born in Mexico and popularized in other Latin American countries. Its movements are centered on rolls, drags, and high flying. There's a traditional American style which favors storytelling in the matches. Puroresu is a Japanese style grown out of the traditional style but usually with less theatrics and heavier on in-ring psychology and legitimacy of the fight. Catch style was popularized in the United Kingdom and involves more emphasis on mat-based grappling and submission holds. There are many other hybrid styles that continue to evolve.

How did you get into wrestling?

I was always fascinated by pro wrestling since I first was exposed to it on television when I was a child. I think most people fall into one of three groups: those who have no interest in the sport, those who have a casual or passing interest at some point in their lives, and then there's the rest of us who somehow can't get it out of our blood. I think I always wanted to play some active part in professional wrestling (the same way I wanted to take an active role in the punk rock community), but it never seemed feasible that someone of my physical stature—not physically "big" in comparison to the stereotypical muscled-up bodybuilder type wrestlers of the '80s and '90s—could actually become a wrestler. I thought more about promoting shows. But the industry changed drastically just prior to the turn of the new century, and suddenly there were more opportunities for nontraditional types of wrestlers.

Last question about wrestling: what's the significance of the mask?

The mask has always played a significant role in wrestling, especially within lucha libre, the Mexican style of professional wrestling where much of my initial training was grounded. Like any wrestling character, the mask allows me to assume another identity entirely. In that sense, the mask *is* my identity and considered "sacred" to who I am. The other advantage of the mask is that it allows me to maintain a completely separate life outside of the ring. I'm very lucky that I have the opportunity to walk the line between two worlds. I have about twenty-four versions of my current mask that I have worn at different periods or for different occasions. I guess it's pretty special to me.

You also play music. Tell us about that!

I have played music with various bands for more than half of my life. However, this is the first time that I have been able to do so as UltraMantis Black. The band has basically been an extension of the character and has intersected all sides of my life. The impetus behind forming the band was the desire to create an avenue that allowed me to vocalize the message of animal, earth, and human liberation in a more expressive way than I am limited to in the ring. Prior to becoming UltraMantis Black the wrestler, I often felt like I had reached a point where I was doing no more than preaching to the choir in the music scene. Wrestling allowed me to begin reaching a completely different audience, in a completely different way, by mixing politics with my performance. It also helped me to grow, to appreciate different perspectives, and to go beyond the superficial. With UltraMantis Black the band, I get to return to my roots, for lack of a better cliché.

In a 2014 radio interview you said that "with the band I wanted to bring social and political aspects of punk rock back to hardcore, where I think it's been lacking in recent years." Which are the aspects most important to you?

Just being more vocal about things that matter and bringing them to the forefront in hardcore again. I certainly wouldn't say that there were no bands bringing their own political activism into their music with them, but it was just so rare to go to a show and to hear a band say anything politically or socially relevant. At least here in the US. Even some of the few bands whose lyrics are blatantly political—no one was talking between songs, no one was trying to spark conversation, merch tables were only being used to sell product. To me, it was disappointing. I've always loved the aspects of punk that made you think, that opened up your eyes. I know not everyone appreciates that and some people don't want to be "preached" at. But fuck it.

How do you feel about the hardcore scene today? Have you seen any changes since you gave that interview in 2014?

Sure, the hardcore scene is never static. Much like pro wrestling and almost all things, it's cyclical and it evolves. There's definitely a number of bands right now unapologetically infusing their political and social agenda into their music. I fucking love that. Maybe it's partly due to the current political climate in this world, but I think kids will always be drawn to and draw from the punk rock ideals that hardcore is rooted in. I will just always believe there has to be more to hardcore than just the music.

How important have hardcore and straight edge been for your personal development?

I don't think it's an exaggeration by any means to say that hardcore helped shape the person I am today. I don't think it's weird or lame. The things

I've learned, the experiences I've had, the relationships I've built, and the communities I've been a part of have all been integral in some way to my development as a human being. Do I love the music? Sure, but hardcore has always been about much, much more than just music and style for me. I'm a firm believer in the personal being the political. Straight edge is incredibly important to me personally, but it's never been the be-all, end-all for me. It has been a gateway to a bigger picture, to bigger issues. But it has always been my foundation and an integral part of my own revolutionary experience.

How would you define your politics?

I used to use terms like anarchist, socialist, etc., but in the end, for me it's less about what I "believe in" as it is what I really am when boiled down to its essence. I'm someone who fights for animals and their home on this planet. I'm someone who fights for oppressed and marginalized people. I'm someone who fights against fascists and oppressors in all their forms. I guess that's about as much as I can simplify it.

How does this fit in with the Order of the Neo-Solar Temple, which I've heard being referred to as "your stable." I don't really know what that means, but it sounds suspicious.

A stable, for lack of a better term, is basically a crew in pro wrestling. I have led several stables in my career: The Dark Breed, The Order of the Neo-Solar Temple, The Spectral Envoy. Pretty much all of them comprised of creepy weirdos on the outside, looking in at the clean-cut mainstream of wrestling.

How do you respond to people who feel that there is way too much focus on masculinity and physical strength in wrestling?

I'd like to think that I'm one of many wrestlers in the current scene that askew that notion to some extent. The ideal in wrestling for many decades definitely focused on big muscles, hypermasculinity, size, etc. But there has been a shift in the past decade, especially in the independent scene, as to what wrestling really is and what it can be. There is certainly a far greater amount of diversity and inclusion. Much more representation from women and the LGBTQ community—both in the ring and outside of the ring in terms of ownership, promotion, organizing, support, etc. Don't get me wrong: there is *a lot* of bullshit in wrestling: misogyny, racism, homophobia—shit is all still rampant. But it's evolving.

UltraMantis Black, ca. 2016. Photo by Zia Hiltey.

I understand you've been involved in the activist milieu in Philadelphia. Do people there know you as UltraMantis Black, or are you taking on an entirely different role?

Even though there is so much bleed-over between who UltraMantis is in the ring and who he is outside of it, I have always kept that identity separate from any direct activism I am a part of in the "real world." I've been involved in that world long before I ever became UltraMantis. Even though I've used the UltraMantis Black persona as a tool to capture attention and to bring awareness to issues to folks within specific subcultures, I've sometimes questioned whether it would actually help or harm the legitimacy of boots-on-the-ground action. It's tricky. I think there's a time and place for UltraMantis Black the character. But more often I think it's just as important to be a nameless voice for the voiceless.

What are some of the projects you've been involved with?

Keeping it general, I've stayed involved with groups and movements working toward animal liberation and justice and the promotion of ethical veganism. Both in the US and abroad. Animal rights has always been at the heart of my interests in working for change. Working more directly now with grassroots groups and sanctuaries has been infinitely more affirming. More recently, due in no small part to the increasingly oppressive regime activity in the US, I've been getting more active with local antifascist organizing as well as the defense of Planned Parenthood, an organization that provides sexual and reproductive health care in the States.

Let's go with a time-tested conclusion: what's next for you?

I'll counter with a time-tested response: I'm still trying to figure out what's next. I'll still keep doing what I'm doing to some extent in some form— whether it's wrestling, music, or activism. As long as my body and/or brain can handle it. UltraMantis Black will never die.

COLLECTIVES

COOPERATIVA STRAIGHT EDGE LIBERTARIA

Julian Vadala was the singer of the Argentinean straight edge band xAutocontrolx. He authored the book *Historias del Buenos Aires Hardcore* (2010).

Can you tell us the story of the Cooperativa Straight Edge Libertaria? When was it founded? Which were its objectives? When did it end?

The Cooperativa Straight Edge Libertaria was founded in 1995. The occasion was the first South American straight edge meeting in Buenos Aires. We had visiting bands from Brazil (Personal Choice, Self Conviction) and Uruguay (Hablan por la Espalda). The intention was to form a group that would bring together the most politicized part of straight edge in Buenos Aires. At the time, a new wave of bands on Victory Records emptied straight edge of its contents, transforming it into something trivial and consumerist, without any clear political position—and if it had any, it was conservative and right-wing. On top of it, they were playing metal!

It was bands like xAutocontrolx and Actitud de Cambio that gave birth to the idea. They wanted to gather bands, labels, and fanzines that identified with straight edge and had left-libertarian politics. A mailing address was established for people from other cities to get in touch. A distro was organized with materials of all kinds, not only about straight edge—there was feminist material, including demands for the decriminalization of abortion, anarchist material, and a bunch of stuff on animal rights. We organized demonstrations against zoos, military exhibitions, McDonald's, and nuclear testing by the French government. We distributed flyers explaining our position and spreading animal and human liberation through veganism.

What was the background to this combination of straight edge and radical left-wing politics? Which were the main influences?
Influences were anarchist theorists, the early-twentieth-century Argentinean workers' movement, the Animal Liberation Front and its direct actions, and the vegan militancy from different groups around the world. Members of the Cooperativa were active in various local projects related to these beliefs.

How was the Cooperativa Straight Edge Libertaria perceived in the wider Argentinian hardcore scene?
Before the Cooperativa, the notion of straight edge was very distorted. Many people thought it was violent, conservative, and right-wing. This changed overtime, but there were always conservative folks with confused ideas in the straight edge scene. We wanted to raise the issue, present other options, and address topics that weren't addressed by the bands that mainly sang about the scene, friendship, and their crews.

Did the Cooperativa Straight Edge Libertaria have any influence beyond Argentina?
Yes, we received mail from all around the world and a lot of support. There was quite a lot of interest in our activities. People sent us material from faraway regions such as Asia, Eastern Europe, and Oceania. Remember, this was before people were using the internet. So, I think we achieved something—especially considering we were all in our early twenties and had no resources.

Was the Cooperativa taken seriously within the Argentinean left? Was there any collaboration with left-wing groups and organizations?
We were nonpartisan anarchists and opposed all forms of hierarchies. We didn't participate in political parties and we never received any support from traditional political organizations. In general, we were dismissed as being anarchists.

What caused the Cooperativa's end?
There wasn't any particular reason. After some years, the bands and zines who belonged to the group were disappearing, and there was a new wave

From *Cooperativa Straight Edge Libertaria* boletin no. 2, 1996.

of straight edge, strongly influenced by the US and very apolitical. Apart from staying sober, their straight edge was mainly about collecting merch from US labels. Although there have always been people with libertarian ideas in Argentina's straight edge scene, no group continued the work of the Cooperativa Straight Edge Libertaria.

Would you say that it left a legacy in terms of having a long-term influence on radical politics in Argentina?

I don't dare say that it left a legacy, but we certainly had an impact. There was very little information about straight edge in Argentina when the Cooperativa formed, and the little that was available was all in English. Today, there is still a strong hardcore scene in Buenos Aires, and straight edge is still alive, too. Bands like Mil Caras and the label Vegan Records stand for an interpretation of straight edge that is close to the one we had in the Cooperativa Straight Edge Libertaria.

What are your thoughts on straight edge today?

I think that straight edge is a good tool to stay away from addiction and the traps of the system. I am still critical of copying any trend from the US, of collecting merchandise, and of valuing fashion more than messages.

Nico was born and raised in Argentina. He founded Fire and Flames Music and Clothing (fireandflames.com) in 2002 while living in Germany. Without him, there might not have been a chapter on the Cooperativa Straightedge Libertaria in this book.

After you read *Sober Living for the Revolution*, you had some nice things to say, but you also wrote on your blog that it was "bewildering" that the Cooperativa Straightedge Libertaria from Buenos Aires hadn't been featured. To be honest, I had not been aware of it at the time. I am trying to make up for it now. What are your memories of it?

I was a young anarchist in the mid-1990s and new to radical politics. The Cooperativa Straightedge Libertaria was among the more visible and active actors in the scene in Buenos Aires. They regularly held concerts that were relatively well attended, there were several bands gravitating around them, and they published one (or several) fanzines. One of the main regular events back then was the Feria del Fanzine, which was held (I think) once a month in Plaza Congreso, and they were always present there as well. It really wasn't just an obscure phenomenon.

Years later, you established Fire and Flames Riotwear. Your collection included a T-shirt that said "Nechaev Brigade: Original Straightedge." Any connection there?

Absolutely. I somehow picked up a copy of Nechaev's "Catechism of the Revolutionist" at a pretty young age (maybe fourteen or so), and, for better or for worse, it was for many years a very strong influence on my views as to what our roles and responsibilities as revolutionaries should be. I believed that there was no morality beyond "is this useful/positive for revolutionary politics or not" and viewed and judged everything from that perspective. I therefore interpreted that the only way to be true to my convictions was to dedicate the totality of my time, my

mind, and my body to revolutionary politics. If your body and your mind are a weapon, then you need to care for them appropriately, and that meant keeping them free of distractions, toxins, and addictions. So while the cultural and political contexts of Czarist Russia and 1990s Latin America were obviously more than a little bit different, revolutionary straight edge seemed like a self-explanatory modern day extension of anarchist self-discipline and politics.

STRAIGHT EDGE CITY: BANDUNG, INDONESIA

Frans Ari Prasetyo

Frans Ari Prasetyo is a hardcore punk veteran, independent researcher, and photographer from Bandung, Indonesia. His interests are the evolution of urban politics, culture and subcultures, artists, underground musicians, and activists.

> Straight edge pride! Hold to deep inside.
> Straight edge pride! True till death.
> —Blind to See, "Today Until I Die" (2001)
>
> SXE is what we are, SXE is what we are
> Painted in My Heart, tattooed in my soul
> —Manusia Buatan, "SXE Is What We Are"(2004)

INTRODUCTION

This article draws on the scene history of HC/punk in Bandung, specifically SXE, traced through collectives, spaces, political communities, music, gigs, zines, and merchandise. I'm trying to weave this into the history of urban youth culture in the city, reflecting both the Indonesian and the global context. My perspective on Indonesian HC/punk is shaped by my personal experience in the DIY hardcore scene in Bandung, in which I have been involved since junior high school, and by my research on the politics of cultural production.

HC/Punk as a global phenomenon provides a toolkit of DIY and subcultural resilience, building and maintaining a community dedicated to its own empowerment, symbolizing a political potential through an aesthetic which is accessible to young people in particular. In Indonesia, the development of punk culture was positioned as part of resistance culture. Indonesia boasts a thriving underground music scene with many punk, hardcore, and metal bands. Underground music continues to provide young Indonesians with a set of alternative identities and lifestyles, providing a route to escape from, challenge, or at least negotiate the dominant frameworks of nationality, ethnicity, and class.

Hardcore Punk in Indonesia

The genesis of punk in Indonesia started in the late 1980s, with a proliferation of bands and scenes across the archipelago during the 1990s. The early development of punk was entangled with the emergence of the opposition movement that toppled Suharto's militarist regime in 1998, in the aftermath of the 1997 Asian Financial Crisis. The punk culture which emerged in the 1990s was considered to be a new phenomenon within the scope of youth culture in Indonesia.

The city of Bandung has always been one of the centers of punk in Indonesia. Bandung has long been associated with modern culture, including music, art, fashion, and design. It is an education and manufacturing center, and thus unsurprisingly also a center of youth culture. A number of prominent rock, punk, and metal bands have emerged from the city's underground scene, as has the distro phenomenon, that is, independent youth-oriented retail outlets which have spread throughout urban Indonesia. Cultural activity is deeply embedded in Bandung and has contributed to its distinctive character.

One of the most significant effects of punk in Indonesia was the democratization of sections of the music and culture industry, with the rise of independent record labels and a wider DIY culture. The most fundamental thing in the strength and sustainability of the DIY HC/punk community is the scene's infrastructure including community spaces, regular events, alternative medias such as zines, and a solid economical base able to support the scene's activities.

Zines have been pivotal in building social and political consciousness among underground youth since the 1990s. The number of zines grew rapidly as the political landscape in Indonesia became more open during the Reformasi period of 1998. Punks in Bandung produced zines covering music and politics, creating an open space to address issues that could not be covered in mainstream media. *SubmissiveRiot* was the first HC/punk zine to come out of Bandung in 1997. While the distro phenomenon has spread to other urban areas in the archipelago, Bandung remains its center to this day. At the height of their popularity, hundreds of distros were operating in the city.

The youth in the Bandung underground music scene have been implementing the DIY ethos by developing commercially independent media and various forms of cultural production. Once a model for independent underground production and distribution, Bandung's distros have expanded and professionalized into a substantial industry based on an integrated business model of underground branding and lifestyle fashion. The implementation of the DIY ethos in the realm of cultural production has also expanded to the production of clothing and merchandise. While DIY production is opposed to the pursuit of profit, it is still concerned with the production of goods and services for sale—in other words, commodities. Underground enterprises often begin as personal projects by young Indonesians driven by a desire for self-expression, to make a contribution to the scene, or to earn some independent income, and this is what happened during the distro boom in Bandung.

DIY is a step to gain personal control during times of political crisis, but it's only a small part of the solution. DIY as an attempt to fight corporate power is also a difficult concept in an agrarian country such as Indonesia, because most people have practiced DIY by building their own houses and growing their own food. They know that practicing DIY does not stop capitalist exploitation. For them, it has not brought equality or created social balance. It is more important to self-organize community, build alliances, and face anyone who is detrimental to common interest.

Straight Edge in Indonesia

Straight edge in Indonesia has always been centered in Bandung. In the beginning, straight edge mainly gained popularity among the urban and educated upper middle classes. It was seen as an alternative to the HC/punk scene, which had a negative reputation in the public associated with what was referred to as the "3M": *musik, mabuk, mohawk* (*mabuk* meaning drunk). Straight edge tried to establish an alternative narrative. It was going against HC/punk hegemony and considered to be at odds with the habits of HC/punk youth at the time. It also influenced scenes that were very distant from HC/punk, such as indie pop. One of the reasons was that indie pop was also popular among middle-class youth and well-regarded by the public. Straight edge became so popular that even artists in mainstream pop bands, for example, Rocket Rockers, X-ed up at shows.

In a sense, early straight edge in Indonesia could be seen as an adaptation to the conservative moral norms of the country. Yet it was also an attempt to salvage the authentic, positive core of punk from the negative excesses of the underground. It was a means of cultural negotiation between HC/punk and the general public.

THE COLLECTIVES

> *Now we're not the same again / We feel the different pain, the different way*
> *Are we still brothers? (3x) / 181 Youth Crew*
> —Manusia Buatan, "181 Youth Crew" (1999)

Riotic

Riotic was established as a distro in 1995–1996 in a private home in Melong Green, Cijerah, West Bandung. It soon opened a downtown store. As the first distro in Indonesia, Riotic served the entire scene. In 1998, it moved to Juanda Road no. 181 and changed its name officially to Riotic 181.

Juanda Road no. 181 was an old colonial house in Northern Bandung. Northern Bandung is a colonial area with magnificent architecture and large courtyards. Being located there gave Riotic a significant boost. It became a melting pot for HC/punk youth and other subcultures such as skateboarders, surfers, BMX freestylers, and graffiti artists. They gathered there after school or work to hang out, buy and sell merchandise, produce and distribute zines and newsletters, and discuss the music scene as well as political activism. Books about anarchism were sent to Riotic by international friends.

Riotic was not a straight edge collective but it was closely associated with it. At the time, straight edgers believed that their individual choices and actions could add up to collective cultural change.

In 2000, Indonesian straight edge received international recognition when Blind to See was one of 41 global straight edge bands to appear on *The X on Our Hands: A Worldwide Straight Edge Compilation* released by Commitment Records in Holland. The compilation was rereleased in cassette format in 2002 by Refuse Records in Poland. It was considered an achievement for the Bandung scene to have one of its bands included. Blind to See were considered pioneers of Indonesian straight edge. Ironically, Blind to See had never claimed to be a SXE band prior to seeing an opportunity to be included in an international compilation based on personal connections. This caused some strife within the scene.

Riotic contributed significantly to the commercialization of the distro phenomenon in Bandung and Indonesia. Today, most of the distros in Bandung are just clothing stores without any connection to underground culture. They carry out economic work without supporting the scene. DIY principles and community spirit are still evoked but only appear on the surface. To understand this development, it needs to be considered that T-shirt raw materials are easily supplied by the textile industry that has been growing rapidly in the East Bandung region since the 1970s. Bandung is today the center of the T-shirt raw material industry in Indonesia, which is linked to the development of a clothing industry that is produced and consumed by youth including the underground scene.

Within the Riotic collective, this caused conflict and division. Some former collective members founded a political movement instead called *Front Anti Fasis* (*Antifascist Front*, FAF).

FAF's aspiration was to overthrow the Soharto regime. Its establishment marked the dividing line between *anarki punk* and street punk. The political orientation of FAF was anarchist, which distinguished the movement from street punks who were primarily concerned with a punk aesthetic. Many straight edgers, who also rejected the street punk aesthetics, found a home in FAF. They often looked like regular guys from high school who wore T-shirts, jeans, sneakers, and had normal haircuts. But they embraced punk ethics and had close connections to the anarchist collective Kontra Kultura.

Sadar 181

The term "youth crew" was used in Riotic 181 as a label for a group of HC/punk youth who gathered there. Out of this group emerged the Kolektif Sadar 181. *Sadar* means "conscious." The collective was named after a Blind to See song by the same name.

Sadar 181 was not exclusively straight edge but had a strong focus on it. Out of time came straight edge band such as Blind to See, Restrain, Komplete Control, Manusia Buatan and Domestik Doktrin. Sadar 181 also issued a zine titled *Bandung Edge News*.

At the time, proper information about SXE was still limited to foreign bands whose tapes or CDs were reproduced cheaply. But the ideas spread, not least veganism. This was a contested and provocative issue. People in Indonesia are accustomed to daily meat consumption. No band was upfront about vegetarianism, veganism, or animal rights. The message was mostly conveyed through zines and interviews. Political messages related to the issue were included in songs, however. "Boycott McDonald's" by Manusia Buatan is one example. In general, the lyrics of straight edge bands focused on being positive and living a good life, both personally and for the community.

Gradually, the political orientation of the straight edge scene became stronger, which also caused friction with Riotic 181, since Riotic became more like a business. Eventually, this caused the Sadar collective to leave Riotic and meet at a different location. In turn, the straight edge scene became more exclusive and separated from the rest of HC/punk. There were also divisions within the scene itself, however, mainly between those who saw straight edge as a political movement and those who stressed straight edge's personal and subcultural aspects. There were also people in Sadar who produced their own merchandise, which was eyed critically by others. Eventually, the collective split into two camps: one group turned into a distro promoting Sadar 181 bands, especially the popular Blind to See; the other formed a more political project, the Stress Distro Collective.

In the HC/Punk scene, each collective must have representative band that becomes the collective symbol. Sadar 181 Collective managed to produce SXE bands such as Blind to See, Restrain, Komplete Control, Manusia Buatan and Domestik Doktrin.

Stress Distro Collective

Stress Distro Collective strictly tied SXE to DIY culture and was outspokenly political. Rooted in anarchism and left-wing politics, the collective saw SXE as a practice of resistance against corporations and global capitalism. It spread the message of anticonsumerism to a large audience, not only the scene. A radical faction assumed the name Bandung Ultra Militance.

Stress Distro served as a meeting spot as well as a discussion group. Straight edge was seen as the basis for political action. The collective was connected to social movements, NGOs, and political groups such as the anarchist collective Kontra Kultura. There was a strong focus on concrete issues that local communities dealt with: food, water, housing, health and public services.

Stress Distro Collective also organized gigs, although they were usually private and not advertised. The collective rejected anything with the air of commercial culture or idolizing particular bands. Gigs were purely seen as community events. Still, there were influential bands emerging from the collective such as Full Error. The zine issued by Stress Distro Collective was *Black Line*.

Clockwise from top left: First issue of *Black Line* zine; first issue of *Lapuk* zine; poster for *Just Do the Edge* launch, Bandung, February 2013; poster for Youth of Today tribute show, Bandung, January 2008. All images courtesy of Frans Ari Prasetyo.

In 2002, the Stress Distro Collective turned into the most influential of all of Bandung's straight edge collectives: Balkot.

Balkot Collective

The Balkot Collective was the successor to the short-lived Stress Distro Collective. It cut all ties to Riotic, which was deemed commercial. The Balkot Collective was enthusiastically DIY. It was also, like Stress, outspokenly political.

The Balkot Collective met on the steps of Bandung's City Hall (*Balai Kota*, or simply *Balkot*, hence the name)—for a long time, every Wednesday at 5 pm. This was considered neutral territory, distinct from the commercialism of HC/punk venues and distros that had spread across Bandung. It was important to occupy public space—a space that would remain even if a collective folded. It was also a convenient meeting place, central and with options for skateboarders and BMX riders outside.

Balkot was organized on autonomous, nonhierarchical principles. It rejected all sponsoring of the gigs it organized. It attracted many new people to DIY hardcore and straight edge and established strong ties to punk activists abroad. Both its location and outlook made it more welcoming than its forerunners who were perceived as more exclusive, even elitist. Many more people from working-class backgrounds could be found in Balkot. Everyone had a voice and skills that were appreciated. It also provided an atmosphere where all sorts of issues could be discussed without pretension or intimidation.

Most of the people who had moved from Riotic 181 via Sadar 181 and the Stress Distro Collective to Balkot were straight edge. But Balkot was not exclusively straight edge. The focus was on politics and DIY culture. Straight edge was understood as a personal choice, while DIY ethics was seen as integral to the scene and the basis of a substantial political movement. Yet due to the majority of its members being straight edge, it was often conceived as a straight edge collective. Therefore, it also helped position straight edge as a counterculture, not just as an apolitical and subcultural bubble. Although less militant than Stress Distro Collective, it associated goals and visions with straight edge and DIY principles. Compared to Stress, Balkot is a looser political formation, more fluid and open. It occupied a space between the commercialized Riotic Collective and the militant Stress Distro Collective.

For Balkot, too, organizing gigs was an important means to create community. They established networks across Indonesia and beyond, allowing bands to travel from city to city, and country to country, playing at DIY venues and fueling HC/punk culture. Gigs in Bandung were organized both in larger public spaces (such as the university building or a sports hall) and privately (a private house, garage, or yard). The Balkot Collective was also the first collective that organized gigs in music studios. Music studios could be rented for a specific time—officially, for rehearsals—with the needed equipment readily available. It was a clever way to get around many of the bureaucratic obstacles for obtaining permits to organize shows.

The Balkot Collective also produced records and merchandise, but it never added more than 10–20 percent of the production cost to the price. Commercial distros could add up to 300 percent. The money generated by the sales was used for the collective's activities, especially for organizing gigs. Balkot Collective can produce stuff cheaply due to the low prices for raw materials, voluntary labor, and its own distribution channels. T-shirts have always been an important part of creating identity in HC/punk circles, and Balkot members have designed various straight edge T-shirts. While the majority of materials related to straight edge (records, magazines, etc.) are still obtained from other countries, merchandise (not only T-shirts but also hats, bags, etc.) has been produced locally. Cheap production costs mean that the products can be sold cheaper than imported ones.

The collective ran record labels such as Inkoherent DIY Nutritionist and Anak Muda Productions. Straight edge bands that emerged from the collective included Freesoul, KxHx, Hooded, Step Right, Fakk Bar Kulture, Morally Straight, Ambush Your Ambition, and Who Will be Next. Older bands that came out of Sadat 181, such as Manusia Buatan and Domestik Doktrin, were also affiliated with Balkot. In 2010, the collective released a compilation titled *Balkot Terror Project*, Balkot-related bands (both straight edge and non–straight edge). In 2013, Balkot initiated the *Just Do the Edge* compilation, which was released by Commitment Records Asia and featured 12 straight edge bands from the South East Asian region.

Balkot members also edited various zines, including *Lapuk*, *Hardcore Heroes vs. Punk Partisans*, and *Beyond the Barbed Wire*. Zine production was so important and prolific that people joined Balkot only because of their interests for zines. In 2012, Balkot organized Bandung Zine Fest, the first zine fest ever in Indonesia. It made a big impact, also beyond the HC/punk scene, as it demonstrated that producing alternative media was possible. It also made it clear to a wider public that HC/punk was about more than just music. Today's International Zine Festival in Indonesia emerged out of the Bandung Zine Festival. Bandung Zine Festival remains, but it is no longer organized by Balkot and has become more commercial. This proves the importance of zines for a wider public.

The Baltok collective still exists. Since 2011, it no longer meets at the Bandung City Hall, but it remains a network of people organizing joint activities, especially gigs, not least of befriended touring bands from across South East Asia. The DIY ethos is alive. Straight edge's golden era has faded, but Balkot is still associated with it and the majority of its members are still straight edge. It remains the most important representative of straight edge in Indonesia, the natural successor to Sadar 181 and Stress Distro.

CONCLUSION

As a political idea, straight edge refuses the decadence of our time and wants to extract itself from society—but not *out of* society. In the Indonesian context, straight edge wants to be part of a society that had strongly rejected punk. Straight edge became a public label, even if it is a personal choice. The straight edge scene, particularly in Bandung, tried to become a part of society by employing musical, verbal, and visual means. In the beginning, this was a big challenge. Today, the situation is very different, since everything is easily available online and through modern communication networks. This opens up space for a more comprehensive and constructive straight edge discourse but also for destructive forms of confrontation. The trace of straight edge in Indonesia is not only seen from the footprints of individuals who bore the X but also from the collectives and bands that have provided the scene with its particular atmosphere.

STRAIGHT EDGE SANKT PAULI

This interview with members of the Straight Edge Sankt Pauli football fanclub was conducted in German by Nic, who lives in Hamburg, and published in the fanzine *xclusivx*, issue 8, June 2017. This is an abbreviated version, leaving out specifics on German football supporter culture.

Hello, and many thanks for your time! Let us start with a little history about your group. Did you meet on the terraces or at straight edge shows?
Most of us first met within Hamburg's hardcore punk scene. Shows at the Rote Flora were of particular importance. Eventually, a small group emerged that spent much time hanging out at the Eisbande, which serves great vegan ice cream. Eventually, we decided to go to the stadium as a crew. There, we were joined by other straight edgers who had been going to the games for a long time. The Südkurve, where we gather, is not so big. People know each other.

When exactly did Straight Edge St. Pauli become an official fanclub?
Some of us had already been active in other supporter groups, such as the Ultrà St. Pauli and the St. Pauli Skinheads. The first time we brought a "Straight Edge St. Pauli" banner to the stadium was on March 1, 2012. That day, "SXE FCSP" was born. After that, we attended home games as a crew more and more regularly, and also went to away games. We brought vegan

caviar and alcohol-free sparkling wine to the chartered trains. In the early days, some of us even X-ed up. We wanted to show that we were part of this, but in our own way.

We had different reasons for being straight edge. One of us has been straight edge for more than 17 years. In the Südkurve, we were soon accepted, since we showed up regularly, brought flags, banners, and stickers, and made a lot of noise (usually right beside the Ultrà St. Pauli drums). For our third and fifth birthdays, we prepared small choreographies. We have also made bigger banners, especially against Nazis. And we have been active in the "Recht auf Stadt" demonstrations against gentrification. In the beginning, we also wanted to organize our own shows, and some of us did, but it's not directly related the fanclub; these are two separate things really.

As a fanclub, what does straight edge mean to you? Is it a "lifestyle" or "sober living for the revolution"?

We are all political and involved in various projects for a different, "better" society: as musicians, as animal rights and antifascist activists, as people working in youth projects. To be straight edge is one aspect of many to change society. What unites us is not a "lifestyle" but a life of principle. We have also "lost" people to consumption. Needless to say, they can no longer be part of the group.

I can get irritated by drunks at games, and they can make me feel uncomfortable. How is it for you as straight edges when you are on the terraces or in a bus with many people drinking and smoking?

Whether you want to be straight edge or not is a personal decision. We are not missionaries. But when someone who is drunk or high harasses others, we have a problem. As long as "live and let live" works, with people maintaining control over their actions, respecting other people's boundaries, and not hurting anyone, they can consume what they want. But when basic consideration for one another is lost, it becomes irritating for everyone, straight edge or not. And, let's not forget, it is also irritating if people are so out of it that they are no longer able to support the team!

About two years ago, we introduced the praxis of taking turns in getting water from Viva con Aqua, the St. Pauli project funding clean water supply in the Global South. We do this both to get alcohol-free fluids and to support the project, not the stadium's commercial caterers.

How important is veganism for Straight Edge St. Pauli?
It has its role but it is not required to be vegan in order to become a member. We define straight edge based on the classical principles of "no drugs, no cigarettes, no alcohol." All else is up to the individual.

Is Straight Edge St. Pauli primarily a fanclub or do you active as a group in other ways, too?
Yes, we see ourselves primarily as a football fanclub, inspired by Ultra culture. Everyone who has ever stood behind us, knows our banners! If we can, we help with choreographies and take on tasks on the terraces, such as collecting donations or selling fanzines. As a group, we are active in and around the stadium, not in the straight edge scene.

In the eyes of many, our club stands for the fight against sexism, homophobia, and racism. But the club's own "Aktionsbündnis gegen Homophobie und Sexismus" quite often reminds us that not everything is perfect on the terraces. How do you perceive sexism and homophobia there?
There is a reason why we gather in the Südkurve. People there share a common understanding of how to be together and treat each other. If people step out of line and violate this consensus, we act collectively. Sometimes, a few words enough, but the terraces aren't a discussion forum; on occasion, you need to be

more straightforward. We don't tolerate discrimination of any kind and if you want to join us in the Südkurve, you have to respect that.

Society at large is, unfortunately, sexist, homophobic, racist, and xenophobic. This bugs us all, not only in the stadium. We have noticed a shift even at FC St. Pauli. Reactionary and "nonpolitical" positions have become more prominent. It's a terrible development.

Anything you would like to add?

Come to Hamburg and the Millerntor Stadium and join us in supporting the FCSP. Because St. Pauli is the only option!

All images courtesy of Straight Edge Sankt Pauli.

SPREADING THE MESSAGE

Warzone Distro is "a zine-creating and distributing project focused on anarchy, insurrection and anti-civilization." It has its own Straight Edge/Radical Sobriety section. Find their catalog at warzonedistro.noblogs.org. The folks running the distro have been involved in radical sobriety projects. I spoke to the founder, Blitz Molotov.

There are three projects that seem to have been very tightly connected: Warzone Distro, Feral Space, and the Black Flag Sobriety Program. Can you explain their respective focus, how they are related, and which ones of them remain?
Yeah, so Warzone Distro was, and still is, a zine-creating and distributing project focused on anarchy, insurrection, and anti-civilization. I originally started it up in 2013 with the intention of creating access to free anarchist information in the city I grew up in. As the years went by, it expanded to include topics discussed within anarchist circles. This distro includes a pretty large selection of vegan straight edge titles from an anarchist perspective.

The Feral Space collective was a vegan straight edge anarchist project started in 2013 with the intention of creating anarchist activity outside the bigger cities. It was an apartment used as a community space for film screenings, Really Really Free Markets, Food Not Bombs, a lending library, and as a general hang out for punks, train kids, and folks from our hood.

The Black Flag Sobriety Program is designed to provide information about addiction and intoxication culture, while also providing support and solidarity with people struggling against drug use, alcoholism and smoking.

Alcohol has played a key role in the epidemic of fascism, racism, statism, imperialism, colonialism, sexism and patriarchy, class oppression, religious superstition, and all the other products of hierarchal authority that has swept the earth over the past few mellenia. It continues to play that role today, as people of the whole world, finally universally domesticated and enslaved by globalized capitalism, are kept pacified and helpless by a steady supply of spirits. These spirits squander the time, money, health, focus, creativity, awareness, and fellowship of all who inhabit this universally occupied territory— "work is the curse of the drinking classes," as Oscar Wilde said. It's not surprising, for example, that the primary targets of advertising for malt liquor (a toxic byproduct of the brewing process) are the inhabitants of ghettos in the United States: people who constitute a class that, if not tranquilized by addiction and incapacitated by self-destruction, would be on the front lines of the war to destroy capitalism.

When: Friday nights at 7pm

Where: The Feral Space in Elgin (email us for address)

Cost: FREE

Doing what: Exchanging stories, discussions, film screenings, physical education etc.

SMASH ADDICTION. DETOXIFY DA HOOD.

Black Flag Sobriety Program in Elgin, Il   Email: xtheferalspacex@riseup.net

Since The Feral Space was a sober space and included zines on radical sobriety, Black Flag Sobriety Program was an idea collectively created to provide support for people battling addiction in the apartment building or in the hood in general. It was also open to anarchists who were interested in using the space as a place to talk about their struggles with substances and/or addiction.

The Feral Space collective ended in early 2018 and everyone disbanded. Warzone Distro still exists via tabling anarchist bookfairs, shows, etc. It has also been launched online, so all zines are available for free in PDF form.

I would say the primary motivation behind all of these interconnected projects was to spread anarchist ideas beyond the borders of the bigger cities, and into the suburbs. We placed focus on vegan straight edge anarchism since we all felt these topics of discussion were lacking in the general anarchist struggle in the US.

In your zines about radical sobriety there has been a strong focus on indigenous voices and the perspectives of people of color. Is this due to the makeup of the collective? Was it a conscious political choice? Or both?

I personally felt it was important to highlight indigenous and POC perspectives on radical sobriety since radical sobriety in a lot of anarchist circles was viewed merely as a "white hardcore kid" thing. I wanted to distribute information that brought light to a struggle against the colonial and domesticating weaponry of intoxication culture that predated the ideas of straight edge and hardcore. For me personally, radical sobriety came before I discovered hardcore and straight edge as a movement. I saw the relationship between intoxication culture, the internalized victimhood mentality and defeatism of those who participated in it, and the brutally repressive state apparatus that followed close behind.

Whenever I hear other anarchists mock radical sobriety, I wonder how much experience they have with seeing how the state utilizes the "War on Drugs" as a sociopolitical method of prison expansion, or how capitalists profit most from impoverished conditions that encourage self-destruction through intoxication. So with that all said, I feel like any time radical sobriety is brought up and shut down via the assumption of "whiteness" and nice neighborhoods, the experiences of those of us in the hood should encourage a sense of urgency towards reevaluating how intoxication culture operates, who it destroys, and who really benefits from it.

Do you feel that there has been growing awareness and interest in sobriety in radical circles in North America?

I want to believe so. It is really hard to tell though. I know based on my experience running Warzone Distro and tabling shows that quite a few people have picked up straight edge anarchy zines and thanked me for having them. There are a few people I know who decided to claim edge after reading zines on the topic. CrimethInc's "Anarchy and Alcohol" is a favorite amongst most people including myself.

Where do you see the main political potential of straight edge? Do you think there will be stronger overlaps between straight edge and radical politics in the future?

I personally see straight edge as a weapon of individual warfare against the normative roles and expectations capitalist society sets for people. There is profit to be made off those struggling with substance abuse and addiction. I see anarchist straight edge as being an avenue of radical support and mutual aid for those who may want or need it, rather than leaving things like AA as the only options. I feel like people don't want to talk about intoxication culture in a critical way because intoxication culture still functions as a social lubricant in a lot of anarchist circles. But I think that if we find the courage to question it and break it down, we can discover new ways of interacting with one another. This can also further the struggle for personal emancipation by allowing us as individuals to discover new ways of viewing ourselves beyond our toxic relationship to the substances that incapacitate us.

As our understanding of how industrial society functions to create and reinforce socially constructed divisions, reducing our livelihood to a mere passive existence, I can only hope that straight edge and anarchy overlap—coexisting as a reclaiming of life once stolen by capitalism and intoxication culture. I would love to see sobriety defended the way anarchists defend their hearts and minds from the brainwashing haze of compulsory worker-ism, representation, and the limits of socially constructed assignments. I personally think there is individual power and courage in rejecting intoxication culture, just as there is power and courage in confronting the state—in court or on the streets. Rather than being distracted and consumed by intoxicants, I hope the overlaps of straight edge anarchy make us more dangerous, more ungovernable as lawless individuals.

IN RESPONSE TO AN INCREASE OF FASCIST AND RACIST ACTIVITY

Midwest Straight Edge Antifa

The following text is from the "About" section on the Midwest Straight Edge Antifa website (midweststraightedgeantifa.noblogs.org), which has been inactive since March 2017.

Midwest Straight Edge Antifa was born on July 31st 2015 in response to an increase of fascist and racist activity in the non-human animal liberation, environmental and straight edge movements. Since these movements have recently gained popularity, their vulnerability to fascist and racist co-opting has increased with newer liberal Animal Rights and environmental groups welcoming and/or associating with fascists and racists. This turns the eco-defense and straight edge movements into spaces that are hostile towards people of color, women, queer and trans folk, the disabled, and others. "Compassion" and vegan ethics do not absolve fascists and racists of their violent ideologies but rather obscures them, allowing them a platform and subsequently de-legitimizing the struggles of others who are oppressed.

Straight edge is a movement open to all. This means that while not everyone embraces straight edge ideology, when fascists and racists turn straight edge into a movement hostile towards people of color, women, queer and trans people, the disabled, and others, support and solidarity with those struggling against addiction and intoxication culture is severed. Midwest Straight Edge Antifa seeks to expose and confront fascists and racists in these movements as well as those who support and associate with them.

Midwest Straight Edge Antifa is a decentralized movement of vegan, straight edge anti-racists and anti-fascists who are dedicated to exposing and eliminating fascism, racism, sexism, speciesism, anti-Semitism, Islamophobia, homophobia, transphobia, disablism and other forms of oppression in general, and within the vegan, environmental and straight edge communities in particular. Towards the destruction of settler-colonialism; we want total liberation.

What we do
1. We Educate:
- by doing serious and credible research on racists and fascists in general, and also on those attempting to infiltrate and participate in the environmental, non-human animal liberation and straight edge movements.
- by sharing information with allies in dozens of collectives, affinity groups and crews worldwide.
- by distributing thousands of copies of all kinds of literature about racism, fascism and oppression for free at shows, schools, conferences, protests, parties and in prisons.

2. We Organize:
- by initiating, participating in and/or supporting anti-racist/anti-fascist demonstrations and actions.
- by hosting diverse, constructive and practical anti-racist/anti-fascist trainings and gatherings.
- by recognizing that racism is a multi-faceted issue entwined with a number of other problems.
- by strengthening our understanding and resolve and working within our communities.
- by defending other anti-racists and anti-fascists across the globe.

3. We Confront:
- by refusing to ignore the violent bigots that comprise racist and fascist groups.
- by directly challenging racists and fascists when they attempt to recruit, organize, mobilize, propagandize, and cause harm to people.
- by using innovative, creative, and highly-effective tactics

• by denying racist and fascist groups the opportunity to monopolize public spaces and by denying racists and fascists the chance to turn the environmental, non-human animal liberation and straight edge movements into spaces that are hostile towards people of color, women, immigrants, queer and trans folk, the disabled, and others.

Why doesn't Midwest Straight Edge Antifa rely on the cops or the courts?
Most anti-racist groups focus all their efforts on creating new laws or getting the police to respond to racism. But the cops uphold white supremacy and the status quo; they attack us and everyone that resists oppression. We stand against the colonial courts, the cops and the prison-industrial complex.

What is fascism?
Midwest Straight Edge Antifa recognizes a number of characteristics of fascist movements. Fascism is an ultra-nationalist ideology that mobilizes around and glorifies a national or perceived racial identity, valuing this identity above all other interests (for example gender or class). Fascism is marked by its hostility towards reason and human solidarity, by its dehumanization and scapegoating of marginalized or oppressed groups, by its use of violence or threats of violence to impose its views on others, and by

Source: no-gods-no-masters.com. (The logo is not directly associated with Midwest Straight Edge Antifa.)

its rejection of supposedly "effeminate" or "soft" values in favor of "manliness." Anti-Semitism and racism are primary facets of National Socialism and most other varieties of fascism. Fascism aims at a militarized society, and organizes along military or quasi-military lines, usually with an authoritarian structure revolving around a single, charismatic leader. Fascist groups may have the facade of an efficient and dynamic organization, but in reality, power structures are arbitrary and ruthless. Fascists use anti-elitist rhetoric to appeal to the "common man," coupled with internal elitism and willingness to accept support from existing elites. Fascism glorifies a mythologized past as justification for its present ideological stances, and as a basis for future organization of society.

What about free speech for fascists?

Midwest Straight Edge Antifa does not use the state to prevent anyone's free speech. The right to free speech restricts the state from censoring ideas, it does not stop the public from opposing hateful ideas.

The fact that people dislike what bigots have to say and want to make that known is not prohibited by the concept of free speech. If bigots actively go out of their way to tell people that 90% of the world's population should be enslaved or that the best thing they can do is kill someone because of their skin color, religion, ethnic background, immigration status, sexual orientation, disability, etc., they can't use "free speech" to silence opposition.

Anti-racists and anti-fascists have an obligation to deny a platform to bigots so that they can't spread their message and recruit. Concert venues, meeting halls, radio programs, and the like make choices about who to host on a regular basis. These choices have a very real impact on bigoted ideas taking root in one's community.

Responding to bigoted speech is important. We believe in being pro-active when it comes to fascist violence, which means confronting fascist organizing before they have a chance to put their ideas into action, and taking fascist threats seriously.

STRAIGHT EDGE RADICALS UNDER FIRE: THE CASE OF STRAIGHT EDGE MADRID

Gabriel Kuhn

This chapter intends to shed some light on the state persecution suffered by Straight Edge Madrid members from 2015 to 2018. The case received much attention among both political radicals and straight edge activists worldwide. I am particularly grateful to Diego and David, two members of the group, who agreed to correspond with me.

NOVEMBER 2015: THE ARRESTS

After suspecting the group Straight Edge Madrid for having petrol-bombed a bank and monitoring them for over a year, Spanish police break into the homes of six members at dawn on November 4, 2015. They take five people into custody and accuse them of "terrorist damages by arson," and "membership in a terrorist organization." Another member, who was traveling during the raids, is accused as well. Three of the arrested are released on bail after three days, another after two weeks. Nahuel, a noncitizen deemed the group's ringleader and an "escape risk," remains incarcerated for a year and a half. The accused are facing up to twenty years in prison according to Spain's antiterrorist laws.

WHO WAS STRAIGHT EDGE MADRID?

Straight Edge Madrid was founded in 2014 by anarchist activists to increase awareness about the political implications of alcohol and drug use. The

Source: Biblioteca e arquivo de José Pacheco Pereira (ephemerajpp.com).

group organized talks and discussions about straight edge, veganism, animal liberation, earth liberation, the social repercussions of drug use, and sobriety in historical radical movements. They put up charity dinners, film screenings, and hardcore gigs. Straight Edge Madrid inspired similar groups around Spain and beyond. The texts "Anti-Fascism, Anti-Capitalism and Straight Edge" and "Antifascist Fight and Drugs," included in their 2015 zine *Sobrios y Alerta: Drogas, Política, Hardcore y Straight Edge*, were translated into English and are available online. They cite

influences from the early twentieth-century anarchist Jules Bonnot to the Cooperativa Straight Edge Libertaria of Buenos Aires. They also list current examples of radical initiatives against drug trafficking from Northern Ireland to Greece to Kurdistan.

BACKGROUND

The persecution of Straight Edge Madrid can only be understood in the context of the general state repression that has targeted radicals in Spain in recent years. There are several reasons for the state's offensive: the need to define a new public enemy following the disarmament of the Basque separatist organization ETA; the wave of popular protests in the wake of the economic crisis of 2008; and a reform of the penal code that included the infamous "gag law," a serious threat to freedom of expression.

The anarchist movement became a particular target of security forces, and a whole series of police operations was directed against them nationwide. These included Operation Column, Operation Pandora, Operation Piñata, and Operation Ice, which Straight Edge Madrid fell victim to. All of these operations were justified by the alleged existence of terrorist anarchist organizations, referred to as "Grupos Anarquistas Coordinados" (GAC), or "Coordinated Anarchist Groups," by the police. The experiences of the persecuted Straight Edge Madrid members resembled those of other activists caught up in the security operations.

JULY 2018: THE TRIAL

The accused Straight Edge Madrid members were finally put on trial in July 2018. With the evidence being very thin, the charges were lowered to "glorification of terrorism." Even that did not stand in court. All of the accused were acquitted. Acquittals, however, are a calculated part of the state's strategy. The main purpose of drawn-out legal proceedings and pending accusations is to demoralize political activists. The Straight Edge Madrid members I talked to confirmed how difficult it was to remain active during the three years they were waiting for trial: "The first few months, we hardly left our homes, and when we did, we were afraid. All of our contacts with activist groups and spaces were compromised. Rumors spread about informants close to us, or even among us, without any foundation. This resulted in mistrust and paranoia. We were left paralyzed."

THE AFTERMATH

While Straight Edge Madrid as a group did not survive Operation Ice, the members I corresponded with expressed no regrets in having been involved: "We were an inspiration for many people. The events we organized marked a before and after in their lives. Not because we were 'enlightened' or we owned the key to liberation, but we opened doors for some towards freer, healthier, more critical, and more revolutionary thinking. That makes everything worthwhile."

I also received troubling news, however. Just as work on this book was closing, Diego and David sent the following note: "We are aware of the recent news about the macho behavior of Nahuel, as well as his abuse of economic solidarity for his own benefit. We have dissociated ourselves from him as a companion, publicly denounce his actions, and sympathize with the victims."

This is a reminder of how the specter of masculine power haunts even the supposedly most progressive anarchist and hardcore punk communities. The following chapter, "Not a Boys' Club/Scene Report," will address this in more detail. Readers are also encouraged to find inspiration in projects such as Portland's No! to Rape Culture, a self-described "action-based organization that aims to dismantle the patriarchal structures within the punk/hardcore/metal 'scene.'"

IS THIS DIY? STRAIGHT EDGE AND SWEDEN'S SOBRIETY MOVEMENT

Interviews with Jens Wingren, Staffan Snitting, Stockholm Straight Edge, and Karin Holmgren

Spearheaded by bands such as Refused and Abhinanda, Sweden, in particular the northern town of Umeå, became a center for the vegan straight edge movement of the 1990s. Straight edge is still a widely recognized subculture, with younger straight edge folks organizing within IOGT-NTO, the umbrella organization of Sweden's sobriety movement. The following four interviews intend to trace this history and reflect on its unique characteristics.

1. IOGT-NTO

Jens Wingren has been straight edge since 2002. He works for *Accent*, the IOGT-NTO magazine.

Can you give us a little background about IOGT-NTO and its affiliates?
IOGT-NTO is the biggest and best-known organization within the Swedish sobriety movement. It was formed in 1970 by a merger between IOGT, founded in 1879, and NTO, founded in 1922. UNF is IOGT-NTO's youth organization. Part of the so-called IOGT-NTO movement are also Junis, an organization for children, and the sobriety movement's scouts. NBV, founded in 1895, is an educational association affiliated with it.

Together with the workers' movement and the free churches, the sobriety movement is one of Sweden's historically most important people's movements. Its influence in the early twentieth century must not be underestimated, not least on the democracy movement. Essentially, participating in people's movements was a learning experience in democracy. People had a voice, they were part of a community, and they took control of their everyday lives.

Sounds almost DIY . . .
I suppose there are similarities. Study circles were also an important part of people's movements. Education and self-empowerment were central.

So, straight edge, a DIY subculture, being today in various ways related to IOGT-NTO, a well-established organization, is not as odd as it seems?
No. It might seem odd for people unfamiliar with Sweden's history, but in this context it doesn't appear strange at all. When Refused was awarded the Music Export Prize by the Swedish state in 2013, Sweden had a center-right government. The band made it clear that it might not even exist if it was for that government's policies. It was rather the numerous local music schools and youth centers introduced by the social democrats throughout the twentieth century that had made their success possible.

What role does _Accent_ play for the sobriety movement?
Accent is what connects the organization with its members. About 20 percent of IOGT-NTO members are active in one of the organization's local chapters. The rest learns about the organization mostly from the magazine. It also has a fair amount of readers who are not IOGT-NTO members, particularly online.

What exactly do you do?
My job description is that of a "reporter." In reality, I mostly work online. I started a podcast and take care of the website and social media. When I write articles for the magazine, it is about topics I take a particular interest in such as the antiracist and feminist work done by the organization.

How well do you fit into IOGT-NTO with your subcultural background?
There are different kinds of people in IOGT-NTO. With my tattoos, I am often mistaken for a recovering addict, which is one demographic. But there are also members from families who've been in IOGT-NTO for generations.

Posters from the IOGT-NTO archives. IOGT and NTO merged in 1970. The posters read: "No hip flask for us: the people's health requires sobriety" (IOGT), and "Fun to be in the NTO."

People know very little about straight edge, but this is slowly changing. We are still a small group, but the organization now has a visible number of straight edge members.

How do other members react to that?

When I started working for *Accent*, the editorial collective consisted of myself and three women in their fifties. Unsurprisingly, there are some differences. But no problems. What straight edge kids do is exactly what IOGT-NTO wants: they create sober meeting spaces. I feel that we are treated with respect. And one thing that pretty much any straight edge person will appreciate is that their choice to be sober is never questioned. That's very refreshing.

Has straight edge's relationship to IOGT-NTO led to a stronger acceptance of straight edge in society at large?

That's hard to say. I'm also wondering whether that acceptance is needed. The term "straight edge" makes little sense outside of the cultural milieu it comes from. If you're not part of hardcore culture and you're sober, then you're simply sober, why call yourself anything else? Yes, "straight edge" might sound cooler, but what does it really mean then?

One could argue that it makes being sober more acceptable if there is a respected subculture that advocates it.

True, but I think we must not overestimate straight edge's significance in mainstream society.

Young people in Sweden drink less today than they did twenty years ago. Does this have nothing to do with the country's relatively strong straight edge movement?

No, I don't think so. It is probably due to other factors, although researchers still seem puzzled as to why young people are drinking less. Guesses reach from new forms of socializing (particularly online) to the current sports and health craze to the increase of the Muslim population. Even if straight edge is relatively big in Sweden, it is still a small and marginal subculture. Granted, it might have been different in the 1990s, when the movement was at its peak.

You've met many straight edge people from other countries. Given the particular circumstances in Sweden, have you found there to be big differences?

No matter where you come from, your experiences will always be tied to that particular place. In Sweden, it is much more common to deal with state institutions and organizations, and this is reflected in hardcore as well. But we've built our scene ourselves, and I certainly feel part of the international hardcore community where this shared experience allows you to make new friends instantly.

Punks face bigger challenges in other countries and this can make the scenes wilder and rawer. There are places where you have to squat to be able to put on a show. In comparison, things are rather comfortable in Sweden. But not everything about wild and raw is good. Squats aren't always the most accommodating places for straight edge people . . .

We've been able to establish a fairly strong, cohesive, and long-standing scene. Drug-free, all-ages shows were always key to us, and we've been able to organize many of them. This is also important for new generations to follow. We have seen this over and over again: as soon as punk and hardcore gigs were limited to bars in a certain town, the straight edge scene largely disappeared. I've heard of eleven-year-old kids attending straight edge shows in Umeå in the 1990s. That's fantastic.

Staffan Snitting (center) at Edge Day in Gothenburg, 2009. Photo by David Johansson.

2. Gothenburg Straight Edge

Staffan Snitting has been a pivotal figure in the Swedish hardcore scene for many years. He was the editor of the zine *Law and Order* (2009–2013) and has played in the straight edge bands Stay Hungry, Sectarian Violence, and Correction. Originally from the south of Sweden, he lived in Gothenburg for many years. For his artwork, visit xstaffanx.com.

In 2009, you were among a group that founded a straight edge club within IOGT-NTO in Gothenburg. Why?
Several reasons. There were about forty straight edge kids in Gothenburg, but they were divided into several cliques of friends. We figured that if we got all of them together regularly, it would be enough to organize good shows. Regular get-togethers also allowed more experienced scensters to pass on their experiences to younger ones. Our goal was to arrange drug-free, all-age shows. IOGT-NTO could not only provide a venue but also funds for a decent PA system and backline gear. In addition, they sponsored shows, which allowed us to keep ticket prices at around USD 5, even when booking bands from abroad.

Quite a few folks would say that it doesn't sound very DIY to have a show sponsored by a 140-year-old organization.

Everyone is entitled to their opinion. But how DIY is it to depend on the alcohol industry to finance your shows? The alcohol industry tears families apart and exploits poverty. IOGT-NTO might be old, but it's a progressive *folkrörelse*, a people's movement, as we say here in Sweden.

No one ever told us what to do. We were in full control. The only rule we had to follow was not to serve alcohol at our shows and to ask intoxicated people to leave. IOGT-NTO venues are designed to be retreats for people who suffer from alcohol or drug abuse around them. This was exactly the environment we wanted to create.

Still, it all sounds rather formal . . .

We had to sit through meetings and deal with paperwork. But that was a small price to pay, as it opened up plenty of opportunities. We organized not only shows, but also film screenings and discussion nights.

Did only straight edge bands play at your shows?

No, that was never a policy. The only thing that was important was that the shows were drug-free. Straight edge bands were in the minority. We always embraced diversity, also within straight edge. At our shows, vegan straight edge kids mingled with youth crew veterans and a new generation turned on by Have Heart. There was a place for all of them.

Did the club have a political profile?

The common denominator of the members was to be straight edge, nothing beyond that. But we put on benefit shows for animal rights groups and supported Rosenlundstödet, a nonprofit organization providing help to street prostitutes who worked nearby one of our venues. I would also think that we opened up a space to discuss various issues within our scene, which included political ones. In this sense, we probably politicized the scene despite not having any outspoken political profile.

How was your club eyed by other IOGT-NTO members?

They were very positive. Not only did we bring new members to the organization, but we also livened up their venues. IOGT-NTO owns quite a lot of property across the country, but much of it lies idle. The venues we had access to were certainly put to good use.

Were there never any problems? Hardcore shows aren't to everyone's taste.

No serious problems. On occasion, people would wonder why there were footprints on the ceiling after a show, or why we had to repair a wall. But they were more baffled than angry. It was very new to them.

Did they ever attend shows?

Sometimes. If they did, they usually had a good time.

A straight edge club within a big organization—did that mean you were able to spread the message far beyond the usual circles?

It gave us a bit of extra exposure. There were a few articles in *Accent*, the IOGT-NTO member journal. In Gothenburg, we made straight edge more familiar and accepted. Unfortunately, some people also felt excluded from our shows because they thought they were for straight edge people only—despite our efforts to make it as clear as possible that this wasn't the case. We just asked people to be sober that particular evening. And I am sure there were times when even kids who were not straight edge enjoyed shows with soft drinks and cookies rather than beer and cigarettes. In any case, we probably had most influence on the straight edge scene itself. Bands were formed because of what we were doing, and similar clubs appeared in other places, including smaller towns such as Norrköping and Eskilstuna.

Did the hardcore kids react to the outside attention?

We all know that there is an element in punk that is suspicious of anyone who has not been initiated. People want to protect their subculture from mainstream influence. But it was never a big issue for us. There were some towns were the clubs caused a bit of tension between straight edge kids and IOGT-NTO youngsters who showed up at shows and objected to stagediving or what they considered to be violent dancing. The reaction was kind of like, "Why do you care? You don't even appreciate the music!" Soft drinks and cookies were fine for them, but a hardcore show without stagediving or moshing was hard to swallow. These kids raised an important question: How are you going to blow off steam and get your frustrations out in an environment that is too restricted? Anyway. There were tensions, yes, but from all I know, they never led to any serious strife.

Your club folded in 2017. Why?

The usual: some of the key people moved away and we were no longer able to book shows regularly. Since booking shows had been the club's main purpose, it seemed pointless to keep it going without having them.

Are there still IOGT-NTO straight edge clubs in other towns?
Yes. The one in Stockholm got really big.

How would you sum up the experience?
We made drug-free, all-ages shows a regular feature in Gothenburg. We were able to create a space free from intoxication. And we brought together hardcore kids from different backgrounds. All in all, it was a great experience. There was a time and place for it, and we tried to seize the moment.

Are there less drug-free, all-age shows in Gothenburg now that you are gone?
Probably, but they still exist. We helped new organizers to establish themselves, and some of our former members are active in new booking collectives.

How would you describe the status of straight edge in Sweden today?
Sweden is a small country, but we had a few renowned straight edge bands. Refused is very well known, even among a larger public. When they appeared in the 1990s, the Soviet Union had collapsed, people were disillusioned with party politics, environmentalism and animal rights gained traction, and personal politics were strong. Veganism and straight edge made the best of it.

3. Stockholm Straight Edge

Daniel and Hannah are longtime members of Stockholm Straight Edge. Daniel plays in the bands No Omega and Mystery Language, works for UNF in Stockholm, and has been active in Stockholm Straight edge since 2010. Hannah works as a teacher, does art, and has been active in Stockholm Straight Edge since 2012.

When was Stockholm Straight Edge founded?
Hannah: Toward the end of 2009. A loosely connected group of straight edge folks in Stockholm who put on shows wanted to get more organized and formed a club within UNF.

Were the experiences from Gothenburg an influence?

Daniel: They were probably a factor. Straight edge folks in Sweden are well connected. You know what others are doing, and if their experiences are positive it's natural to adopt them.

Hannah, you said you joined the club after about a year or two. Before that, you had been to many of the shows it put on. Why did you get involved yourself?
Hannah: I pretty much knew everybody, and when someone asked me whether I wanted to join there was no reason not to. I never had any regrets. It's one thing to meet people at shows on a regular basis, it's another to be actively involved in putting them on. The sense of community becomes stronger.

Many subcultural projects come and go. You've been booking shows for a decade now, involving up to 100 bands a year. What's your secret?
Daniel: The formal structure helps. It gives our work a solid frame. In addition, we have a core of people who are very dedicated. And we are in Stockholm, which makes it relatively easy to maintain a steady membership. In smaller towns, key people often move away, it's hard to replace them, and projects fold.

Doesn't a core of dedicated organizers make it difficult for new members to take on responsibility?
Hannah: It is a problem we are aware of, and we have introduced different ways to help new people find their place. Every new member has a "mentor," who introduces them to everything and who they can turn to with questions. This has worked really well. It is also important to make new members understand how much commitment it needs if they are serious about booking shows.

Do you only book straight edge bands?
Daniel: No, our focus is on sober, all-ages shows. Only our shows on

Edge Day feature exclusively straight edge bands. Otherwise, it is not important whether the bands are straight edge or not, as long as they accept our booking policies, which include that everyone—artists and audience—have to be sober on the night of the show.

Hannah: We must not forget how rare sober, all-ages shows have become. Many touring bands we book get very excited: "Wow, finally, we aren't playing in a bar!"

I read that you've introduced a project to strengthen gender equality in hardcore. Can you tell us about that?

Hannah: When we started out, many of the group's key members were dudes. In hardcore, this is not unusual. This was discussed often, but not much happened. We realized that we needed to be proactive to make a change. A few years ago, we started with a conscious effort to avoid all-male shows. Today, this has become routine. We never book shows that only have men on stage. This has had an impact on the audience as well. Representation is very important.

Daniel: We also did a survey to find out what was needed to make women and transgender people feel more comfortable at our shows. It confirmed how important representation was. It also confirmed that the aggressiveness at hardcore shows was often associated with masculinity. This is not so easy to deal with. We've been trying to make people aware of how their dancing impacts others, but you can't expect everyone at a hardcore show to just stand there and tap their feet. It's challenging to find the right balance.

Hannah: We've also made a conscious effort to reach more women and transgender people who might be interested in joining Stockholm Straight Edge. We put more thought into the design of our flyers and where we would distribute them. Me and others made a flyer in 2016

Stockholm Straight Edge recruitment flyer, 2016: "Are you sober? Curious about music, concerts, and how to organize them? Hang out with us! We meet every week, all are welcome. Get in touch if you want to know more!"

that we put up at known feminist meeting places in Stockholm. This contributed to the group becoming more diverse.

Speaking of representation: is it correct that the number of men on your board must not exceed 50 percent?

Daniel: This is mainly a formality since our organizing structure is flat and based on anarchist principles: everyone has a say. But we need to appoint board members, and, yes, we make sure that not more than 50 percent of them are men. What's more important in terms of getting everyone involved, however, is to make sure that everyone really *can* get involved. It's easy to say that everyone is allowed to do everything, but it's worthless if people aren't enabled to do different things. That's why we organize workshops on how to work the PA system, how to book bands, and other relevant topics.

What is "Stockholm Safe Edge"?

Hannah: It's a platform built by women and transgender people in our group. Most importantly, it allows people who feel unsafe at our shows—be it because of a band we booked or because of the behavior of people in the audience—to get in touch and discuss this. The platform allows us to deal with these matters better than before.

You have also canceled shows, which caused a bit of controversy. What happened?

Daniel: This was several years ago. In 2012, we had booked Fallbrawl for Firestorm Fest, a show we organize every year on Walpurgis night. Some of us already had mixed feelings about it, and when they released a video recorded in a strip club, we dropped them from the lineup. In 2013, we canceled a show with Kickback after we became aware of sexist comments they had made.

How important is your relationship to IOGT-NTO?

Daniel: First and foremost, it allows us to do all-ages shows. And that's not just because it provides access to venues that we can use, but also because it helps us make tickets affordable for teenagers. I've heard people complain that we use IOGT-NTO sponsoring to undersell other bookers, but that doesn't make much sense to me. First of all, hardcore is not about commercial competition. Secondly, other books make a lot of money from selling alcohol, a source of income we don't have. If us collaborating with a well-established people's movement allows us to organize all-ages hardcore shows, I'm all for it. Sure, someone might think it's cheesy to have their logo on our posters, but if that means we can sell tickets at a price everyone can afford, I'll accept that cheesiness. No one has ever told us what to do. Other people in IOGT-NTO might not always get what we are about, but there is genuine interest and curiosity. Some of our most active members today discovered hardcore only because we became a part of the organization.

But how DIY is the bureaucracy?
Hannah: Honestly, it's not that big a deal. We don't push papers all day. The weekly meetings are very important socially and for the continuity of our work. We only have to hand in a few documents every year. It is easily worth it and nothing that interferes with our love for hardcore.

4. Straight Edge and the Popular Movement Archive

Karin Holmgren is the head of collections at the Folkrörelsearkivet (the "Popular Movement Archive," or "Archive of People's Movements") in Sweden's Västerbotten region. The archive is located in Umeå, the region's capital. Umeå was known as a center of the European straight edge movement of the 1990s. In 2011, the archive opened its own straight edge collection.

What's an archive of people's movements?
The Swedish term *folkrörelser* refers to popular movements that organize apart from governmental institutions in order to bring about social change. The biggest Swedish people's movements emerged in the nineteenth century, and some of them have been very influential, the sobriety movement being one of them.

In the 1960s, various organizations tied to people's movements expressed the desire to document their history, based on the thousands of records and other material they had accumulated. This resulted in the founding of related archives all over Sweden. The one in Umeå opened in 1969. It is important to note that the archives were originally conceived and financed by the people's movements themselves. Only later did provincial governments provide funding as well.

Today, we serve two main functions: we provide a service to the movements by archiving their history, and we enable researchers to study it.

What were the origins of the straight edge collection?
I first discussed this idea in 2007 with my colleague Susanne Odell, who is also an archivist. We had both come of age during the 1990s when straight

edge was very influential in Umeå. In 2010, when I became the director of the archive of people's movements, we saw the possibility to put this into practice. Susanne was hired to lead the project, and we went to work.

Source: helalf.se.

Why did you feel that the collection was important?

First, there was no documentation of a period that we had experienced as very significant in Umeå's younger history. Secondly, we were intrigued by the challenge to document a modern form of a people's movement. Straight edge had no organizations or official records. Documenting its history required an approach very different to the ones we were used to.

Is straight edge a people's movement?

The main characteristics of people's movements are that they are grassroots-based and have an impact on society: they want to bring about social change, they provoke debate, and they influence public opinion. All of this was true for Umeå straight edge.

Abhinanda performing at Ålidhems Ungdomsgård, 1994. Photo by Linda Åström Svedin.

There were also concrete connections to the historical people's movements. IOGT-NTO, for example, lent out venues to straight edge bands. So did one of the Pentecostal churches. In fact, a Pentecostal priest produced two albums of Abhinanda, apart from Refused the most influential band of the era.

You said that documenting Umeå's straight edge history required a different approach than the ones you were used to. How did you go about it?
Susanne did numerous interviews and reached out to people who had been involved in the scene. We were lucky by getting a lot of material from David Sandström, the drummer of Refused. He had a big private collection of hardcore-related material and always wanted to make use of it in some way. He was very happy when his hardcore treasure chest became the basis of our archive.

It was also helpful that David was such a respected figure in the scene. It gave our project credibility and encouraged others to make donations as well. We also got plenty of important material from the youth center Galaxen, which was an important meeting point and venue for straight edge kids throughout the 1990s.

What kind of material do people find when they visit the archive?
Most importantly, hundreds of video recordings and thousands of photos, but also fanzines, newspaper clippings, tapes, records, even clothes. The collection looks very different from most of the other ones we have.

In 2014, you organized a bigger exhibition. Can you tell us about this?
The European Union had named Umeå the 2014 European Capital of Culture. This coincided with a new museum opening in town: Guitars—the Museum. We were invited to do a straight edge exhibition for the opening. We saw this as a perfect opportunity to show how important straight

From the "Umeå—the European Capital of Hardcore 1989–2000" exhibition at Guitars—the Museum, 2014. Photo by Marcela Faé (fotostrasse.com).

edge had been for the town's cultural development. The exhibition was called "Umeå—The European Capital of Hardcore 1989–2000." There is also a catalog available under the same name.

No one gave you flak for this being a pretentious name?
Haha, no. I suppose most people understood that it was a tongue-in-cheek reference to Umeå having been named Europe's Cultural Capital that year. Furthermore, Umeå was indeed commonly referred to as the hardcore capital of Europe in the 1990s, not only in Sweden. And the legacy lives on. The exhibition was visited by people from all over the world. There was a kid from Canada who also visited the archive: he was very young and could have only been a child in the 1990s, but he was very familiar with the history.

Did no one ever criticize you for wrecking a lively DIY movement by confining it to an archive and putting it in a museum?
There was some skepticism early on, but it never turned into a big problem. When we started out, we made it very clear that we specifically wanted to document the period from 1989 to 2000, the heyday of Umeå straight edge. We didn't want to interfere with the existing straight edge scene, and we certainly didn't want to suggest that its history had ended. We simply thought it was important to honor the significance of the 1990s, and to keep the memory alive.

You suggested that Umeå straight edge had a big impact on life in Umeå overall. In what way?
To begin with, it involved a lot of people. The straight edge movement of the 1990s was built on all-ages shows held at youth centers and the like. The audience was very young; some were in their early teens. A whole generation was influenced by the scene. It was considered a cool thing to be straight edge.

If we look at the specific consequences of the era, the spread of vegetarianism and veganism was probably the most important one. Pretty much overnight, many students demanded vegetarian and vegan meals in school. This caused a huge public debate that became particularly heated when people related to the straight edge movement engaged in militant actions against McDonald's, Shell, slaughterhouses, and animal testing labs.

The sobriety aspect was overshadowed by all this, but it also provoked folks, which is perhaps ironic: people worrying about teenagers not doing "typical teenage stuff," rather than being glad about a sober and politically aware youth.

Straight edge youngsters hanging out at Ålidhems Ungdomsgård, 1995. Courtesy of Folkrörelsearkivet i Västerbotten.

Participant at a meeting of the syndicalist SAC in Umeå, 2012. Photo by Jan Abrahamsson.

Finally, the scene caused quite a lot of people to move to Umeå. They were attracted by straight edge and/or the music. Many of them stayed on and became an integral part of life in town. It has changed the place in many ways, even if the straight edge scene is no longer as big as it once was.

Why is that?
That's hard to say. Both Refused and Abhinanda dissolved in the late 1990s, and their members went on to play different kinds of music. This was certainly a big factor. The scene was more than the big bands, of course, but there is no getting around them having been very influential. Galaxen closing down in the year 2000 also had a big impact. As a physical space holding the scene together, it could never be replaced.

For more information about the archive visit umeahardcorearkiv.se. The catalog of the "Umeå—The European Capital of Hardcore 1989–2000" exhibition can be ordered at info@folkrorelsearkivet.se.

LEFT, RIGHT, "UNPOLITICAL": THE STRAIGHT EDGE MAZE OF RUSSIA

Sergey, Ruslan, Vitalik, Anton, and Evgeny

The straight edge scene in Russia has received a fair bit of international attention in the past fifteen years. Unfortunately, it has been for all the wrong reasons, since right-wing adaptations of straight edge have been particularly pronounced in the country. Robert Matusiak talked about this in *Sober Living for the Revolution*. More recently, I've been trying to revisit the debate with voices from Russia itself.

The narrative voice is that of Sergey, the person I've corresponded with most extensively. He has played in the bands Namatjira, Preface to the Dead Sea, Homemade, and Proschai. The other protagonists are the Antifa straight edge activist Ruslan; Vitalik, who has been involved in the band Haram, the Hard Times record label, and the online portal sxe.ru; the musician and label owner Anton; and Evgeny, guitarist in the band Partybreaker and one of the organizers of Russia's Edge Day.

I'd say that the first sXe-related movements in Russia were noticed in Moscow in the mid-1990s. The band Skygrain was only active for a couple of years, but with the development of heavy music and more information from other countries, other bands appeared. The best-known sXe-related band of that period was Unconform, who played at Fluff Fest in 2001.
Ruslan: Football hooliganism subculture had a significant impact on the Moscow hardcore scene. As well as its followers with ultra-right, Nazi, and

nationalistic ideas. Therefore there were a lot of conflicts at the gigs. The first day I visited hardcore show, there were two fights in a club (between Antifa and Nazis), plus a fight after the gig (between two football supporter groups).
Vitalik: *When all my peers from school started to try alcohol and soft drugs, straight edge seemed like a great alternative: the music, the gigs, the bands, ordering discs and merch through mail, the whole philosophy. I thought that this was much more interesting and much cooler than what my peers had to offer.*
Anton: *It's only when internet access really kicked in that things jumped to another level. I guess it holds true for other countries, too. Myspace and message boards back then made it so much easier for people to get into music and ideas and just get in touch with other people.*

But the "golden era" of the Russian sXe-movement started in the mid-2000s with the band Proverochnaya Lineika. Petr "Pit" Silaev, the band's vocalist, is considered by many here to be a Russian Ian MacKaye! You see, before him (and, unfortunately, after him and his band) straight edge in Russia was rarely connected with activism. It was a personal choice and it stopped there. Pit, however, was very active. Along with others, he started the sXe zine *IMHO* and the website sxe.ru. Both had a huge impact on the development of the scene. Pit promoted direct action, from Food Not Bombs to ALF to Antifa. And even if not all of the people in involved in these activities were straight edge, the sXe movement became very closely connected with them.
Vitalik: *Proverochnaya Lineika was the main combative force of our crew. They played shows under bridges in Moscow, in the forest, and in other strange locations, always without a permit. They became very famous within the scene. Pit's lyrics were strange but deep and funny at the same time. You could hardly call it music, but there was no lack of aggression in how these guys played. The main focus was on crazy performances and ideology. A whole crew of straight edgers and antifascists formed around the band. All other bands were "just the bands."*
Anton: *Where did the straight edge movement start here in the first place? Within the musical movement. Where did the straight edge movement had the most momentum here? Within the antifascist movement.*

Moscow and St. Petersburg have always been the centers of the movement, but it spread to other cities in Russia as well—often, it was more interesting there. There were also differences between Moscow and St. Petersburg. In Moscow, straight edge was more closely connected to antifascist activities, in St. Petersburg more to veganism. In Moscow and St. Petersburg, there

Petr "Pit" Silaev performing with Proverochnaya Lineika in Krasnodar, Russia, 2006. The crowd celebrates fighting off a Nazi attack. It was the third during Proverochnaya Lineika's 2006 tour. Courtesy of Petr Silaev.

were also more subdivisions within the scene, as it often is in bigger places. In smaller cities there were hardly any divisions.

Ruslan: There was a very strong and big scene in Kirov. Maybe even stronger than in Moscow. Kirov is very special. As far as I know, there is no such thing in other cities. The problem of movements in provincial cities is that they are short-lived because people strive to live in big cities, so the movement fades away. But in Kirov, they have their own atmosphere even now.

During this period, hardcore/punk gigs were regularly attacked by Nazis. Pit, along with other great guys from different scenes (like the late Ivan Khutorskoy), united people to fight Nazis at the gigs and on streets. The Nazi attacks led to the deaths of several guys from the hardcore/punk scene—and not all of them were Antifa, some just liked the music. This was terrible. But there was also strong unity within the DIY community at the time. There were gigs, where hardcore, street punk, metal, and screamo bands played together, sXe or vegan or not—there was no strict division.

The end of Proverochnaya Lineika (and the activism related to sXe) came when Pit got involved in the 2010 protests against the government's decision to remove the Khimki Forest near Moscow in order to build a motorway. Pit scheduled a gig to support the protesters. At the show, he said that music was not as important as direct action, and he suggested to go to the Khimki administration and show them that people were against their decision. Several hundred people, mainly anarchists and antifascists traveled to Khimki from Moscow by train. They reached the Khimki administration building with almost no resistance from the local police and, within three minutes, they broke the windows, fired air guns, and spraypainted the walls. It probably became the most famous and biggest direct action that Russia had seen.

After that, Pit was forced to leave the country as he faced criminal charges. He wrote a book about his Antifa activities and currently lives somewhere in Europe. Since then, the sXe movement in Russia has almost exclusively been associated with music. Straight edge is, once again, seen as

Under the name DJ Stalingrad, Petr "Pit" Silaev wrote about his experiences in the Russian antifa movement in the book *Exodus*. It has been translated into several languages. This is the cover of the Finnish edition.

a personal choice. But nowadays, everyone in hardcore/punk knew what straight edge is.

There have been bands, both in Russia and the CIS countries, and there was a bit of a youth crew revival. Ten years ago, there was a very strong sXe revival in Ukraine. In Belarus there was always a really strong political hardcore scene, but not sXe-related. Relations to Ukraine have become more complicated because of the political crisis between Russia and Ukraine, but I hope this will pass and the shithead politicians will no longer affect our scenes. Known Russian straight edge bands of the past decade have been Engage at Will, Flawless Victory, High Hopes, Haram, Partybreaker, Apache, and Nashi Nadejdy.

Ruslan: There was a huge hardcore and sXe movement in Ukraine. We were often going to them and vice versa. But after Maidan, Crimea, and Donetsk/ Lugansk everything changed. People from both sides started to support their own government blindly, nationalism started to rise, there are people from both sides who went to war, sometimes even sharing the groups with Nazis. Bands supported the current regimes on stage. It was total bullshit.

Evgeny: I'd like to name the Ukrainian band Aspire, which, in my opinion, is one of the most significant bands of the entire post-Soviet area, both musically and lyrically. It perfectly matches my concept of straight edge: eternal search and strive to learn about yourself and the world around you. Too bad this band broke up.

There are women involved in straight edge and they are usually into feminism and women's rights. But there is a lot of sexism in the scene and they are often ignored—like almost all feminist groups in the country. Often, they are integrated in the hardcore punk scene only verbally, but not in reality. When stories about sexual abuse within the scene surface, many guys question the survivors or think that "feminists are going too far." It reflects a deeply sexist culture, and any change in the scene will require a change in mainstream society, too. It will take a long time.

I should mention the Vegan Club in St. Petersburg that was active for a couple of years in the early 2010s. It had a policy of no animal-derived materials, no smoking, and no drinking, so it was a great place for vegans and straight edgers to meet, listen to lectures, watch shows, etc. People who were involved in the club are still active in St. Petersburg but are mainly concerned with veganism and environmentalism. Still, St. Petersburg is not only the Russian vegan capital, but it's also the center of a small vegan straight edge scene. There are much more vegetarians among straight edgers than vegans, though.

I remember an Integrity gig at the Vegan Club. The Integrity members didn't like the rule of not drinking there and their singer, Dwid, called the people who ran the venue "vegan pussies" during the show. It was disappointing to see someone with so much status within the scene disrespect the efforts of people to create a safe space, especially after they invite you to perform there.

Very few people in the straight edge scene stay for ten years or more. Most of the "oldtimers" are gone, and they are not interested in telling their story. They seem to think of their straight edge days as a youth period that they have outgrown. Some of them once shouted "Young till I die!" It can be

MOSCOW EDGE DAY

21.10. «ШАГИ», 500/700 рублей

PARTYBREAKER · LOSS · OUTXSET · XSUPREMACYX
RESURGAM · REBROUKA · VURDALAK · XLIFTEDX
The HERD · X-RAY · TAX ON JOY · HAWKxHADESxDOG

disheartening when people who once were very active in the scene start to live a life like everyone else. We all need energy and inspiration to go against the flow. That's why it's good to go to Fluff Fest and meet people like Greg Bennick, Kurt of Catalyst Records, Robert from Refuse Records, Andy Hurley, or other guys who are still true to their ideals. I always tell them how I play their records or read their interviews when I feel down and need some emotional support.

But also people who are still straight edge are hesitant to talk about it. It reflects the attitude of it being a personal choice. Not many activists are straight edge today.

Russian reality, especially in small cities, leaves you with two choices regarding substance use: either you decide that alcohol and drugs help you to survive all of the darkness and depression around you, or you shake off the dirt and decide to take life into your own hands. The latter is the more active way, and it implicates that you start thinking about what you consume and why.

Ruslan: Life in our country is very hard when you are sober. You have to relieve the stress somehow. Alcohol and weed are the most affordable methods of relaxation. Watch the numbers: bottle of beer = 0.50 EUR; a bottle of vodka = 1.50 EUR 1.5; a book = 5 EUR; a ticket for a football game = 10 EUR. So what will be the choice? The cinema can compete with alcohol, but there are so many shit movies that drinking is preferable!

Evgeny: Russian reality, especially in provincial cities, is one of total poverty, lack of prospects, and, as a result, problems with alcohol that serve as escapism. For many people here, straight edge has become a way to remain human, and serves as a protest against the surrounding reality. It's not so much about what they want to be, but about what they don't want to be.

What makes the situation in Russia special is that Nazis have attempted to use straight edge for their purposes, probably more so than in any other country. The situation is similar in some Eastern Europe countries, but here in Russia there were times when it looked as if the majority of the scene was fascist. That's why people in Russia who know nothing about the hardcore scene think of straight edge as a right-wing ideology. In recent years, the Nazi adaptations of straight edge have subsided a bit, but they are still prevalent, especially in smaller cities. It has also been affected by the divisions within the extreme right around Russia's annexation of Crimea.

Anton: I think right-wing interpretation of straight edge is pretty simple and doesn't vary that much. Just the standard bullshit about "keeping your blood clean" and uniting against punks/foreigners/people in power.

There is also the problem of straight edge being confused with a popular movement called ZOJ (*zdorovyi obraz jizni*, or, healthy lifestyle), but it's not the same. ZOJ is very popular now among young people in Russia. It is mainly connected with sports, working out, etc., and somewhat with nutrition. The concept already existed even during Soviet Russia, but it experienced a boost in the last several years. It has no particular ideology apart from being healthy. It might entail some personal protest against the advertising of alcohol/smoking/drugs. Followers are often despised by other young people. They are seen as preachy and of thinking of themselves as superior.

The confusion between straight edge and ZOJ is illustrated in the short film *Outcast.* Supposedly, it is about straight edge, but it really is about ZOJ. It propagates being healthy, that's all. The protagonist does nothing to solve the problems around him. He is living in a bad neighborhood (which is typical for Russia), and he is bullied by others. But the only thought he has is to be healthy; not to make your neighbor-

Russian straight edge antifa youth showing their colors at a May 1 rally in Moscow, 2010. The banner reads: "No weaknesses, no prejudices. Without justice there is no peace!" Source: redskins.ru.

hood a better place; not to have a talk with others to explain why what they are doing is wrong. Okay, they might stop to bully him now, because he is strong, but they will simply find another victim. That's the reality of kids into ZOJ. They see no further than their nose. No surprise that many Nazis seem to like this movie. Nazis use ZOJ a lot for their propaganda.

Evgeny: It's no wonder that Nazis have adopted straight edge. It fits their crazy ideas of super humans, race supremacy, and other bullshit. Nowadays it is mainly promoted by steroid freaks on YouTube who propagate ZOJ.

To illustrate the difference to straight edge, let me share a story. When I did one of my straight edge tattoos, the artist asked me what straight edge was. He pointed at some guys doing pull-ups in the yard and asked if they were straight edge. I said, "No," and explained that I didn't even know whether they were drinking or smoking. "Okay," he said, "let's suppose they do not drink or smoke, and they don't do drugs—are they straight edge then?" "No," I said again, but now with less certainty. However, I think you should at least know the history of straight edge as a movement to be considered straight edge. You don't have to wear that label to be sober or drug-free.

But straight edge is more than just a name for those choices. Straight edge is a movement. ZOJ is not.

Ruslan: Straight edge cannot be based on just a healthy lifestyle. It is an integral part of the hardcore scene, a protest against things that put a person inside boundaries and put a label on them Addiction to alcohol or drugs, pressure from society, aggression, and discrimination. Straight edge makes you free from all that. Without prejudices!

Evgeny: Since 2016, we have been organizing annual Edge Day shows in Moscow, trying to have bands from all over Russian and, if possible, from neighbouring countries. During the last show, the art director of the club came to us and asked: "Why do people not drink? Is this some sort of sports club?" We think that moments like these prove that our shows are successful. There are a lot of young people and this is great. Almost everyone who is into straight edge comes to our shows, but this is not the most important thing for us: everyone is welcome!

The way I see it, the Russian straight edge scene has been more influenced by straight edge in the US than by the current European scene. Sometimes, it might seem as if the Russian scene has taken only the worst parts (for example, an apolitical "music for the sake of music" type stance). Nonetheless, I strongly believe it has been changing the lives of many kids for the better. And I don't just mean that it encourages them to abstain from drugs and alcohol. In order to be straight edge in Russia, you need confidence and inner strength. Social pressure and the ever deteriorating political and economic situation leave you with few options to sustain yourself. Under these circumstances, a simple personal choice can make a difference; a personal example can demonstrate to other people that a different existence is possible. This, in turn, can be a motivation to change the world around you.

SCENE REPORT

THE FUCK HARDCORE
SHOWS PROCLAMATION

Jen Twigg

Jen Twigg has played in several punk bands, including The Ambulars, Attendant, and Fraktur. This text is from a guest column in *Maximumrocknroll* no. 336 (May 2011).

It's one of those things where you avoid something you take issue with for a while, and then suddenly find yourself in the middle of it, and it catches you off guard, ill-prepared, and you start fuming.

I went to see Envy at Reggie's back in October (amazing, by the way!). One of the opening bands was Trash Talk. It was funny, because the first two bands were some instrumental band from Belfast and Touche Amore, and although kids were going nuts and singing along, it was no big deal. Then Trash Talk came out. Immediately, a huge pit formed in front of the stage, squishing almost everyone else back against the back wall. And then the familiar scene began.

Pacing back and forth, posturing aggressively, stomping, kicking, punching, violently flailing arms. Two dudes accidentally knocked into each other and started posturing at each other and shit talking, needing to be separated before a fight. Kids crisscrossed the room, performing one of the most extreme versions of macho masculinity ever to dilute the political bases of punk rock. Because this violence isn't even raw and reactionary; it's planned, staged, practiced. It privileges machismo unquestioningly.

It privileges the antiquated notion that dudes can't control themselves and need to blow off steam violently because men will be men. It's such an obvious fucking farce.

THE FUCK HARDCORE SHOWS PROCLAMATION.
It's one of those things where you avoid something you take issue with for a while, and then suddenly find yourself in the middle of it, and it catches you off guard, ill-prepared, and you start fuming.
I went to see Envy at Reggie's back in October

When I watch this shit happen, I think to myself, of course I felt like a weird outsider a lot during a certain time of my growing up in punk . . . almost all of my friends were dudes and we always went to hardcore shows. I couldn't win, because there was barely any room for a different way to enjoy shows; you either had to perform the type of violent masculinity going on in the pit, or stand in the back and be accused of being a punk rock girlfriend who only holds coats and can't hang with the big boys (or find a way around that which is still privileged, like taking photos or tabling). And either way you're pitted in competition against other girls, because the dudes compare you to the other girls involved on a scale of who's conforming to hardcore dude standards the best, most worthy of being accepted into their group on their level, on their terms. The prevalent thread at hardcore shows is a dichotomy of macho fucking bullshit.

The thing is that I love a lot of hardcore music. I love listening to it, and I always have, especially amazing bands like Sick Fix, which subvert these standards as much as possible from within the genre. I just can't fucking stand how this stuff is often acted out at shows.

Pop punk dudes may often be sad misogynists and have their own set of issues deserving dissection, but at least I can go up to the front where I can actually see a band during a pop punk show and sing along and know I'm not going to get punched in the head by some beefy posturing asshole who probably has a Nike shoe collection and is an aloof jerk to the women he dates. That's why I got into punk, to get away from that mainstream dude mentality of entitlement and privilege and to be critical of that kind of performance. To be faced with it is a slap in the face, literally. And I'm not fucking interested.

I know that people who like going to hardcore shows will read this, and may disagree with me or be super offended. That's fine. You should think about why exactly that is though. You might think, Jen doesn't know what she's talking about; she just doesn't get it. Wrong, I do know. I've been going to hardcore shows for ten years and I've performed all of these roles at some point, and seen them performed. I'm interested in subversion and revolution, but not the kind that involves dick measuring contests. Radical counterculture politics like veganism and straight edge lose meaning when they are performed in such an oppressive environment without questioning it.

ALCOHOL AND SOLIDARITY

Ane V.

This article is taken from the zine *Sjølstyrt liv* no. 6, Winter 2010. As the author states, it was written "in the context of a debate regarding alcohol being served at the Bodø Hardcore Festival; the arguments, however, are relevant to many other contexts as well."

Ane V. is a transgender person from north of the Arctic Circle. They live in a small village, make comics, illustrations, zines, and sometimes texts and music, mostly autobiographically inspired. They like a lot of black ink and work that has a political tone to it.

Bodø is a town of fifty thousand people in the far north of Norway. The Bodø Hardcore Festival has been organized since 1999.

There are a thousand reasons to explain why alcohol contradicts the principle of solidarity. I could write a lot about this but can't be bothered. However, I want to say a few words about why I find that drinking alcohol at the Bodø Hardcore Festival (BHCF) contradicts solidarity.

First, BHCF is an all-ages festival. Creating different age categories, and excluding a significant number of participants from parts of the venue, has nothing to do with solidarity. It goes against any commitment to overcome age discrimination. Furthermore, alcohol being available for people over 18 has led to people under 18 trying to smuggle in alcohol or get drunk beforehand in order to join in the "fun."

Art by Ane V., 2018.

Second, the alcohol industry stands for everything that BHCF is supposed to stand against. The alcohol industry stands for consumer culture and makes money off of people getting drunk and feeling insecure. It contributes to folks thinking that they have to be drunk in order to be social. Alcoholism is a huge problem not only for those directly affected by it, but also for their families and friends struggling alongside them. Serving alcohol at BHCF shows no solidarity for alcoholics (sober or not), children of alcoholics who are reminded of a difficult childhood, and partners of alcoholics who are reminded of abuse, and perhaps physical and psychological violence, in connection with alcohol. Pretty much any restaurant and shop reminds them of this, and it would be nice to provide a space where this is not the case.

Third, I have attended BHCF for a few years now, and I have seen patterns of growing alcohol consumption. I have heard from several women about inappropriate comments and being groped by drunk men. There are always people spreading bad energy, using offensive language and behaving poorly. In my experience, events without alcohol and an audience that is there because people want to have a good time and listen to the music have a much nicer feel and better atmosphere. People are more considerate, more responsible, and they have genuine fun, rather than being drunk or high on other drugs. In my opinion, those who are primarily interested in drinking can go to a bar and allow the people who come to the festival because of the music to dance to it in peace.

Fourth—and this is perhaps the most important bit (in any case for me)—many people feel unsafe and uncomfortable around others who drink. They are afraid to go out, and they avoid places where alcohol is consumed (parties, concerts, restaurants). It has been shown again and again that sexual abuse occurs more often when people are drunk. The same is true for psychological and physical violence. People under the influence of alcohol have less control over what they say and do, their motor skills are weakened and their reactions are delayed. It is more difficult for them to interpret others, to understand what they want and what makes them feel uncomfortable. They act in ways that offend and intimidate others. Many people also become more aggressive when they drink, and some look for physical contact without realizing that the person they touch might not want to be touched. In short, it contradicts solidarity to sell and consume alcohol at BHCF because it makes many people there uncomfortable and excludes those who feel unsafe. Defensive rights are always more important than offensive rights, and there is no excuse to act in ways that hurt others.

I don't know how many times I have decided not to go to a party or concert because alcohol was served there. And I have talked to many people who feel the same. Alcohol is excluding.

Fifth, drinking means a lack of solidarity with those who have worked their asses off to create a nice festival only to be forced to take care of people who are out of control because they are drunk. It forces them to take on the role of security, to try to reason with people, to throw them out, etc. Plus, they need to clean up the mess that always comes with a night of drinking. BHCF is what it is because many people are willing to help as volunteers, and we should make what they do as easy and pleasant for them as possible.

Yes, I know that there is always a lack of solidarity in our lives in one way or another (child labor, privileges, etc.), but we should still try to act in a spirit of solidarity, reflect on what we do, and make sure it doesn't offend or hurt others. Solidarity!

WHEN STRAIGHTEDGE WALKED THE EARTH / STRAIGHTEDGE MEANS I HAVE NO FRIENDS / NOT GOING TO THE EARTH CRISIS GIG

Laura Synthesis

Laura Synthesis started the zine *Synthesis* in 1996, and Synthesis Zine Distro a year later. She has organized gigs, campaigns, demos, and film events. In 2003, she was involved in opening a vegan cooperative café. She currently works in a homelessness charity and volunteers as a legal observer with Green & Black Cross. She lives in South East London with her partner and two little terriers. This is a medley of three of her essays.

When Straightedge Walked the Earth (2004)

NB. The purpose of this article is to put forward my belief that alcohol is solely destructive. I am not advocating any kind of a ban on alcohol.

So sxe has all but died out in Europe and is it any wonder? Its popularity was established as a trend rather than as a movement and so of course people are going to find it difficult to hold on to something so superficial. Maybe we need to be reminded that straightedge ethics are actually very radical, revolutionary and progressive. Being straightedge means I am saying no to some of the most manipulative devices that the Powers use to keep us from being free individuals. They want to drug us into ignorance and passivity. They want us to have artificially constructed desires and to make us forget our desire for freedom. They want to make money from these constructed desires.

All the above things concern me of course but lately I have been becoming more and more conscious of *straightedge as a feminist choice*. The feminist aspect is mostly about alcohol but I will mention the "don't fuck" aspect very quickly first.

DON'T FUCK

When I first heard Ian MacKaye's lyrics I really was impressed to hear a man talking about sexuality in a responsible way for a change. The truth is that men are taught to be consumers of sexuality and consumers of women in the same way as they are taught to consume everything else in capitalist society. More recently of course women have been brainwashed the same way. We do not learn how to interact with other human beings, we learn how to use people's bodies and forget that those bodies are part of a complete individual. Men with this attitude behave hatefully toward women and occasionally they need to have their behaviour pointed out to them if they are ever going to try to behave differently. Sexual consumerism poisons all interactions between women and men. It is also another way men gain power over women in our patriarchal society.

DON'T DRINK

Alcohol has one purpose. A friend of mine recently pointed out the one possibly positive aspect of intoxication, the fact that we all occasionally need to temporarily escape from ourselves to stay sane in our mad world. The way I see it though, we have healthier ways of doing this and at any rate I cannot think of a single person I have come across who has a moderate approach to using alcohol as a temporary escape in this way. I have however come across many forms of alcoholism.

VOMIT ON THE STREETS OF LONDON

I live in an alcoholic society. Sometimes I think that almost everyone in Britain is alcoholic. The whole of working class culture is built on having a drink in the pub in the evening. Pubs are not for meeting people or spending time with friends. In a pub or bar one is constantly pressured to drink alcohol and to have more and more of it. Living in Britain is very expensive yet people spend huge proportions of their income on drink. Often of course they are getting drunk because they are depressed about their financial problems!

VIOLENCE ON THE STREETS OF LONDON

For the record, I do know that alcohol does not create violence. Alcohol simply brings out the truth; it uncovers the emotions we usually keep under controls. Some people are jolly drunks, some are affectionate drunks, some are loud & obnoxious drunks, some are sad drunks. The most visible drunkenness for most of us though is probably violent drunkenness. Every Saturday night on every high street in Britain there are men of various ages whose lives are full of repressed fury. They have been raised to live down to masculine stereotypes of toughness and power-seeking. All their artificial desires are constantly frustrated (as they are supposed to be if we are to continue to spend money on satisfying them). The only emotions they have learned to express are destructive ones. So obviously the problem goes deeper than just alcohol, but as long as people use alcohol as a crutch, an outlet, and an escape they will never find constructive, positive solutions to their problems.

PROFITING FROM MISERY AND VIOLENCE

Most of us have probably had bad or even horrible experiences with drunk people. Some of you may have even been raised by one or more alcoholics and lived in constant dread of what happens when a family member starts drinking. Drinking drains family incomes. Drinking turns people we love into violent monsters beyond the reach of reason or sense. Drinking is a huge factor in people's (let's be honest, usually men's) violence against their partners and children. Alcohol is the number one drug used by men to date rape women. The manufacturers of alcohol know all of this. They really do not care.

PROFITING FROM RAPE

The definition of "rape" should be made clear before we go any further. Many people still do not know what rape is. Rape is when someone manipulates or forces someone to have sex without their full consent. Rape can happen even when the rapist believes that the other person has consented. Everyone has the responsibility to clarify their sexual boundaries and their partner's sexual boundaries. If one partner wants to limit the sexual boundaries at any point the other person must respect this; no exceptions. Being drunk is not an excuse for crossing someone's boundaries.

I see the production of alcoholic drinks as overall an evil and unethical industry. Alcohol capitalists make their profits by selling something which is chemically a poison. This poison is used by people to make themselves

Laura Synthesis in the midst of the Brexit turmoil, London, 2016. Photo by Sam Challis.

insensible and while they are drunk this generally prevents them from taking a positive role in the world. A drunk person is at best a passive consumer and at worst a thug, rapist and committer of domestic violence. Alcohol advertising revels in sexism and misogyny. Drinking will make you more feminine and more masculine. Drinking will enhance your ability to be a sexual consumer. Alcohol will get you laid. Alcohol companies are perfectly aware of the use of alcohol as a date rape drug and they market their product to men with the promise of sexual results.

Personally I find it shocking that so few campaigns exist to inform women of the dangers of drinking. Right now there is a pretty good poster campaign in bars in London warning women about accepting drinks from strange men or leaving their drinks unattended because of the use of drugs like Rohypnol. Men drugging women however is relatively rare. Men using alcohol as a date rape drug is common and accepted because of course no one acknowledges that this is what is happening. The only campaign I have ever heard of about this was by the Women's Campaign of the National Union of Students in the UK. New students at UK Universities are constantly pushed to drink when they first arrive and most end up drinking to excess. Many women end up having drunken sex in this situation which often is not safe and/or fully consensual. Unfortunately the NUS Women's Campaign attempts could never achieve a very high profile in the face of all the pro-drinking propaganda. Many students' unions only survive on the profits from the alcohol in their bars.

THINK ABOUT IT

Every alcohol manufacturer in the world
Every bar in the world
Every bar employee in the world . . .
. . . must get some percentage of their profits from the use of alcohol to rape women.
. . . must get some percentage of their profits from people who beat up their partners and children while under the influence.
. . . must get some percentage of their profits from alcoholics who drink themselves to death.

This is the industry you are supporting when you buy alcohol.

I do not feel smug to be straightedge. I feel sad and frustrated about the effects that intoxication has had on the world and has every day. I also feel afraid for my own safety when I walk streets where drunk people are likely to lash out with violence against me or my friends at any time.

In a World Without Alcohol

There would be one less excuse for rape.
There would be one less tool for rapists.
Many more people would be forced to confront their demons.
Just think of the relative peace in our streets and homes.

Straightedge Means I Have No Friends (2008)

Do straightedgers hang out in crews because nobody else will have them? Is that even a bad thing? I believe that straightedge is a Very Good Thing for each of us and the wider society (though I won't go into the reasons now; check out my website for the essay "When Straightedge Walked The Earth"), and I'm calling for more social solidarity between edgers, even if that implies crewism.

I think we all know that most people who temporarily call themselves "straightedgers" do so for self-esteem, peer pressure or social status reasons. These are also the main reasons people drop the edge and indeed leave the hardcore scene altogether. What could be more ridiculous than sticking to a youth counterculture when you spend all day with proper grownups at work and can't collect records because you have babies to support? In Europe, 92% of straightedgers drop out at by the age of 26 (I just made that up, but it's not far off). Now in my mid-30s, I can inform those edgebreakers that staying true would have gotten no easier at the age of 27.

Social pressure in adulthood is more insidious than when we were youths. Life gets more complex so destructive life choices have more niches and cracks to insinuate themselves into. Speaking personally, peer pressure to drink has no effect on me whatsoever, but I do feel the social repercussions.

I live in the famously sozzled United Kingdom, a society so alcoholic that drink isn't just the facilitator or basis of all social interaction, but its proxy.

"What are you doing this weekend?"

"I'm going out drinking/getting pissed."

If you don't drink, it can be assumed that you aren't interested in socialising at all. I'll present a couple of scenarios to demonstrate how difficult it can be to extract alcohol from everyday life.

Scenario 1:

The English way of starting a sexual relationship is to snog an acquaintance when both parties are drunk. There is simply no language for approaching the physical/emotional hurdle that people in this society are prepared to use.

Scenario 2:

People do notice, and comment, if one drinks non-alcohol at the pub or a party no matter how low key one is about it. Misery loves company and drinkers may feel anything from discomfort to anger around someone more sober than they are. They know it puts them at a disadvantage.

If anything, situations like those above become more common after 30 as everyone's lives become so boring they can't do anything together but sullenly sip pints.

One of my sxe contemporaries is certain that by not drinking socially during one's late teens and early 20's, one ends up a "cranky old loner" with no friends. When I think of the straightedgers my age who do have tight bonds of friendship, it is with other straightedgers (whether or not they use the term). On the other hand, I just as often see straightedge adults who hate each other and have been talking shit since the '90s. We carry the Ieper Fest in our hearts (proper name: the VortNVis Festival—annual gathering popular in the '90s where sxe and other hardcore kids would come together and make enemies).

It can be positive that many sorts of people are attracted to the straightedge lifestyle, but it's not much of a basis for friendship in itself. On the contrary, and I am guilty of this, one can be more annoyed by straightedgers who are, for example, anti-abortion / support commercialism in hardcore / are evangelical christians / all of the above than by non-sober HC folks with these beliefs. Nevertheless, I wish we could find more common ground. When a friend loses the edge, I don't feel stabbed in the back. It's when a straightedger is too cool to want to know me that is the real betrayal. When I meet a straightedger who is also an anarchist and into screamo, I almost can't believe my luck though I know from experience that this is no guarantee of an ongoing relationship. Hardcore kids can be such social fuckups. Dammit people, shared understanding and values, even over something as superficial as straightedge, is a precious thing and these connections need nurturing and maintaining.

Since thinking about these things, I've gained a greater appreciation for the idea of "straightedge sisterhood"—a term that never has amounted to much and is pathetically rarely associated with feminism. I've had great experiences of fun, mutual support, friendship and empowerment with women through the punk/anarchist scene, but sometimes it seems the explicitly sxe corners of the scene bring out the worst in insecure girldom (eg. popularity competitions and shit-talking). Nevertheless, the phantom of an idea like a sisterhood based on soberness in a world infected by drunk/drugged male violence has potential.

In conclusion, just because the '88 crew style has the tinge of cultish, macho, chauvinism about it, doesn't mean in the 21st century we can't reclaim and redefine it. Social solidarity is healthy—it gives us roots and comradeship in an atomised world and can be a base for building or cooperating for social change. When I meet a fellow punk, sober or otherwise, I'll keep trying to build those bridges because we all need each other and the better world we can create together.

Not Going to the Earth Crisis Gig (2018)

"When the militant thing came about, obviously these people's issues were not just about being sober. They were about power and violence and anger, and how to get that shit out of their system."
—Ian MacKaye

Amazingly, the band Earth Crisis have a gig at the end of my street tonight. It's a surprising venue to say the least. It's not one of those midsized Camden Town venues where all the commercial hardcore bands of a certain size play, but a pub in South London with weekly open mic nights. Not only that, but it's the only nonfestival gig they seem to be playing in the UK on this tour. I've never seen them live and I won't be buying a ticket to see them tonight. Surprisingly, there are still tickets left. I'd expected this show to be sold out in minutes. Clearly things have moved on in terms of numbers who will turn out for this stuff.

The stuff itself hasn't changed sadly. I had a look at the support bands—UK straightedge bands! In 2018! The first video of the first band I looked at was a live gig in which the focus was on the violence in the pit. Looking at that video I felt embarrassed for the participants and thought I saw embarrassment in the violent boys themselves. Here we have young white men who clearly aren't comfortable in their bodies, in their attempts to move their bodies or in their masculinity. To move that way, they clearly have some issues they feel the need to work out, but the movements are forced and awkward. It's the same moves kids like them were doing 20 years ago—choreographed, deliberate and executed poorly.

It's a relief to find I have an ironic distance from violent dancing now. Fifteen years ago I felt a more intense repugnance. I used to think I could be friends with anyone in the punk/hardcore scene. In fact, I felt as if we all were friends already. Metalcore showed me that the scene could produce music I don't like. More than that I found that this subgenre was home to values and practices a spectrum away from what I thought we were about in the underground scene. Suddenly, most straightedgers in Europe were these violent wankers with reactionary politics. One of these boys saw the word "feminist" on the cover of my zine and dropped it back onto the distro stall like a hot coal.

They were boys. Deeply homosocial, ignorant about the complexity of the world, hung up about their relationships with their fathers. Anti-abortion because they'd not actually accidentally knocked someone up yet. And drunk by the time they were 26/28/32 years old. Karl from Earth Crisis apparently isn't though, to give him credit. It's likely that the vegan revolution that has taken over the world is partially a result of the popularity of vegan metalcore. Not to forget of course that vegan metalcore is an inheritor of the vegan and vegetarian punk and hardcore that came before it.

In four days' time I'll have the honour of visiting Penny Rimbaud and Gee Vaucher at their home Dial House in Essex. It'll be my second visit and the result of my Argentinian sister Flo's friendship with Penny. There's a direct line from Crass to my radical politics and veganism. I'm fairly confident that the influence of Crass on the world has been at least 99% positive. I wouldn't say that for the violent, political reactionary, macho metalcore scene.

BLOCKHEAD BY BLOCKHEAD
How many people got pulled into that subgenre who could have received a radical political education and some emotional intelligence from any other part of the hardcore scene? How many were put off alternative culture completely by the posturing nonsense? Worst of all perhaps, how undermining was it of our noncommercial global network of friends that this bloated subgenre so forcefully pushed profiteering attitudes and practices where they weren't needed or welcome?

A friend I've known for 20 years said to me recently that he regrets how we all treated each other in the 90s. He meant the intolerance for each other's approach to commercialism in the HC scene among other things. Admirably, he had managed to be friends with everyone and I suspect he was chiding me for my tendency to be in conflict with the H8000 types. I'd like to think I can meet on common ground with anyone, but reactionary and capitalist attitudes tend to colonise and destroy, and so even neutral ground has to be defended and the rebel alliance has to push back to not be overrun.

WE'VE GOT A BIGGER PROBLEM NOW
When I saw that 2018 video of the boys windmilling and elbowing each other in the head, I found my body reacting in the same way I do when I hear news of fascist actions. Macho insecurity and toxic masculinity are key to fascism, the "alt-right" and the H8000-type mentality. It's not to be excused or ignored. There are a range of methods in the political and social

organising repertoire to deal with all of these. None of them has been wholly effective. As important though is building the alternative society we want to live in. Just a few minutes away from my home in Southeast London is DIY Space for London—a social centre run by a collective of volunteers that has been the dream of so many punks in London for so many years. It's got an "Accountability Agreement" and is a genuine safe space. You feel it when entering the building—this is a good place that is good to be. Its existence and the events that happen there are an example of the positive change our scene can bring to the world. We can achieve when we bring our collective dreams together, show each other comradeship, act with good faith and address problems openly.

> *"We need to learn, or re-learn, how to build comradeship and solidarity instead of doing capital's work for it by condemning and abusing each other. This doesn't mean, of course, that we must always agree—on the contrary, we must create conditions where disagreement can take place without fear of exclusion and excommunication."*
>
> —Mark Fisher

NOT FOR ME

Elina

This text was taken from the Swedish zine *Sober Coven 1: Nykterhet* (2015).

My first contact with self-chosen, active sobriety was through the hardcore scene. I was one of the crew, I knew the right people, I helped organize gigs. I belonged to the community. It was a community that that made me feel safe and that was in many ways rewarding. Us. Together.

But there were cracks in the unity: obvious differences between myself and those who were accustomed to taking up space, to being listened to, and to being seen, physically, verbally, and musically. If they fucked up, they just laughed it off. Their self-image was not dependent on how others saw them. Straight Edge. Sobriety. Brotherhood. Dudes.

Straight edge, so they say, requires you to be true till death. Some people are straight edge for their own sake, some out of solidarity with others. No drugs, no alcohol. Never. There are, of course, not only dudes in hardcore and straight edge, but they are the vast majority. They set the norms.

I never chose to "claim edge," as it is called. I can't apply the concept to myself. It sounds wrong and weird. Not because I plan to start drinking next month or because I'd like to use other drugs; it is more about a fear of disappointing people or of losing their respect should I "fail." Hatred against dropouts is everyday stuff. Even worse is the casual hatred against drug users. It makes me feel very uncomfortable. They could be talking about who I was.

From *Sober Coven 1: Nykterhet*. Art by Majja.

I have long struggled with low self-esteem, even self-hatred. I was prone to self-destructive behavior, self-punishment. Alcohol and drugs meant many things to me at the same time: destructiveness and reward, pain and escape. I still get tempted. Sometimes more, sometimes less.

In order to live up to expectations as a "girl," it feels like I have to be so much better. I have to have so much more to offer not be doubted. Doing your best is not enough. You have to take yet another step, be better than all of bloody humanity (read: all men). You have to strive after perfection. You must not make mistakes. You must be a "good girl."

I refuse to be forced into an identity only to be taken seriously by a group of dudes. I will no longer allow their patriarchal despise for weakness undermine my self-esteem. I am sober—for me, for everyone—but I also understand what it means to be human, and I will no longer hate myself. I am not perfect, and I don't want to be part of your bloody macho crew.

I don't dare to claim something. Or let's say: I don't want to claim a name that is tied to hatred against those who suffer from all the shit brought upon them by society, patriarchy, and capitalism. I don't want to be in the same category as the dude-bros who laugh about jokes at my expense—or, indeed, at the expense of those for whom things have turned out worse.

SPECIAL INTEREST

STRAIGHT EDGE
AND RELIGION

Interview with Francis Stewart

Francis Stewart is from Northern Ireland, and a longtime participant in the straight edge hardcore scene. She is the author of *Punk Rock Is My Religion: Straight Edge Punk and "Religious" Identity* (2017) and teaches at the Bishop Grosseteste University of Lincoln, England.

You've written a dissertation about straight edge and religion. Can you give us a short summary?

The PhD thesis was both a sociological examination of how sXe has manifested and is performed in the UK and Ireland compared with parts of the USA, and an exploration of the role that religion as a concept and as praxis in the West has had on that. It was also a consideration of what we mean when we use the word "religion," and in what ways religion as a concept and a construction shifted in a postmodern, increasingly globalized, technological world. I argued that subcultures such as sXe punk have emerged as forms of implicit religion (using Edward Bailey's definition and analytical categories/tools) and as a surrogate (in the original sense of the word, meaning "successor") for more traditional forms of religion, such as what we problematically call world religions or institutions such as the church. Using the voices, ideas, and experiences of the interviewees I demonstrated that within such surrogates it was not dogma, institutions, answers, or even a divine being that mattered, but questions of authenticity, selfhood, self-responsibility, DIY, and community that were the core.

You interviewed a lot of people. How did you find them?

The interviewees were found in multiple ways. Some I found through friends who put me in touch with their friends, or friends of friends, and so on. Others I found during fieldwork at gigs/shows/events; I would tell them what I was doing and ask if they wanted to be a part of it in some way. A small number were found by putting announcements in fanzines, also online, with means of contacting me. In two subsequent projects—one on Dharma Punx, and one on Anarchism, Religion and Animal Advocacy—I have expanded that by doing similar outreach on social media closed groups. Often those interviewees would then put me in touch with friends who they thought would want to be a part of it. In the later stages of the PhD project, I came across groups such as the Punk Scholars Network and the Anarchist Scholars Network, which were amazingly helpful in finding contacts. Finally, as I would present my work at academic conferences, a very small number of other scholars would come up and tell me they were involved with punk or had a friend who was and give me contact details from there. In some ways, it was not unlike how it used to be pre–social media, mobile phones, and the internet, when you tried to set up a tour for your band or your mate's band or book bands for your venue. Punk, in the broadest terms, has developed really effective networking tools through simply having to figure them out as it went along.

I held the rule, and still do, that in order to try and maintain some distance I would not interview close friends or family as there is always the concern that they would unconsciously try to shift their answers and responses in such a way as to help me with whatever they thought I would want to hear. Not out of malice, but simply because it is human nature to want to help those we care for, to want to do what we can to help them achieve their goals or dreams. I also didn't want them to be exposed to any accusations of being a set up (for lack of a better term) or to have their experiences and ideas dismissed by other academics because of their relationship with me. This was particularly a concern because I was also trying to deal with the insider/outsider quandary that many researchers have to cope with.

How did you negotiate that tension? You are straight edge yourself.

The honest answer is: not very well sometimes. It was something I struggled with, and still do, a lot. You can read all the academic books you want about conducting field work, maintaining a distance, and so on, but in reality you frequently have to deal with situations in which all of these boundaries are blurred. There were times—such as the first time I walked into 924 Gilman Street—where the distinction between you as a punk on the one hand, and you as an academic researcher on the other go completely out the window. At that moment, when I walked in and saw for myself the graffiti, the images, the stage that I had previously only ever read about in band interviews or in Brian Edge's book *924 Gilman: The Story So Far*, I was completely an insider. I don't think I could even have spelled the word "religion" in that moment!

I did try and put strategies into place to help maintain the distinction—not interviewing close friends for example, or not holding interviews in places I frequented as an audience member (this was something I had to limit in the end to specific venues in Glasgow and Belfast). I also used my own body to remind me of the distinction: I let my hair grow naturally and stopped dying it black or bright colors, and I removed facial piercings and let them close over. On the other hand, I didn't make any attempt to cover up tattoos (in fact, I got more as I went through my fieldwork and used the experience in my thesis), and I did not stop wearing band shirts (although I do that now when teaching).

I also tried to hand over a lot of control and ownership to the interviewees as a way of honoring my own punk ethical codes and a sXe sense of self-responsibility. Each interviewee determined how they wanted to be identified, each interviewee received a full transcript of their interview with the right to veto any part of it prior to it being used. I refused to edit the interview selections, so hesitations, repeated words, self-corrections, silences are all included within the quotes. I think that listening to how people talk, to the rhythm, cadence, and struggle of articulation is a key part of the job of an ethnographer and it is very revealing with it comes to dealing with categories such as religion, secularity, spirituality, etc. It also means that you have to focus very carefully on the insider/outsider tension so as not to allow those voices to become smothered or over-explained by academic analysis.

Probably the hardest part of dealing with the insider/outsider tension is emotional. You have to accept that in doing this study and analysis, you are going to have to withdraw to some extent from the very thing that gives you your identity, your moral code, your enjoyment, your sense of self. You can no longer be fully within the sXe scene, but at the same time you are not separate from it, and so you cannot really find refuge within the academic world either. You exist in this hinterland, and that can take its toll. The other emotional aspect in being an insider is that you have to honestly face up to the problems within your own subculture—within my own work I had to listen to and deal with instances of sexism, homophobia, and violence. sXe remains very male-dominated, as is evident in the ratio of male-identifying to female-identifying among my interviewees.

As a woman, I was often alone while interviewing men, which was normally a fantastic experience, but when instances of sexism or homophobia occurred, I really felt the insider/outsider tension being heightened by my own positionality. Do I react as an insider and call them out on it? Or do I behave as an outsider and let them complete the interview and then just analyze the problematic nature of it? More often than not, I surrendered any sense of detachment and reacted to it as an insider and challenged their statements at the risk of losing the interview.

I can see in my own writing when that has happened, as I tend to then try and regain some control over it by over-analysing or over-labouring the points. When I was editing the thesis into a book for publication and gathering the permissions for lyrics, I approached Ian MacKaye to use some Minor Threat songs, and he asked to read the chapter they would be placed in. He had no way of knowing that there were sections of that chapter that were drawn from interviews and encounters with violent hardline sXe individuals who would often espouse really vile views. To his credit, he quickly picked up that I was over-writing about them to the extent that I was diminishing the sXe individuals who try to live a more positive life. In drawing my attention to them, he actually made me far more aware of what I was doing and why and how much of that was drawn from the emotional impact of the insider/outsider tension. Forcing me to deal with that actually made it a much better book in the end, and a much stronger text than the thesis was, so I am incredibly grateful for that.

Why did you focus on religion in your work?

I grew up in Northern Ireland during the second half of the Troubles, that is, during the 1980s and '90s. I was aware from a very young age of how divisive religion can be, but also how it can function in such areas of civil war as a means of creating community, identity, and safety. I realized that religion—Catholicism and Protestantism, in this instance—gave markers of belonging and a way for some people to cope with utter devastation and horrific loss of life, but that it was also used to control lives (areas we could live in, schools we could attend, even jobs we could have) and to maintain a cycle of hatred because it provided a convenient language that explained a civil war without having to look at other causes such as centuries of colonial rule and brutality, civil rights violations against Catholics, corrupt politics etc.

As a young adult, I grew increasingly curious as to what replaced religion as I had understood it in Northern Ireland for those who rejected it, didn't belong, or were rejected by it. I was very struck by the linear nature of the concept and wondered what was to come next. At that point, I was reading a lot of Nietzsche and was very influenced by that in terms of his thinking about death and rebirth in cultures and times.

As I began to approach the PhD I was annoyed at a number of things: the way sXe is so often ignored or only mentioned to be ridiculed in a lot of punk books (really there was only Ross Haenfler, Brian Peterson, and yourself that were fighting against that tide, and I wanted to be a part of that fight because it was something I strongly believed in); the way religion is assumed to have specific meanings as a category and descriptor that really serves only to consolidate the authority and position of certain groups, especially in relation to violence as William Cavanaugh so eloquently outlines in *The Myth of Religious Violence*; the way in which it is assumed that to be a punk is to be antireligion without any consideration as to what religion actually is or how it is experienced in a myriad of ways by people and communities. I wanted to find a way to explore and bring to light the experiences that my friends and I, and others like us—the quiet audience members, those not typically written about—were having within sXe punk. Those annoyances, combined with increasingly seeing aspects of more traditional "religious" behavior appearing at shows, as well as spirituality arising once again in lyrics in a way we hadn't seen outside of the early Krishnacore scenes of the 90s, led me to focus on religion.

In *Sober Living for the Revolution*, I wanted to highlight the progressive and radical elements of straight edge culture. After much back and forth, I decided against including religious currents. But it wasn't an easy decision, as the politics aren't always clear-cut. For example, Hare Krishna devotees have contributed to compassion, a respect for human and animal rights, and a critique of consumerism, but they also espouse an ideological framework characteristic of most religions, including patriarchy, authority figures, and a sense of elitism. If I had had you as an adviser for the book, what would you have told me?

Not really sure I would have told you anything other than go with your instincts. The book is fantastic as it is, I have returned to it many times and no doubt will do again in the future. However, I do applaud you for noting

"Mother Edge." Art by Phoenix X Eeyore.

that there is no clear distinction between religion and politics. The reality is that these are all constructed categories and so we use them in ways that best suit our own agendas—consciously or unconsciously. The persistent artificial separation of religion and politics is really just a furthering of the artificial binary of religion and secularity that doesn't hold true for the life experience of most people.

The question to ask is always two-fold: a) Who benefits from me knowing this information in this way? And b) what really motivates the actions of the individual? In the example you provided of the Hare Krishna devotees, those in the upper echelons of power within ISKCON benefited in multiple ways from a very particular narrative constructed around compassion, respect for sentient life, and anticonsumerism. However, that benefit was not all good, it enabled (and perhaps, I am only guessing, emboldened) them to continue child sexual assaults, inappropriate relationships with women, authoritative positions, sexism, elitism, and greed. In *Evolution of a Cro-Magnon*, John Joseph outlines how they were able to hide this from common devotees. Mike Dines has also done some important work on Krishnacore, which I think he is hoping to publish as a book fairly soon.

Whether we like it or not, religion—as in organized, institutional religion based upon interpretation of a text or dogma or creed—has been a huge part of social development and construction for thousands of years. It is inculcated within us and shapes how we think, much as constructions of gender are. It forms a part of who we are and the way we interact with others. There is no getting around that. The problem is that its influence on us and our thinking is often subconscious. Therefore, we do have to question motivations. To return to your example of the Hare Krishnas: do they engage in patriarchy because they are Hare Krishnas, or do they engage in it because they grew up in a society in which being a man is privileged in multiple ways, whether the male is aware of that privilege or not? Or is it that they do it because of some combination of both? This is where I think examining the role and influence of punk and religion upon one another, and trying to tease out that relationship further, can be really revealing and, I hope, really helpful.

In what way?

In two areas: the community they provide, and the tools they can potentially provide to shape society for the better. Human beings have a need for belonging, companionship, friendship, and acceptance, and most people find that only partially in family—we need communities outside of our family to make that whole. Those communities nurture us, challenge us, and shape us. Some people find that in religious communities, others within punk, including sXe, communities. The two may be very different creatures politically and aesthetically, but they fulfill the same function and thus have a strong progressive potential because of the necessary care they provide. It is worth remembering that traditionally both communities have attracted some very damaged and broken people. Nearly 80 percent of my interviewees came from a background or childhood that had drug and/ or alcohol addiction and the attendant problems that can occur with that: domestic violence, mental health issues, poverty, instability, lower access to employment, education, etc. They often talked of sXe, and especially the community, as having "saved" them in one way or another, and of being itself "sacred." This is really interesting use of theological language that again indicates just how much religion (traditionally understood) has shaped and remains a part of our thinking and our societies.

The second potential is the tools. Both religion and sXe provide strong moral codes to live by, guidance on behavior, some indication of a sense or notion of right and wrong (although these can be somewhat black and white while appearing didactic), and a continual means of connecting with something larger than oneself. However, these tools are at best potential because they are in the hands of people, and people are messy and complicated. The tools can only work as well as those using them. If those individuals are not willing to examine and check their own privilege and positionality, and to think intersectionally, then those tools remain underused, or, at worse, become a means to insulate oneself to your own failures.

I am thinking here of some individuals I interviewed in relation to Dharma Punx (known in the UK as Rebel Dharma), who repeatedly articulated attitudes that revealed orientalism at the core of their thinking, or who unwittingly made sXe punks of color feel unwelcome and unwanted at their sittings—while simultaneously complaining that they were losing their space to nonpunk university students. There were interviewees who discussed some horrible experiences of sexist behavior or even assault being carried out by audience members at sXe shows, whom one assumes were self-identifying as sXe. One interviewee who was selling merch was repeatedly harassed by young men wearing shirts with slogans such as "No Clit in the Pit." They tried to take the stock and to grope her. A lot of women told me how disheartened they were that men who would speak with great passion about the sanctity of the lives of animals, and act accordingly, could not see how their behavior and attitude to women directly contradicted that. What I am trying to say is that in those instances, the tools are underused or used in such a way as to make the sXe'r feel superior and justify themselves. The potential of the tools was not realized. The same is true for some individuals within various different religious groups. We know only too well of the judgment and treatment meted out to unmarried mothers in the Magdalene Laundries for "fallen women" in Ireland, the sexual abuse and rampant patriarchy within some leaders/teachings of the Hare Krishnas, Buddhist violence in Sri Lanka, and many more examples that could be drawn on in much smaller scales.

Some of the individuals I interviewed were wrestling with the potential cross-over between religion and sXe, trying to find a positive way to make it work for them. They strongly felt a desire to have something in their lives that connected them within a larger purpose, provided a sense of enchantment, and enabled some element of mystery. This desire for "a reenchantment of the world," as Christopher Partridge calls it, is a growing force amongst a range of people. My interviewees were often disillusioned with what, in their eyes, science had become (they would often conflate all of science into a discussion of the new atheists), or in relation to what they felt science had taken from them in terms of finding mystery and magic in the universe. At the same time, they understood the importance of scientific advances for medicine, quality of life, technology, and so on, so they were trying to resolve a conflict within themselves. In many ways, in their discussion of science and this inner conflict, what they were often struggling with was the widespread assumption that religion and the secular should and must indeed be a binary. They had absorbed that assumption throughout their lives (as we all have), but they were finding it less and less accurate or reconcilable with their own experiences and needs. They valued sXe and what it gave them, how it shaped them. It remained a key part of their identity but was unable to provide all that they needed in their lives, so they sought to find ways of successfully binding it with forms of what we would often consider traditional religion, particularly Hare Krishna, Buddhism, and Islam—I really struggled to find sXe individuals who did this with Christianity, although Ibrahim Abraham has done work amongst those who consider themselves punk Christians (but not sXe punk Christians) to create their own spirituality (or faith, as it is more commonly called in the UK). They articulated that Krishnacore, Dharma Punx, or Taqwacore gave their lives more meaning, better structure, and a way to understand the moral code they wanted to live their life by. Of course there were interviewees who found no such solace or reenchantment through such groups, and instead tried to locate it within sXe itself. This manifested itself through really interesting religious language such as referring to spaces, bands, and individuals as "sacred," calling the abstinence rules of sXe their "beliefs" or "moral code." One interviewee actually referred to it as their "dogma." In so doing, they found that having that sense of reenchantment, or something to construct a life around, had helped them deal with or seek out help for mental health issues, suicidal thoughts, addiction issues, and life choices. One interviewee talked at length about how it had helped her deal with a violent domestic abuse situation. It is in these real-world situations that the greatest potential can be drawn in an interaction or conversation between sXe and religion.

Are religions as ideologies necessarily conservative and reactionary?

No, I don't think they necessarily are conservative, I think that the ones that are choose to be for one reason or another. That may be cultural context, interpretation of text, faith, or desire to control—again, this is why it is always so important to consider the motivations of people. For example, the antiabortion laws in Northern Ireland are supposedly drawn from the religious beliefs of the people, specifically the religious conservatism of both the Irish Catholic Church and the conservative Free Presbyterianism of Ian Paisley who founded the Democratic Unionist Party that still follows much of his teaching. The reality is that the majority of people in the country have never been asked their view on it in regards to being allowed a vote or referendum. If one takes seriously the views put forward on social media, letters to newspapers, and public protests it would seem that the official stance of antiabortion is strongly at odds with broader public consensus. Therefore, one must ask what their true motivation is in maintaining such tight control over the bodies of women. Would those politicians still hold such conservative views if there was no such thing as a religion or religious text to draw upon for justification? I suspect they would be, because they would draw on another ideology, because it enables them to control a specific group of people they want to control or believe they have the right to control. Historically, religious conservativism in the West occurs in cyclical patterns when groups of people feel under threat (real or imagined) that change in society limits their influence, their privilege, or their future. As it is an attempt to regain some sense of control, it is not surprising that they seek to further that control by gaining positions of power and/or authority. Perhaps it is the ugly reality of human nature.

In regards to being reactionary, that's the more interesting consideration because reacting to something can be positive or even vital. For example, the liberation theology of Latin America that wove Marxism in with Catholicism in attempts to help people live in a very difficult and dangerous situation. Another example can be found within the development of Black theology, which is varied in what it is reacting to: for some traditions, it is a reaction to slavery and its continuing impact in the US. For others, like Thomas J.J. Altizer, it was a reaction to the Holocaust and a serious consideration of the death of God. Altizer actually received death threats for his work, and this was during the '60s in the US when it was the midst of the cultural revolution—and yet an idea put forward by scholars responding to and trying to understand issues such as the Holocaust, slavery, and the treatment of persons of color sparked such an intense, extreme and vile response.

We could spin this in a really interesting direction and consider whether sXe is an ideology and, if so, whether it is a conservative and/or reactionary one? Traditionally, ideology is understood as a system of ideas and ideals, especially one which forms the basis of economic or political theory and policy. Does sXe fulfill that criteria in some way? An argument could be made that the three core tenets of sXe—voluntary abstinence from alcohol, drugs, and casual sex—are a systemic set of idea (or a temporary set of ideals for those who later break edge) that form the basis of economic theories and actions, and political theories/understanding/potential actions in the individuals who undertake it. Many older sXe'rs develop a strong statement that their abstinence is at least in part driven by a desire not to contribute to the economic well-being/profit and continued power of certain companies, be they alcohol, tobacco, or companies with unethical practices or dominance in global markets. A lot of interviewees discussed how their motivations to maintain their edge had shifted from a desire to break family cycles of drug and/or alcohol abuse, or a desire to avoid putting poisons into their body in an attempt to remain more alert and self-responsible, to a strong sense of broader social responsibility and activism through individual action; this included to economically ensure they hold companies to account. Likewise, a significant number of interviewees also talked in depth about how sXe had shaped their political theories and positions. Most interviewees credited punk, often directly sXe, with opening their eyes through lyrics, band interviews, and on-stage discussion to political realities, theories, and positions. This was particularly the case with those who self-identified as anarchist (however they understood it). It also became very clear that it was their interaction with sXe and other forms of punk that created a much stronger sense of the necessity of intersectional thinking and acting. They held these views with the same level of conviction that many religious people hold to their religious ideologies. They talked about their edge as being akin to a wedding vow, used phrases such as "commitment," even "faith," with regard to their edge, or their following of the three tenets. Some of them even expressed disappointment in those who broke edge in ways very similar to how a Christian would describe a former Christian, talking of them as having "broken something sacred"—in Christian parlance, this would be a "backslider." I would argue that these interviewees demonstrated that ideologies adhered to in a similar way as religious ideologies need not necessarily be conservative.

However, by no means was this a unanimous approach. There were interviewees who vehemently claimed a sXe identity and expressed views and opinions that would be considered very conservative. For example, some openly opposed abortion arguing that being sXe was about supporting life and that included the life of the unborn child. Others stated very conservative views on women or immigration that would not be out of place within various conservative religious traditions, and in a similar way they often used the justification of it being their interpretation of sXe, akin to interpretation of a religious text. I would argue that these interviewees demonstrated that ideologies can be conservative. But putting both together demonstrated that both stances, conservative and/or reactionary, are choices not inevitable or necessary. What we perhaps need to do is shift our thinking on what an ideology is and on how we categorize it. When used in relation to religion, it is often uncritically negative, whereas the ideology of the state is not considered at all or is seen as uncritically positive. But is it really any different dying/fighting for one's country rather than dying/fighting for one's god?

So, is straight edge itself a religion or not?

This was the question I concluded my book with, and it was in some regards the hardest question to answer. Ownership of religion has been historically held through the ability to define it, and thus decide what it is and what it isn't—and, by extension, who is and who is not religious. We have, of course, seen that develop into the very notion of what an acceptable (usually white, Christian or Jewish) and an unacceptable religion is. This plays out in really interesting ways, such as determining which religious sounds are allowed to permeate our soundscapes (church bells) and which are deemed a public nuisance (the adhan, in the West often referred to as the Muslim "call to prayer"). So, in trying to answer, or maybe even ask, such a question, there is the danger of reinforcing troubling norms and power plays—but there is also the possibility to open up space for wider conversations about religion, norms, and such power plays in a way that can helpfully change or overcome them.

I reject the notion that sXe is a "quasi-religion" of some kind. I really despise that term, no matter what it is applied to. The word "quasi" is Latin and means "as if" or "almost." If we are to take seriously what people are doing as well as their reasons for doing it, then calling it something that is less than complete or only second best is deeply problematic and comes from a place of (often unacknowledged) privilege, enabling the dominant to speak over/for the weaker or smaller. If we are doing this in relation to religion, then we are forcing the very notion of what a religion is, or can be, into a very narrow, and therefore tightly controlled, definition. "Quasi" as the precursor reinforces this, as it effectively denotes that the group being examined is close to a religion, but not quite there yet. It falls short and is only being used because the individual cannot, for whatever reason, access actual religion. (The implication, of course, always is that "real" religion is to be preferred.) This reduces the capacity of what people have turned to or created, the very thing you are studying, to be taken seriously, because it has failed to meet some mythic or spurious idea of what a religion is.

The second thing I would note is that there was a marked difficulty amongst the interviewees in defining religion or specifically answering this question—and it was asked of all interviewees. This was slightly less so, but still evident, in those who aligned themselves with or self-identified as Krishnacore, Dharma Punx, or Taqwacore. These interviewees would often say that while they considered it a natural extension of being sXe, they were not sure if sXe was actually a religion or not because it was in addition to the interpretation of Hinduism, Buddhism, or Islam that they followed. Others who were sXe but not Krishnacore etc. were more inclined to qualifiers or hesitations such as "kinda like a religion," "it sorta is my religion," and so on. They would then spend ages trying to explain or justify it, but often what they were doing was trying to work with a language that was too constricting for their life experiences.

No interviewee claimed sXe as their religion in terms of how religion is defined within social sciences such as the sociology of religion. But then again, as I have been arguing throughout this interview, and indeed throughout my book, that definition is very problematic and highly contestable. In trying to talk about it in religious terms, the interviewees have shown how much religion is a part of our everyday experiences and of how we think, including subconsciously. But they have also shown that they are putting their faith, hope, or belief in sXe in a manner analogous to those who choose to place their faith within a particular religion, and that deserves to be taken seriously.

Do I personally think sXe is a religion? No, I don't. William James argues that a religion must contain that which cannot be located elsewhere. There is nothing within sXe that has that. All of it can be found elsewhere, it is simply that for those individuals who select sXe—or are selected by it, as many asserted—this is where it works best for them. But it doesn't work for those outside of the subculture. What I think sXe is, is something else: it is the surrogate to religion, its successor, that which comes next. I think this, because sXe functions successfully on a collective level enabling adherents to create a familial bond they often experienced as fractured within their own home lives. Furthermore, sXe is linked with political and social issues in a way that encourages action and enables people to see beyond a selfish view of the world. It promotes thought and justification that, spurred by suspicion of authority, in turn promotes the challenging of one another and of oneself. In offering sXe as a surrogate, I am asking something I cannot yet answer but really want the scenes to talk about: can sXe go beyond religion rather than just repeat or even master it? It hasn't yet, but does it have the potential to do so? If so, what shape and potentiality does that hold?

THE JOYS OF ZINE-MAKING

Kat grew up in a small village in the Black Forest in southern Germany. She was the editor of the fanzine *xclusivx* (2013–2018). Feeling like an outcast all her life, to Kat zine culture became a big family.

At a time when zines became increasingly rare, you started one. Why?

We sat in the backstage area of a local venue in southern Germany where we helped with the catering. It was Edge Day 2012. Me and my life partner Phil were joking around and said that we could do a zine with a cover like all the gossip magazines and call it *xclusivx* due to all the exclusive content.

In a former life, I was a radio host. I had my own show at an

Kat and cat, 2018.

independent radio station from 2002 to 2004. When talking to Phil that night in the backstage room, I remembered how the rock and metal bands that I interviewed would tell me how "great" and "different" my questions were. This gave me the confidence to attempt to recreate this energy in print, focusing on the bands we loved: punk hardcore combos with much to say. And for all those who think that I am this kid you "cannot trust" because I have a metal rather than a punk background: where I grew up, the punks were the drunks and the metalheads the edgers. I claimed edge at the age of sixteen as an act of rebellion against rural village life.

In hindsight, was it a good decision to start a zine?
Of-fucking-course. I don't do regrets. It's a coping mechanism as well as a survival mode. Crying over spilled milk is not my way of life, I would not stop crying at all if I lived that way. Those five years and ten issues were a blast and I would not want to miss the them for the world. I met so many great folks and felt a connection to the vegan straight edge scene like never before. And readers told me the same, from all over the world. Apparently, a feminist vegan edge zine that is pro-intersectional filled a gap. We were able to connect readers who were isolated in Australia or rural Colorado (you know who you are, folks!) to vegan straight edge people from different backgrounds. I am so happy this happened.

xclusivx developed from a twenty-eight-page, black-and-white publication into a one-hundred-plus-page, multicolor one. This is not an unusual development. But it seems the contents also changed a little. You always retained a strong focus on food and veganism, but as the years went by you added interviews and articles on all sorts of topics. How did the zine develop from your own perspective?
A zine can be everything it wants to be: eight pages or a hundred, loosely put together or properly bound. That's what I love about zine culture: you can do what you want. After issue five, we were often told that we were a "real magazine" on the outside but a fanzine on the inside. But many of our readers liked that and encouraged us to continue on this path.

The way our zine developed was based on the feedback we received. Wishes for better readability led to more pages, poor picture quality lead to full color, and requests for covering certain topics led to more content. We got lots of shit for becoming "fancy" and making use of crowdfunding, but we stand by it. We always pumped money into the zine, and in the beginning we could afford it, but we needed extra funds for the last three issues. More pages, thicker paper, and full color made things more expensive. It was hard to ask for something, but I won't feel ashamed for it.

As far as the topics are concerned: vegan straight edge is not an isolated theme, it touches upon so many other subjects of life. And, to be honest, just eating plants is not veganism, it is simply a plant-based diet.

On your website, *xclusivx* was presented as "DIY. Ad-Free. Non-Profit. Self-Published." What did that concretely mean for your work?

DIY meant that we did everything ourselves apart from printing and assembling, which was a reaction to the feedback we got. The ad-free bit was really important. Many hardcore zines are financed by advertising. We never opted for that because we felt the ads disrupted the flow and because it felt weird to get paid for advertising stuff. Besides, we would not have found many advertisers that stood on the same ground as us. Having principles is not always helpful . . .

The zine was edited by the "*xclusivx* Fanzine Collective." Tell us about that!

In the beginning, it was just Phil and me, and we remained the core of *xclusivx* until the end. Others shared a little part of the path, some writing for the zine and the blog for quite some time. But the commitment that was required was not for everybody. As the editor, I was holding everything together, arranging the topics, and reminding others of their deadlines. It grinds you down to some extent.

I'm wondering about the blend of hardcore punk, vegan straight edge, and progressive/radical politics that has characterized the zine. Did these interests develop at the same time, or did one come before the other for you?

It was always the ground we stood on. The challenge was to find artists, bands, activists, and topics who fit our convictions and our way of life, as it is reflected in the zine. We were often told that we were "neither fish nor fowl." (Vegan fish and fowl, of course.) But we did what we wanted to do. Just being straight edge without giving a shit about feminism? Living a vegan lifestyle and thinking racist views are okay? Being a feminist but still eating animals? Fighting against oppression while having antisemitic views? Not caring about politics, just being here for the music? Our aim was to present perspectives that allowed readers to connect the dots. The people we interviewed and our articles were not telling others how they should live their lives, but they shared ideas about how we can all change aspects of our lives.

Over the years, you have used many attributes to describe *xclusivx*, from "vegan" and "drug-free" to "antifa" and "atheist." One term that appeared repeatedly was "intersectional feminism." Can you explain what you mean by that?

In fact, the wording got changed into the correct phrasing of "pro-intersectionality" and "pro-intersectional." Kimberlé Crenshaw introduced the term into feminism in 1989, arguing that the experience of being black and being a woman cannot be separated from each other. Let me quote Wikipedia here: "Intersectionality is an analytic framework which attempts to identify how interlocking systems of power impact those who are most marginalized in society. Intersectionality considers that the various forms of what it sees as social stratification, such as class, race, sexual orientation, age, disability, and gender, do not exist separately from each other but are complexly interwoven. While the theory began as an exploration of the oppression of women of color within society, today the analysis is potentially applied to all categories (including statuses usually seen as dominant when seen as standalone statuses)."

Dr. Corey Wrenn of the Vegan Feminist Network is a real inspiration to me, challenging thoughts about norms and stereotypes. Let me quote her, too: "Given that species, class, race, gender, and other identity categories are all historically constructed using similar mechanisms (such as animalization, objectification, sexualization, depersonalization, denaming, and so on), it is important to apply an intersectional perspective to achieve a more accurate understanding of oppression for nonhuman animals and humans alike."

Dr. Wrenn also, rightly, points out that although "most animal rights activists and vegans are women...patriarchal norms endemic to society and social movements push men (especially hegemonic ones) to the spotlight."

We were criticized by some who thought that our zine was "all over the place." But in a puzzle of oppression, no piece is isolated. Intersectionality is not a single-issue fight. All of this is very relevant for straight edge: I don't know about you and your surroundings, but where I am, straight edge is very white, cis-hetero, male, and macho. I'm not trying to diminish the high number of vegan straight edge grrrls I personally know, but I'm talking about the overall perception of the "straight edge club."

A pro-intersectional approach includes language, too, and we always tried to make everything as accessible as possible, not speaking in an academic voice or publishing texts and articles that were hard to follow. I know myself how alienating an academic voice can be: even though I have a degree in English literature, I often found it very difficult to read feminist zines from the US. I just could not follow their train of thought. It felt particularly frustrating when my depression was acting up, and I wanted to make sure that the people reading our zine would not have to endure highly complicated texts.

The antifa part we eventually dropped, because there are many parts of the antifa movement we do not want to be associated with. We are antifascists through and through, but toxic masculinity, antiveganism, or the Boycott, Divestment, and Sanctions campaign against Israel are not our way to be antifascists. It's the same with straight edge: we do not want to be associated with pro-lifers or boys' clubs protecting perpetrators.

I believe you once said in an interview—sadly, I forget which one—that you considered vegan straight edge to be the "only true straight edge." Can you elaborate?

We say that whenever we get the chance! Being straight edge is a personal choice for personal reasons, and veganism is a political choice for political reasons. You should be vegan if you are living without mental pollution by any kind of drugs, since your body is not a graveyard either. I cannot verify this scientifically, but I think it's a killer combo.

You must have interviewed close to a hundred people for the zine, some well-known, others less so. How did you get in touch with them all? Was it easy to convince them to contribute?

Oh right, I never counted them . . . For starters, let me say that the internet is a brave new world. With all its horrible aspects, it is still the best way to connect with people on a global scale, in a fast and easy manner. Most of the time, I found people through doing research on people I already had decided to interview. Like, when one cool band played with another cool band on the same bill. Or when talented artists worked for an activist organization. It's all connected in our little feminist vegan straight edge world. And once you find people, it is easy to contact them online. Over the years, my selection process worked a lot better than in the beginning.

There are people in one issue or the other that I wish we had not interviewed. But that's water down the river, we made those choices to the best of our knowledge at the time and cannot influence the past.

I think I never really needed to convince anybody. The bigger problem was to get the interviews back in time. And contributors assuming they would get a free copy of the zine. Sometimes, there were more than twenty-five people contributing, and we simply couldn't afford to send everyone a free copy. I guess we should have made that clearer from the start.

RATS IN THE WALL
EVA GENIE IS NOW 'MORE CYNICAL AND HATEFUL' THAN IN GATHER

justin smith
A MAN VERSUS HIMSELF

CLAES NORDIN
LIFE AFTER ANCHOR

XCLUSIVX

FANZINE COLLECTIVE × ISSUE NO. 6

ROBBY WALLACE
BREAKING FREE
WITH PHOTOGRAPHY

6€ · $6 · 6SFR

Eva "Genie" Hall on the cover of *xclusivx*, issue 6, July 2016.

My two biggest disappointments were that Ceremony (after we had personally spoken to them in Amsterdam—but I'm still a fan!) and Gaz Oakley, who runs the Avant-Garde Vegan website, did not answer very long, detailed interviews that took me days to create. I am okay with it not working out, it is just frustrating when you put in hours of work after they agreed to do an interview before they chose not to. And if you never hear from them again, you ask yourself what the reasons might have been, and the first thing you do is question your own work. But then you think they might simply not have had the time, and that your little fanzine is not big enough, and then you let it go. It's not about ego, it's about lost time you could have invested in someone else.

But not to be misunderstood: while there are burdens involved when making a zine, it has been an awesome experience and we have met super rad people!

xclusivx was a bilingual zine, German and English. This is rather unusual. There have always been people outside of the English-speaking world who decided to do English zines to reach a broader audience, but to combine one's mother tongue with English is rare. Why did you make that decision? How was it received by your readers?

This, too, has to do with accessibility. It is arrogant to assume that everyone in Germany, where we are based, speaks English fluently. That might be the case in academic circles, but, as I pointed out before, we don't want to restrict our message to that audience. At the same time, German is limited to Germany, Austria, and parts of Switzerland . . . It's a catch-22 you will never get out of, so in the last issues we simply let people who present their work in English express themselves in English, and people who present their work in German express themselves in German. We were happy to receive emails saying, "I wish I could speak German," and we happily translated or summarized the texts for people who were interested.

Once, we tried to do an issue with every text in both English and German, but it went terribly. I had to do all the translations, it took me forever, and in the end the issue was no pleasure to read since we had to sacrifice font size for page volume.

I might add that we've had offers from people in Indonesia and Latin America to translate the whole zine into their languages in order to make it more accessible, but we didn't know how to manage the distribution.

If you look at the last decade: What other straight edge zines—or blogs, for that matter—would you recommend?
Concerning online resources, I already mentioned the Vegan Feminist Network by Dr. Wrenn. I also recommend the website by Dr. Breeze A. Harper whose work is amazing. Music-wise, I frequently check out *DIY Conspiracy*, *IDIOTEQ*, and *Brooklyn Vegan*. I also follow the journey of *Esther the Wonder Pig*.

As far as fanzines go, I would always highly recommend Dominic's zines, which you can get at Fluff Fest: *It's the Limit* is one of them. He's a joy to be around, and his zines are super cool. Sadly, the Riot Tea Club collective retired, but they also did amazing zine work. The zine which everything started for me was *Back to the Bins*, which I purchased at Fluff Fest 2011. An up-and-coming zine I like is *Amused*. A great book is *Aphro-ism* by Aph Ko and her sister Syl.

Anna Vo says in an interview in this book that the zine *Fix My Head* ended with issue 10 because that's a round number. Did you apply the same logic when you announced the end of *xclusivx* in May 2018?
Of course, 10 can be seen as a caesura, but not a quiet one! More like a loud breaking point. I was simply at the end of my energy. It just happened to occur after we released number 10. Proud of the double digits!

The passion is still there, but I am mentally so exhausted that I cannot continue. The email feedback in response to our announcement of calling it quits almost broke my heart, but I also felt overwhelmed by joy and gratitude for having produced something that came from our hearts and went right into the hearts of others, some of them living on other continents. That is incredible.

When you announced the end of the zine, you wrote: "It's time for something different, something new, something else." Are you able to make this more concrete yet?
It will be a while before my batteries are full again for anything new. The perks of the internet are balanced out by its dark sides: haters and trolls drain much-needed energy in the fight against fascism, racism, patriarchy, animal abuse, rape culture, toxic masculinity, and street harassment. If you use a certain hashtag or wording, "Men's Rights Activists" will find you. If you post vegan memes, meat-eaters will spam the comments. You need social media to communicate with your audience, but you have to deal with all this shit, too.

Activism is a lifelong struggle, everyone does it differently, and all of us have to channel our energy to make an impact. Being angry and sad may be the starting points, but in order to keep fighting you need positive resources within you. Maybe there will be another outlet for my activism. I loved making this zine very much, and I will find a way to produce something from my heart again that also touches others. In the meantime, I am grateful and go with Baz Luhrmann's line from "Everybody's Free to Wear Sunscreen": "Remember the compliments you receive, forget the insults!"

STRAIGHT EDGE AND DESIGN

Jan Tölva sang in the hardcore band Kurhaus and played bass in the deutschpunk band Halbstark. He organized shows, published zines both in print and online and, for many years, had a regular column in the fanzine *Trust*. Jan studied sociology, toiled as a forklift driver, and is currently working for a vegan shoe company. He lives in Berlin and has been vegan straight edge for more than seventeen years.

Jan, as far as I know you had the idea for the Berlin Straight Edge logo, which was then copied by several other straight edge groups. How did you come up with the idea?

A few years ago, it became quite common to drop the vowels from words in graphics, first in advertising, then in popular culture, where it was quickly combined with ripping off the legendary Run-DMC logo. FCK NZS or FCK CPS might be the results best known among political radicals.

At the time, there existed an informal group of straight edge folks in Berlin. Inspired by Stockholm Straight Edge and similar groups in Sweden, we wanted to give the group a more formal character; we felt it would send an important message, not least in a city known for its party and drug culture. Hence, we did our own variation on the Run-DMC logo: SXE has long been used as an abbreviation for straight edge, and BLN is a fairly common abbreviation for Berlin. I liked the idea because it combined urban aesthetics with a secret code; the logo is instantly recognizable for those in the know but somewhat mysterious for others.

Your version was then used as a template by various straight edge groups...

Yes, there were quite a few that used it. The most visible copy was perhaps SXE MAD for Madrid, but similar logos also appeared in Leipzig, Barcelona, Tel Aviv, Quito, and other cities.

Were you surprised?

Not really. We live in the digital era. Memes are all the hype: you take something, you change it, and others do the same.

How much design work have you done?

I've always designed in a DIY context. When I lived in Chile in 2008, I sold homemade buttons at shows. I did zines and designed posters for events. At the moment, however, I don't do any of that. I also stopped playing music and writing my column for *Trust*, the longstanding German hardcore/punk zine. I am close to forty now and feel I need to create space for something new, although I haven't figured out what that could be yet. I first need to get rid of a few things, for example a thousand records, hundreds of books, and the instruments I got for the electro-punk career I never started.

Are the graphic dimensions of straight edge underrated?

Punk, which hardcore grew out of, has always been a visual movement. Take the Sex Pistols' cover for *Never Mind the Bollocks*: it's iconic. Imagine someone spotting it on a record store shelf in 1977 between the latest of Yes and Genesis! Visual aspects remained important in hardcore, even if they

"Youth of Today fist" smashing the swastika. Courtesy of Jan Tölva.

Straight edge tattoo. Courtesy of a modest friend.

were obviously tuned down. In the case of straight edge, you even ended up with a clean-cut jock style reminiscent of a sportswear catalog. But particularly in the early days, the punk element was very strong in straight edge graphics. Take the black sheep on the cover of Minor Threat's *Out of Step*: it's a very simple, very clear image that still works today. Later, the bands of the late 1980s to mid-1990s developed a pattern for T-shirt designs that has passed the test of time and has been replicated hundreds of times: a photo from a live show combined with a succinct slogan (everyone remembers "True till Death") and the band's logo font. And then there is, of course, the X! The tattoos alone are countless . . .

How have straight edge graphics changed with digital culture?

The most important thing is that anyone can do multicolor designs now. This is very different from both the black-and-white aesthetics and the two-color printing of earlier eras. Now, we can already see the opposite trend, where people use digital means to create cut-and-paste designs. As long as you have a bit of patience, you can pretty much do whatever you want with today's programs. At the same time, there has been a professionalization of design, not least in hardcore circles. If you're in a hardcore band, it's quite likely that you know someone who works as a graphic designer. It's interesting to see this parallel development of democratization on the one hand

and specialization on the other. The results are intriguing. Ripoffs are very common, whether it's making a poster inspired by the *Dance of Days* book cover, or a flyer reminiscent of a CBGB's show in 1982. Straight edge designs are full of references and quotes, even if they aren't recognized by younger folks. There is also plenty of variety. You can get a back patch from Iron, a Swedish queer vegan straight edge band, that would fit right on any metal denim vest.

The three knives are reminiscent of the logo used by the German antifascist "Iron Front" in the 1930s. Courtesy of Jan Tölva.

You never ended up being a member of Berlin Straight Edge . . .

Well, it's not like there's an official members list. But, true, I was never too involved. I guess I have never been much of a group person. I think they do great things though and they have strong ties to antifascist politics. I have been involved in the Antifa movement since I was 14, and this is still much more important to me than any subcultural identity. Berlin Straight Edge also has great

Iron back patch. Design by Thomas Rosén. Courtesy of Iron.

T-shirts playing with old designs, for example a Youth of Today fist smashing a swastika. In the end, the reason I never became more active myself was probably that I already have way too many other hobbies. Groundhopping and birding top the list.

SOBER BUT NOT STRAIGHT EDGE

Interview with Jon Active

Jon Active founded Active Distribution, Europe's largest anarchist distributor of literature and "stuff" in the late 1980s. For thirty years, he ran the distro out of his London home. Jon has organized punk gigs, helped set up squats and activist spaces, supported the animal rights movement, and argued for the anarchist cause continuously. He now lives in Croatia.

Thanks for agreeing to the interview. Are you worried about being outed as straight edge now?
No, because I'm not straight edge.

But you're punk and you're sober.
It's not the same thing. I was teetotal before I even knew that straight edge existed.

Me too. But discovering straight edge was very exciting: I was no longer the odd one out but belonged to a worldwide community.
Good for you. I love being the odd one out! I don't need an American label to guide me. To me, it's all about individual integrity. Straight edge took everything I disliked about hardcore and made it even worse: conformity and regimentation to the extreme. Not doing drugs is a personal decision one should come to through questioning stupid norms, not following new ones.

What's wrong with hardcore?

At first, I didn't understand the difference to punk, especially musically. Eventually, though, I realized that hardcore was punk for kids who were too scared to be different.

Because they didn't look punk?

That's part of it.

Some people would claim this as a strength of hardcore: by looking like everyone else you don't scare people away and your message spreads more widely.

To me that just confirms that these people don't dare to truly challenge society. Whatever you want to say about the origins of punk, there was creativity and individuality involved. Rejecting conformity was central to the punk idea. People risked something, not least by the way they looked. You only need to hear the stories of what happened to The Slits to know how reactionary society was—and still is—to abnormal dress code. That's a very strong message in itself: the individual expressing themselves against the "status quo" of how people dress and think.

Many straight edge folks might have stopped drinking and smoking, but they are still jocks. What message does hardcore want to spread with its indecipherable lyrics that often don't mean anything anyway? The macho poses, dancing, and attitude of hardcore was always a turn-off for me.

Straight edge has certainly made it more acceptable for people in punk to be sober. Is that a bad thing?

No. And I'm not writing off the entire scene because of its extremes. But there are very disturbing elements. Take the whole thing about sex: what on earth is wrong with sex? It's a very natural and very fun part of life, or at least it should be! By taking a stance against sex you join the ranks of sad religious ideologues and patriarchal fools. Women's sexuality especially has been—and still is—sickeningly repressed by patriarchy, religion, and tradition. It's incredible that a subgenre of punk rock, however far removed, can espouse such prudish puritanical poppycock!

I suppose that most straight edgers who care about the sexuality bit would say that they are against "irresponsible sex."

Well, that's easy to agree on, but it doesn't explain the Krishna offshoot!

Perhaps there are other things to agree on: why are you sober?

Me and my mate used to steal his dad's cigars and my parents alcohol because we knew we weren't meant to have those things. I got drunk three times when I was a teenager and, on the third time, I ruined my friend's bicycle. At the time, I tried to rationalize it away and excuse myself, but I came to the conclusion that if I was gonna fight the forces of state control, both within my mind and in society, I would need to be in control of myself and not intoxicated. I stopped drinking then and there. I also clearly remember looking out of my chemistry class one day, thinking I wanted to get out and have a "fag," but that very moment I understood that this was the wrong reason to get out of school and that I was about to get hooked on something stupid. I've never smoked since.

All the boys desperate to prove themselves were smoking and bragging about getting drunk, yet it was just "normal" behavior, nothing clever or rebellious about it. At school, at university, *and* in punk rock, drinking and smoking were clearly tied to violent macho behavior. I had no interest in that culture. I have never regretted my decision, not once. On the contrary, I have experiences all the time that confirm my choice. The drinking culture I have been witnessing worldwide has done nothing to make me want to "try a sip" or "celebrate just this once." Never!

What experiences are you referring to?

It begins with subtle, everyday life type of things. If you're in a foreign country and you hang out with friends, they are usually very considerate. They will speak English if they can, or someone will translate for you. But as soon as they start drinking, the consideration gradually slips away till you are left sitting there wondering what the fuck they are going on about (and wish it was easier to learn foreign languages).

Then, there are the effects drinking has on organizing. It just drains way too many resources, and I don't mean just financially. Just think of all the energy that goes into senseless fights, both verbally and physically. And the consequences can be very serious: jail time, unwanted pregnancies, etc.

For many years, I helped organize benefit shows around London. There was a great community space I used regularly, Chats Palace. About a decade ago, we had a benefit gig in memory of a dear friend, with a Slime cover band from Germany. Halfway through the show, an audience member was laying unconscious on the floor. Why? He had gotten punched and kicked by some punk who was upset over his beer being spilled. The folks from the venue had to call an ambulance and the medics called the police. Things like these give the police ammunition to use against venues when they reapply for their license to operate. I was so sad that my event had put the venue at risk, I stopped putting on shows altogether. These are minute examples of thousands I could quote.

Coming out of the British anarcho-punk scene, is it true that drugs were everywhere? At least that's one of the stereotypes when people juxtapose that scene to straight edge.

The drinking was pretty obvious. Beyond that, I personally didn't see much in the way of drugs, but maybe that was just because I didn't partake. Reading the personal accounts of the era that we distribute through Active—*Not Just Bits of Paper, Some of Us Scream Some of Us Shout, Tales from the Punkside,* and *And All Around Was Darkness*—it seems that drug use was indeed more widespread in the political punk scene than I had realized.

You've been distributing radical literature for about thirty years. Have you seen any increase in publications on alcohol and drugs?
No.

Really? I feel there's been an increased interest in the subject among activists, at least in North America.
Maybe. But, personally, I feel that straight edge can put people off as much as help encourage folk to be drug-free.

Because people are afraid to be thrown in the straight edge box if they address the issue?
Yes. I myself have kept quiet often enough to avoid being misunderstood as someone out on a straight edge crusade. At least when it concerns drinking. I'm less tolerant when it comes to smoking. Smoking in the presence of others affects everyone much more directly and is about the most unanarchic thing I can think of.

People from the scene always assume I am straight edge once they discover I don't drink, which is kinda annoying to me. I don't get vocal about

such things because I don't want to be lumped in with the straight edge mentality. I tend to let my own abstinence speak for itself, unless, of course, I get asked. I do the same—mostly—with my veganism.

Well, I'm glad I asked. Final question: You've recently relocated to Croatia, enjoying life in the countryside. What does that mean for Active Distribution?
It continues. I gave it to some friends in Bristol. I myself now focus on Active Publishing. We are printing in Croatia and distributing through Active and other outlets. We do reprints of radical books that are hard to get in Europe, and also publish our own stuff. You can find a list of our titles at activedistribution.org.

DEBATE

THE XO HEARTLINE
OX MANIFESTO

Anonymous

This text was written by two vegan straight edge feminist anarchists after the 2006 Fluff Fest in the Czech Republic. It was published on Myspace.

We are anarchists. That's the most important thing. Everything else follows from that. We are anti-capitalists. And as anarchists we believe in total liberation and direct action. This includes the liberation of all humyns and non-humyn animals. We are against the destruction of the world. We are vegan and drug-free because we can only fight the world being sober.

As anarchists we are against all forms of discrimination. There are no topics that have priority. We believe that all oppression and discrimination should be fought together. With any means necessary.

We are feminists and pro-choice because we believe that there shouldn't be any rules, and humyns should decide for themselves what to do with their bodies. We are against laws and rules of any kind. We don't like conservative ideas within hardcore. That's why we are against hardline and homophobia. We don't accept traditional gender roles nor care about sexual orientation.

We like the ideas of straight edge but we don't like it when people see it as a kind of religion and a set of rules.

We fight for self-determination but we are against all nations and therefore cannot support any people's fight for a nation. Nor are we willing to show support for any existing state. All nations and states need to be abolished!

Drawing by Emily. Source: sett.com/flashbang.

We love hardcore/punk and the political message behind it. But we don't like tough guys. We love to dance without getting hurt ;)

We enjoy our lives and have a positive outlook.

And we believe we can change the world!

WHAT IS XO HEARTLINE OX?

xo HeartLine ox started off as a spontaneous idea of two friends. We felt the need to say something against fascist ideas within the vegan sXe scene.

It is not a set of rules. It's something very personal. We are against strict rules as hardline sets them. We are against BBP (Bring Back Prohibition) because it's ridiculous to want a law telling people what to do and what not. We don't believe laws of any kind can bring about any positive change. Laws are not the answer and will definitely not lead to the goals we want to achieve. And we are against slogans like "Vegan Jihad" because we hate that this word actually always stands in a fanatic religious context. We are against religions! No matter if institutional or not. People should start thinking and making decisions on their own, and not let a higher nature lead them through life.

We want to build up a drug-free veganarchist movement! So if you want to help us, come and join us! Write comments, blogs, whatever you like! Spread the xo HeartLine ox message! Let's fight those conservative ideas together with love and fun! :)

ANARCHO-STRAIGHT EDGE

This article was originally published in the first issue of *Hold Your Ground* zine from Melbourne, Australia (ca. 2010).

A friend once said to me that they were "an anarchist first and a straightedger second," but I don't think the two are mutually exclusive or that one should have to be prioritised over the other. The connection between anarchism and straightedge varies from some of the most obvious issues such as capitalism and consumption to more indirect issues dealing with addiction as a community and rebelling against the socialisation of alcohol. Some of these issues are contentious but in no way am I trying to say this is what straightedge is about or that to be an anarchist you must be straightedge. I am just drawing upon common ground, explaining how straightedge is inextricably tied to anarchism for me, and trying to help people understand straightedge from an anarchist perspective.

In its most basic element refusing to consume alcohol and drugs is an anti-capitalist statement. It is the logical extension of keeping consumption to a minimum and questioning the necessity of the things we buy. However, it is also much more important than reducing unnecessary consumption because of the role alcohol has played in perpetuating capitalist oppression and fascism. The role of alcohol is that of pacification; stealing our time, money, and emotional, physical and mental energy. Energy, time and money that if spent on dismantling the current system of oppression (instead of destroying ourselves, our health and our capacity to fight back) could destroy the capitalist system. It is not a coincidence that the very companies and governments (don't forget those heavy taxes) that profit from the sale of alcohol and drugs are safe and relatively unthreatened by the pacification and intoxication of society.

I know that alcohol and drugs are not the only things that steal our time, money and health. TV, consumerism and perhaps the biggest culprit of all, work, also steal our time, money and health, and you could still be straightedge and not make better use of your time. However, as a straightedge anarchist I'm fighting against alcohol and drugs as inclusive of all forms of escapism and repression in an effort to reclaim my life from this system. This doesn't mean that I spend 100% of my time fighting the system, we all need to relax and escape sometimes, but as a straightedger I'm just committed to finding more positive and constructive ways of doing that.

By refusing to buy alcohol I am also refusing to support the often sexist, racist, and homophobic advertisements and tactics of the alcohol industry. I am also refusing the Nihilistic attitude of some punk music particularly chaos punk (life's fucked so let's get fucked up) and the social laws of conformity that would have all my social interactions and relationships dictated by alcohol. Even organising or attending a punk show that isn't in a bar is rare and that's exactly where the idea of straightedge came from—divorcing punk from alcohol by making sure that everyone could see shows regardless of whether they were of drinking age.

I feel that a lot of people draw the line between straightedge and, for example, being vegan because eating animals and their by-products is a choice that clearly causes suffering to others but consuming alcohol is seen as a personal choice that only affects yourself. But anyone who has ever tried to help their friends, family, loved ones or themselves through an addiction would know that the line between choices that only affect yourself and choices that affect others is not so clear. I think we all could agree that addiction is a serious issue that needs to be dealt with by everyone not just straightedgers.

Not only do companies and governments financially benefit from our addictions but they create our problems, sell us the "cure" and count on us getting addicted. This may sound a little far-fetched to those unfamiliar with capitalism but think about it . . . most people who commit "crimes" do so due to the desperation of poverty, a condition exclusively created by the capitalist system. Governments and corporations market and sell us alcohol

not STRAIGHT as in hetro but EDGE as in DRUG FREE

From *Hold Your Ground* zine no. 1.

and drugs to escape and to "take a break" from the very conditions of life that they created and when we get addicted they provide little help. They sell us nicotine gum and patches, methadone, naltroxone, valium, and institutionalised psychiatric programmes that leave us little control over how we actually kick our own addictions and often result in yet another addiction. Anarchism removes the condition of poverty that creates that majority of addictions and forges a community response that empowers individuals to combat addictions. Straightedge also does this but as a preventative measure by recognising this capitalist scheme and taking back control of our own lives.

As an anarchist I'm against any connection between straightedge and religion and any fucked up anti-sex attitudes. If someone abstains from alcohol/drugs/sex and they are religious it's because they are religious not straightedge, and if they happen to be into hardcore and religion (they obviously missed the point completely so go back and listen to Minor Threat again) they are religious first and straightedge second. Religion and straightedge are incompatible just as religion and anarchism are because there is nothing positive about religion. Organised religion has contributed to thousands of years of rape, sexism, queerphobia, and abuse. Anarchism is sex-positive and since straightedge is positive it should be sex-positive too.

There are many fucked up attitudes in straightedge or held among straightedgers that I think are sexist, queerphobic and at the least irrelevant to straightedge. One of the most common attitudes that I have encountered recently is that in order to be respectful to womyn straightedge men should abstain from having casual sex. The idea here is that by refusing to engage in casual sex straightedge men are adopting a pro-feminist attitude that refuses the male conditioning of treating womyn as sexual objects. Although it is good to challenge gender conditioning, this attitude is far from being pro-feminist; in fact it is the opposite. Although men may have been conditioned to treat womyn as sexual objects, womyn have been conditioned to deny their own sexuality and sexual agency and reserve themselves for loving relationships and husbands. This "pro-feminist straightedge" attitude continues the sexual repression of womyn by not allowing them to experience sex without love and meaning, and is the same repression of marriage and other sexist institutions that womyn have been fighting against for decades. This attitude is also very heteronormative (the assumption that everybody is heterosexual) and queerphobic as it doesn't even consider the gender conditioning or roles of queer relationships and leaves no room for anyone to experience sexuality, regardless of sexual and gender orientation.

All gender conditioning needs to be addressed and the best way to do this is not to just do the opposite of what you're conditioned to do, but to question, redefine and forge your own positive relationships. This takes a lot more effort but is exactly what straightedge and anarchism are all about. As a straightedger I don't refuse drugs and alcohol just to do the opposite of what's socially acceptable but because I see positivity in having control over my own life and making better use of my time. Anarchism is obviously devoted to ending sexism and other gender/sexual oppressions but is also positive in the same sense as straightedge as we search for a better way of life by making demands and forging positive solutions to our problems. Therefore having a sex-positive attitude is a part of an anarcho-straightedge perspective.

Straightedge hardcore kids and anarchists definitely share positivity in common. Straightedgers often talk about seizing life and having a positive outlook which is an attitude anarchists must embody in order to overcome the pessimism of many who believe anarchism is idealist and to keep fighting for a better life in the face of so much opposition. Our hardcore punk scenes and social spaces also reflect the way we want to live our lives, whether it's counteracting homophobia, racial supremacy or drug use in the scene. Many anarchist social spaces host punk shows with many straightedger and hardcore bands playing fund raisers for a range of political issues. Straightedge hardcore kids help create a kind of microcosm of the equality anarchists try to create on a larger scale.

Anarcho-straightedge combines the anti-capitalist, anti-consumerist, pro-feminist, queer-positive politics of anarchism with straightedge ethos of clear thinking, positivity and substance-free living. It is a complementary relationship where straightedge can add clarity and positivity to the political struggles and seriousness of anarchism and anarchism can bring political direction and meaning to a largely apolitical straightedge scene. However, anarcho-straightedge is not a movement and not all people who identify as such will agree with these ideas.

IDENTITY CRISIS: RECLAIMING AND REASSERTING RADICAL VEGAN STRAIGHT EDGE

Anonymous

This article was originally published in the second issue of *Out from the Shadows*, an "irregularly printed zine, compiled and edited by one extremely odd kid from the Northeast Ohio region," ca. 2006.

It never ceases to amaze me how the majority of people, particularly in the context of the contemporary radical punk milieu, get so terribly uncomfortable (even angry!) when even the phrase "vegan straight edge" gets brought up. If the topic actually gets pushed past all the initial objections and barriers it rarely gets farther than a wholesale-dismissal as an ideology, as if the stances of those who are not vegan straight edge are some how more radical than ours, or that ours are silly and to be disregarded.

But what is more frustrating and disheartening than these non-participants and their refusal to be open to discussion is the retreat by many of our comrades into obscurity, afraid of reproach or the consignment of pariah by the group-at-large. In many of the places I have traveled, at many convergences and conferences, I have had to coax persons out of the vegan straight edge closet. When, at one gathering, I asked if any person who identified themselves as vegan straight edge kids would like to meet up and discuss our potential in the resistance community, I was very well going to have to run for my life from the 40 oz-toting majority, with eyes of fiery drunken vengeance, only later to have nearly a dozen persons come up to me and express a desire to talk and with a relief that there were other vegan edgers present because they "felt like no one-else here was down." When some of us finally sat down and talked, the reluctance to talk—about sober spaces, about civilization and our discontent with it, about veganism and what sucks about it (the idea of a rigid morality based on diet, not the diet itself silly!), about the role drug culture plays within the punk and activist community effects the struggle—vanished. It seemed that all we needed was a little support from each other and a collective push to open up and we had so much more to share. It seemed pretty obvious to me at the time that *we, the radical vegan straight edge, suffer from an identity crisis*, forced upon us by the larger (and in some eases dominant) punk and activist culture.

The main argument against, the routine dismissal, and the first attack to suppress discussion of radical vegan straight edge is almost always in some way, shape, or form linked to an aversion to the Hardline Movement. For starters, *being vegan straight edge does not equate to being hardline.* Does being non-sober mean being an addict? Certainly not. This "if you are x then you are y" type of mentality is prejudice, plain and simple. I would think that through the statements and actions of members of the modern radical vegan straight edge community it would be apparent that our intention is to create a new culture of resistance, based on total liberation for all, not revive a rigid moralistic movement based on ignorance. However, while we're on the subject, I think we should clear the air surrounding the Hardline Movement. I've seen too many tiptoe around this, so I'm just going to lay it all out for everyone. Here's how the ever-useful wikipedia.com defines it:

"The Hardline movement grew out of the more politically conscious sections of the Southern California hardcore and punk scenes in 1990. Although one of the basic tenets of Hardline was that it had existed in various forms since the beginning of time, the ideology was largely formulated by Sean Muttaqi of the band Vegan Reich. The Hardline philosophy was said to be rooted in one ethic (the sacredness of innocent life), but in reality the ethos rested on that base and on an idea of an immutable Natural Order. Put in more specific terms, Hardline can be described as a synthesis of deep ecology, straight edge, animal liberation, leftism, and Abrahamic religion."

Now, to elaborate more on Hardline's history, one should most certainly check out Wikipedia's extensive and detailed profile, but to sum it all up, Hardline, in its short time, started as one person's zine and ideology, seemingly based on the beliefs of the MOVE organization and small handful of bands, which as it grew in popularity began to move hardcore kids from the basements and into the streets, so to speak, as they formed the Coalition to Abolish the Fur Trade and were connected to an undoubt-edly large yet undetermined number of ALF and ELF actions (graffiti such as "S.E.A.L."—Straight Edge Animal Liberation—was found at arsons, van-dalizings, and liberations, and while it is certainly conceivable that many of these actions were performed by vegan straight edge persons outside of Hardline, many Hardline members served time for actions), and eventually broke from the hardcore and punk community and moved towards radical Islamic beliefs, and have since seemingly vanished into obscurity (hopefully for good). Throughout this evolution, their basic tenets remained, and thus were widely criticized for their sexist and homophobic stances. Rightfully so, I'd like to add. These attitudes were based on little more than ignorance and the inculcated prejudices passed on from the dominant culture and its mythologies. Especially considering that the natural world Hardline idolized and fetishised is full of diversity and survival activities that were somehow distorted as unnatural and criminal in the context of humanity. I want to make it clear that *any group or person that stands in the way of total libera-tion for all as Hardline and in turn Taliyah Al-Mahdi did, should be criticized and openly resisted.* Today, we as radical vegan straight edge persons have worked far too hard to be marginalised and silenced because of a former movement with ties to our identity. We are no more responsible for the Hardline Movement than any white radical person is for the Ku Klux Klan, and much like that white radical, we have a responsibility as vegan straight edge persons to work against such organizations, beliefs, and activities in our communities.

History being clarified, and that point being made, I'd like to quote from an Interview with Mack Evasion, a rather infamous vegan straight edge fellow in the anarchist community, to effectively deflate the arguments against radical vegan straight edge, and the dismissal of our community via Hardline:

> When people criticise Hardline (generally for the stance on abor-tion or homosexuality), I always ask them: What do you think of the Black Panthers? Of MOVE? Of course amongst radicals the response is positive, "I support them," etc. There is a certain obligation as an "anarchist" or whatever, to dis on Hardline, just as there is an equal obligation to support the Black Panthers. But I have to point out that high-ranking members of the Black Panthers made openly sexist and homophobic statements. MOVE was openly homophobic. Why do we discriminate? Because we assign "fashionable" status to some groups,

THIS IS NOT
A FASHION SCENE

STRAIGHT EDGE
IS POLITICAL

RESIST, WITH EVERY OUNCE OF LIFE, WITH EVERY BEAT OF MY HEART

From *Open Minds* zine, issue 1, June 2011.

and "unfashionable" status to others. There is no pause for objective consideration. As a person belonging to a certain counterculture ("anarchist," etc.), you are simply obligated to support one and condemn the other.

I really couldn't have put it better myself. The radical punk community yearns to find solidarity with other communities and to move beyond its history as a "white movement," and in the process has a tendency to all-too-quickly align itself with movements, organizations, and persons from outside communities whose views and goals are incompatible with that of resistance. Whenever the discussion of the role punk plays in the larger movement gets past this, it usually (conveniently) stops at the contributions of early punks like the Crass collective or the recent radical punk phenomenon and anti-movement known as CrimethInc. These are, of course, excellent examples of punk's momentum and potential (not to mention that many active participants in CrimethInc cells are vegan straight edge), but to disregard the contribution to radicalism in hardcore and punk that Hardline provided and the inroads into the larger resistance culture that it created, and to keep trying to fit other cultures' movements into the context of our own, demonstrates a serious problem that we as a community must face now. *We need to critically approach our history and weed out the praxis from the pitfalls.*

Another common dismissal of the radical vegan straight edge is that we are taking a "superiorist" stance amongst and against the larger group-in-question. This is a defensive move used by the dominant culture when its attitudes and perceptions are being outwardly opposed by a certain group (such as "reverse-racism" accusations by those whose cultures have perpetuated hundreds if not thousands of years of race-based hatred, etc.), and it is used in a similar context here. I have not yet encountered a radical vegan straight edge person asserting themselves as superior to any non-sober people. Those who claim such a position are not radicals, frankly. *We as members of the radical vegan straight edge are working against morality and its constraints, not reinforcing false dichotomies*—although it certainly seems our opponents would have it this way. It's also been my personal experience that this is usually an argument presented by those who are very insecure about their own personal choices and who are concerned that their hypocrisies will be revealed by a change in the group's dynamic or perspective. This is another indicator of a serious lack of critical thought within our community. *We need to open up.* We're all hypocrites, and it is time to be honest about our shortcomings and personal struggles, and we need to begin to build support networks to counter these.

We have every right to express and celebrate our identities, and anyone who opposes our doing so should ask very serious questions about themselves and their role in resistance culture. To celebrate one's identity should never be hindered, but in fact encouraged, as such expressions can create solidarity and support in communities that are largely dispossessed and discouraged. A wonderful example of such empowerment is Anarchist People of Color. I can't imagine anyone in the anarchist community condemning or opposing APOC based on the negative aspects of former movements by people of color, or calling the group "superiorist" because it seeks to create a safe space for persons of color to identify and organize. Aren't we as the radical vegan straight edge merely asking for similar space and opportunity?

How much of our community's potential has yet to he realized because of this imposed disenfranchisement? How much longer will we allow ourselves to be marginalized? Will we disappear into obscurity within resistance culture because of "vegan straight edge shame" or will we break through this identity crisis with strong bonds of solidarity? Only time will tell, but in the meantime those of us who are out there should be outspoken in our identification as the radical vegan straight edge, asserting ourselves and our identity within the larger resistance movement both within and outside of hardcore and punk.

STRAIGHT EDGE: AN ANARCHIST POC PERSPECTIVE ON RESISTING INTOXICATION CULTURE

Hellrazor xvx

This article was published anonymously in the second issue of *Riotous Incognitx: a queer, insurrectionary anarchist, vegan straight edge zine* (ca. 2013). Hellrazor xvx is named as the author in a reprint in the 2015 zine *Straight Edge Resistance*.

Anyone who lives in a low-income community of color knows that when jobs are scarce, survival happens by any means necessary. Drugs are a product with endless demand in the hood. Where people are suffering, escapism facilitates a toxic market. From nicotine to alcohol or weed to heroin, somebody poor enough will find a way to get it to sell or use to escape. As a kid I remember folks would be stumblin' around the block tweakin' out daily on different shit, and every once in a while one would sit down next to me at the park and spill guts about their pain. Seeing the misery of being a drug-addict in their eyes and face never leaves my memory. To hear some of these folks speak to me like an adult and vocalize this misery left me asking the same questions: Why does this happen to people? Is it merely the choices they make or are there bigger factors that play key roles in cultivating a life of oppression and neglect? As I got older I realized that as human animals caged by civilization, private property ownership, and the armed gangs who protect those in power; intoxication culture is escapism. In many cases it is self-destruction due to internalized and repressed anger. It is fucked up that most families live on scraps while others sit on more than they need. When the survival rate drops and hunger consumes your patience, "crime" becomes an inevitable option. Some folks use that five-finger-discount but others continue to suffer in fear of getting caught and

From *Straight Edge Resistance* zine.

locked up. So, what else to do when fear reinforces a cage of its own within the mind and heart? Some concede and self-destruct. Others sell poison to their own people, either to survive or get rich. Intoxication culture thrives where folks are angry and poor Pacifism and apathy co-operate with escapism by discouraging direct confrontation with the underlying causes of such misery.

I first claimed straight edge when I was 16. It wasn't just the music, the unity at shows, or the X's (which weren't easy to see on my hands). For me, being straight edge was primarily a personal political statement. I had seen what intoxication culture and addiction did to people in my community. I saw what it did to my own family and seen how the "War on Drugs" was used to brutalize and imprison people of color. It was obvious that the white supremacist capitalist system profited from intoxicated people of color. The prison-industrial complex swells as the state uses addicts as snitches. There was a full blown market for nicotine and alcohol consumption in the hood. As long as we we're distracted with addiction and poor health, questioning the origin of our misery came last. All of this including the lose of friends and family to overdose left me with the anger to reject intoxication culture. I embraced straightedge after deciding I would never use or depend on that shit. Why the fuck would I ever put money directly into the pockets of those who don't give a shit about us, our health, the environment, or the non-human animals caged up in their testing laboratories? Just so I could "get wasted" or catch a break with a hit of nicotine? But while I had the determination to reject intoxication culture, not everyone is the same. I can only speak for myself for this decision.

One thing that I have found problematic with both the anarchist and straight edge community is the lack of support groups or sober safe spaces

Source: overthrowxoppression.bandcamp.com.

offered for folks struggling with addiction and intoxication culture. While traveling I had seen so many anarchist collectives filled with cigarette smoke and swimming in alcohol. Most anarchist collectives get shy when questioned about a sober safe space and supporting comrades fighting personal battles with addiction. I personally feel that radical sobriety is important in radical circles, and that support for those tryin' to kick toxic habits is necessary for opening more avenues of solidarity. While many other folks are straightedge for many other reasons, I use my sobriety as a weapon of war. To me, straight edge is more than just X's and tattoos. To the industries, tobacco companies, drug cartels, and everyone else getting rich by enslaving addicts, my straightedge is a black flag. Personally, straight edge means no surrender and the refusal to be pacified by the system's weapon of internalizing defeat. Solidarity with all those who are struggling against addiction for self-liberation. All power to the families and community folks rising up in arms against drug lords and cartels in their towns.

AN INDIGENOUS ANARCHIST AGAINST INTOXICATION CULTURE

Sarambi

This article appeared in 2015, both in the zine *Straight Edge Resistance*, edited by the Feral Space collective, and—together with another piece by Sarambi, "Deconstructing Myths Surrounding Veganism and People of Color"—in the Warzone Distro zine *My Vegan Straight Edge Is Anything but White: An Indigenous Anarchist Critique of Speciesism and Intoxication Culture.*

The process of refusing intoxication is one that is long and arduous as a queer indigenous POC. The intense interlinking and bound together issues of being indigenous to land known as South America, a land being ravaged by major crop production of monocrops, but also of tobacco, coca, marijuana, and other chemicals being taken at a large rate out of context and out of balance like how people from off that land treat ayahuasca and other plants. As a queer individual now in the gilded, imperial terminal capitalist monstrosity known as the US, I see for what reasons our lands are being destroyed: it's for temporary pleasure, to numb from our suffering, because we have been told that how we exert liberation, freedom, and our sexuality and gender fuckery is at the bottom of a glass or end of a rail. I have also had to bear witness to the history of alcoholism en mi campesinx, mixed indigenous but not mestizx, familia. I have watched too many people end up in the clutches of the state for abusing or pushing drugs only because they had nothing else to gain or lose in their eyes so they listened to what was given to us. I speak to folx about why them spending what energy, resources, and capital on substances is not liberation, it is continuing genocide, ecocide, extinction, capitalism, colonial imperialism, and is keeping them from moving beyond themselves to actually get free.

This is a message for my indigenous relations and others: stop listening to the colonizer, stop trying to please our oppressors in every form they take. They feed off of our dead lives. We have resisted for 523 years, and often that has included abstaining from the intoxicants they push on us so we are easy and don't feel our destruction. We tell them to keep alcohol away from us, and though people die from saying no, we go on. We push governments, no matter how "leftist" or down they seem they are all gaming on maintenance of keeping nations/labor/trade for capital/systems that benefit them and must not be trusted, and narcos from lands, and even with armies against us we persist in the name of not having the substances destroy our land and people further. They have already written and foretold their demise.

To everyone else who is not yet on the same page: this is for you. You who seek to end the world and dance in the quick wild waters ready to erode the mutated fallowed earth. Why does your liberation cost the planet, other species and other humans far from you and your spectacle? Why are you seeking out making the spectacle yours instead of shedding it to embrace a real existence as an individual and collective instead of a walking dead existence? How do you justify your revolutionary revelry, subversions, or social revolt when you are still not embracing the agony and suffering of your own life let alone what your choices to consume do away from you? If you're not about capitalism, why are you acting as a consumer? If you are about decolonization, why are you promoting colonial land grabs, genocide against indigenous bodies, and destroying our connection to the environment we have always learned from? What is your cognitive dissonance with seeing suffering, extinction, and factual affects on things that you do see like the war on drugs and the incarceratory state, the military and medical industrial complexes, white supremacy, colonization of the land we are on in the US, etc.?

This is real talk. This is the problem. There is no conscience consumerism, as we all know hopefully, because of the mechanisms that make capitalism flourish. You cannot promote use of substances without participating in the justification of capitalism, you cannot produce many of the recreational substances used in North America, Europe, and amongst those with the capital ability to use without the exploitation and genocide of an ecosystem. We as humans in this age have seen it in both the proxy colonial wars through the Fertile Crescent and colonially termed Latinoamérica within the last 30 years. Within the warfare against US defined "terrorism" and hunting for oil in Iraq, what gets left out is the US's want of the opium poppy fields in Afghanistan when they entered. It also happened to coincide with the increase of opiate painkiller prescriptions doled out to Americans by primarily pharmaceutical company backed doctors and the continued rise in popularity of opiates as a recreational drug. This market still exists, as does the continued occupation, where people of the land are growing and being "raided" by the US but the opium gets overseas. Similar drug pushing and coerced production for the US was seen anecdotally in the Golden

Triangle as the US was fighting in Vietnam, and committing secret operations in neighboring Laos and Cambodia. Drugs benefit the US as an empire, sorry.

But if it wasn't clear enough, look just south of the US colonial line from Mexico to Argentina—the US controlled and backed War on Drugs is not only meant to create the conditions to justify genocide in the US against Black and Brown, Indigenous and arrivant bodies, it is also a strategy to continue the legacy of the Dirty Wars, juntas, and white supremacist/Casta driven, colonially based neofascism that not even Leftists in charge and adored by American and European socialists can be found not falling under. Many people are no longer able to access their generational homelands due to violence related to the purest capitalistic motives of those who have "moved up," forced to take work as runners, pushers, guards, etc. since there is nothing else because the land is poisoned or monocropped, the water is poisoned from mining residue and pollutants or is stolen to produce alcohol or soda or to be bottled as is for resale, and all other avenues are limited due to racially backed classism and anti-indigenous sentiment, strict morality, gender and sexuality guidelines brought out by colonizers and neo-colonizing missionaries from the US (I see you Mormons, Jehovah's Witnesses, and Evangelicals), and purposefully underdeveloped status in the world. When we are given nothing, we turn to what we are granted, it seems. But we do fight back, Xyha people kick marijuana growers off their land before the paramilitary can come into their territory. The Emberá of Panamá, the Purépecha of México, the Bribri of Costa Rica, the Nahua of Colombia all have fought back and have even kicked out other foreigners or outsiders as they are aware how they could be blindsided by cartel movement if they are interfered with. Autodefensas and Zapatista communities throughout Mexico not only abstain from intoxication but also fight off cartels and the paramilitary government forces who are hand-in-hand with the cartels and the US. This type of armed resistance and pushback has history in the Americas to even earlier colonial periods and to this day, even in North America, autonomous and/or sovereign indigenous lands fight and die over preventing more damage and death done by intoxication. Though this has not always been and does not need to be the case either in indigenous lands producing or in occupied lands where it is consumed.

We can choose, and some of us do, to negate the existence of these intoxicants for political and decolonial reasons. By refusing to play into not only what pacifies but what comes up and promotes systems that are inherently based in imperialism and capitalism as well as used to bolster kyriarchy all around, one feels all the agony they should: for themselves to do what they chose or must for existence without being lulled into any false pleasure of this civilization, for other beings and the planet being destroyed near and far from them, and for the future as this continues. When you actually feel every painful aspect of living, you are more apt to resist at your fullest because you are able to sense how unyielding and sickening parasitic everything is. If you can feel that, and feel it always at the level as it is, then you have a stronger will built up to fight back as nothing is cushioning the blows any longer. Nothing is keeping your head above water, until you take the boat that civilization has given to some and smash it to bits, and float on a board. Nothing is numbing you, making you forget, making you feel pleasure when you, those around you, and other on the periphery are dying or are already dead as you are walking dead. In a framework that is against all oppression, against all control, against all passiveness, it continues that one should negate the interests of civilization and gilded pleasure at the cost of everything you think you fight for. You cannot destroy your masters without going all the way.

STRAIGHT EDGE ANARCHY: THE DANGER OF A SOBER INSURRECTION

Anonymous

This is a reprint of a 2014 zine written by "some insurrectionary queers of the sober kind."

INTOXICATION CULTURE

Intoxication: derived from the Latin word *intoxicatio*, meaning "to poison one's self." Intoxication culture is a set of institutions, behaviors, and mindsets focused on the consumption of drugs, alcohol, and tobacco use. Intoxication culture facilitates the anesthesia promoted by those in power who seek to disempower and pacify the enslaved. As an antithesis of self-liberation, intoxication culture promotes defeatism through the internalization of self-hatred and pity.

On a global scale capitalism not only manifests its destruction environmentally but also in the form of

STRAIGHT EDGE ANARCHY
The Danger of a Sober Insurrection

self-destructive actions and behaviors which have become normalized as a traditional development of civilization. As a coping mechanism, intoxication becomes an accepted part of daily life, whether it be as a reward for a long hard week of wage-slavery, or a self-prescribed sedative and so on.

Intoxication culture is self-perpetuating and captures the idea of rebellion through self-destruction. Often an individual manifests depression and anger cultivated by preexisting oppressive external forces, through a variety of self-destructive actions. Rebellion in this sense is internalized as self-hatred, apathy, and self-pity. As self-hatred, depression, and feelings of inferiority become exacerbated by addiction, profits soar for capitalists. Rather than directly confronting problems that exist in one's life, an individual becomes dependent on a source which provides temporary escape. Escapism becomes an alternative life of apathy through toxic consumerism. As nourishment for self-pity, hopelessness, and apathy intoxication acts as an agent of consolement.

The deprivation of self-respect coupled with feelings of inferiority has and continues to be an obstacle in the way of insurrectionary attack. This short pamphlet was written in hopes of presenting a critical view of toxic pacifism while highlighting the urgency for sober attack.

CHEMICAL WARFARE AND COLONIZATION

Alcohol was an integral part of the colonization process. Everything from creating alcoholic abusive behavior within what used to be peaceful Native groups and tribes to pacifying slave revolts. European Christian colonists used alcohol as a chemical weapon of warfare in their genocidal and ethnic cleansing, mistreatment, and exploitation of indigenous peoples. Alcohol and tobacco became tools of privilege creating hierarchy as those who had more access to these could sell them for the labor of others. Once tobacco became known for its profit, indigenous people, slaves, and indentured servants were put to work on lands that were taken by brutal force from the Natives. Alcohol and drugs were used for their pacifying and numbing effects. As the wild and free became more intoxicated and distracted from the reality of their rapidly changing existence, they began to internalize the hatred imposed upon them. With the development of an identity crisis the process of assimilation took place as many indigenous and other people of color became a target for capitalists who profit from social intoxication.

DISTRACT AND PACIFY

Capitalism relies heavily on distracting people from the reality of its oppressive control. As long as people are ignorant and docile, capitalism and its destruction can remain unchallenged and operational. Through toxic submission capitalism normalizes the monotony of social disempowerment. As long as the casual exchange of labor for capital, capital for inebriation takes place, there is no threat to the civilized order. While a local punk benefit show rages in clouds of cigarette smoke, Reynolds American (a $19.5 billion corporation) takes much of the profit. Empty beer cans and hungover anarchist punks litter the floors of squats and rented spaces as the US casually continues its military domination of other countries abroad.

In a system of psychological warfare, pacifism is defeat. It is the neglect of one's self as a result of the civilized disconnection from wild raw emotion. Emotional suppression induced by inebriation cultivates the pacifist role of allowing external forces of oppression to exist and dominate without confrontation and attack.

Intoxication distracts an individual by complicating preexisting stressful circumstances to the point of emotional exhaustion. During this time of anesthesia spaces of emotional and physical vulnerability are opened and exploited. These complications and distractions allow capitalism and those in power to oppress without conflict.

By impairing and debilitating the emotional and physical arsenal foundational to self-liberation, intoxication culture is an obstacle in the way of revolutionary organizing and attack. The revolutionary act of overcoming these obstacles and addictions in pursuit of self-liberation is nothing less than an outspoken refusal to be tamed and pacified. It is a refusal to promote and participate in a culture which aids the destruction of others.

WHY STRAIGHT EDGE?

Straight Edge is the politics of regaining control over one's self, and of taking back from those who wish to enslave and control. It is the politics of rejecting the "values" and toxic traditions that have been instilled in civilized society. In a system dependent on the intoxication and ignorance of people, the abstention from these tranquilizers is a refusal to comply with, and rebellion against the system.

As people have been drowned and chained by capitalist traditions, Straight Edge is embraced by anarchists as a firm rejection of a culture promoted and perpetuated by a system seeking total physical and psychological control. As a rejection to the assumption that all will participate in the intoxicating consumerist routine of passive obedience, self-disrespect, and toxic submission, the Straight Edge movement has increased. This has occurred as anarchists extend solidarity with freedom fighters globally, understanding that cognizance and sobriety are a combined expression of resistance to the self-indulgent, apathetic ethos that defines mainstream US culture.

"WAR ON DRUGS" = WAR ON PEOPLE OF COLOR

As a result of the state-operated "War on Drugs", communities of color are targeted for police harassment and mass incarceration. Crack and other drugs remain as large sources of profit for the white supremacist system. By keeping POC communities passive and politically indifferent, the state is able to warp public perception with the delusion of progress with incarcerations. Straight Edge anarchists understand that the state is never an option for fighting intoxication culture. The state is not only the colonial, repressive apparatus protecting private-property ownership and the white supremacist order but also an accomplice of intoxication culture. One does not have to look far to see how the state uses intoxication culture to fuel the prison industrial complex. The state has used drugs to orchestrate the destruction of the Black Panther Party and has made multiple attempts to undermine the cohesion of the Zapatistas with alcohol. Due to their destructive counterinsurgent effects, there is a total absence of consumption or sale of drugs and alcohol in the Zapatista autonomous communities.

Alcohol manufacturers, coca and marijuana syndicates, and "chemists" have created a colossal destructive industry based on both "legal" and black market demand. Philip Morris and Anheuser-Busch, although both household names, are just as responsible for community destruction and murder as the Sinaloa Cartel (Mexico) or the Noorzai Organization (Afghanistan). From an economic standpoint radical sobriety reduces the demand for their "goods" and limits their power at an individual level. As a whole, the Straight Edge movement maintains not only a threat to these businesses by disrupting their flow of income, but also to the normalcy of emotional suppression, obedience, and apathy. In this sense sobriety is embraced not only as a rejection of submission, but also as a declaration of war.

SOLIDARITY

Attacking intoxication culture means individual resistance and collective support. Civilization is a prison of misery, coercion, and oppressive inequality. Institutionalized racism, sexism, and other forms of oppression create feelings of severe depression and isolation. Intoxication culture thrives in areas dominated by poverty, depression, and isolation. This explains why communities of color are often affected by addiction and intoxication where the state takes advantage carrying out murders and mass incarceration.

Support and solidarity are important in helping to strengthen the struggle against addiction as well as developing an intersectional attack on all oppression.

Radical sobriety support groups and spaces help replace religious groups that rather than addressing addiction as a natural response to an oppressive environment, seek to replace one form of codependency with an authoritarian one. Providing revolutionary sober-safe spaces that are open for recovering addicts, community discussions, and radical support help aid the struggle against intoxication culture. Being inclusive rather than rejecting those struggling with addiction is of utmost importance as well as encouraging self-empowerment in those who feel powerless against their addiction.

Straight Edge identifying anarchists stand against religion, homophobia, sexism, racism and all forms of oppressions and should not be confused with "hardline" ideology. Radical sobriety is not only a self-liberating act of rewilding one's self, but also as a form of solidarity and support with those struggling against addiction. Embracing an intersectional struggle against all oppression and authority means solidarity with all who struggle for freedom—including freedom from addiction and the pacifying force of intoxication culture.

Towards the destruction of civilization, all prisons, and the domesticating globalization of capitalism. For human, nonhuman animal and earth liberation.

HOW TO MAKE SENSE OF STRAIGHT EDGE NAZIS

Extreme right-wing adaptations of straight edge have been haunting straight edge culture for a long time. In *Sober Living*, I discussed relevant developments in Eastern Europe with Robert Matusiak from Refuse Records. By the time the book was released, the phenomenon of neo-fascist and neo-Nazi groups advocating straight edge, and using its symbols, had spread to other parts of Europe as well as to North America. The following is an excerpt from an interview that the collective La Terre d'abord invited me to do in the summer of 2010. The French version appeared on the website laterredabord. fr, the English one on ZNet (the page is no longer available, but the interview is archived on the PM Press website). I cut the parts about *Sober Living*, but the discussion about different political interpretations of straight edge seems to remain relevant, not least in light of the attention that far-right groups advocating straight edge have received in recent years, such as the Rise Above Movement.

La Terre d'abord: **How do you see the evolution of the straight edge movement?**

Gabriel Kuhn: I think that straight edge has developed in many different ways, which is good—although I could do without the conservative elements.

In particular the last ten years have brought real diversity, also on a musical level. Straight edge is no longer tied to the youth crew style of the

1980s or the metalcore of the 1990s—today you have straight edge acoustic acts, straight edge power violence bands and everything in-between. There are also different definitions of straight edge—the most contentious issues are veganism, sexuality, and the exact understanding of drugs/intoxicants— and there are different political adaptations, reaching from anarchist to neo-fascist straight edge groups.

As I said, the conservative elements I could do without, but in general diversity is good—it enriches and stimulates.

We think that straight edge is a form of *désengagement*, of refusal of the hegemonic values. So, it is connected to social commitment, against any oppression, and so to veganism also. How do you see it and how do you think straight edge people see it?

I like the notion of *désengagement*, I think it describes one of the political dimensions of straight edge very well. As you say, there is a rejection of hegemonic values and norms. So if you are opposed to the political and economic system that produces these values and norms, being straight edge marks an opposition to it. However, the political direction that this takes is not necessarily clear at first. Fascists reject the current system too, so a mere gesture of opposition is not enough to claim straight edge for left or radical politics. I don't think there is an automatic connection between *désengagement* and social commitment or the fight against oppression. Something has to be added to allow straight edge to head that way: social and political awareness, a commitment to a just and egalitarian world, empathy and affection. To some, veganism will be an obvious choice to make; others might make other choices with respect to their diets. I don't think that this in itself is decisive. What's decisive is that you fight for a better world *for all* and that you engage in respectful and comradely dialogue with others who want to do the same. No single individual has the answers as to which exact forms of behavior or conduct will get us there—but a common effort will guide us in the right way. And what applies to veganism applies to straight edge too: to some it will be an important part of this journey, to others it won't. Some people might prioritize other forms of *désengagement*. After all, complete *désengagement* is hardly possible in a world dominated by nation states and capital. In the end, it is the solidarity and the mutual support that counts. For us straight edge folks this means to prove our ability to contribute to this struggle in positive and constructive ways.

So this is how I see it. How do other straight edge people see it? I'm not sure. I suppose that some see it similarly, but there are many different understandings of straight edge, including those that reject any connection to politics. As I said before, there is a lot of diversity.

In the last years, some far right movements, especially in Russia and Germany, try to integrate the straight edge culture in their ideological models. In France these last months, some people try to follow this pattern. What can you tell us about this tendency making straight edge a social Darwinism?

Straight edge in its very basic definition has no clear political content—it merely indicates a refusal of drugs/intoxicants. The political connotations of straight edge come from the context it appears in and from the ideas and notions it is linked to. It is easy for the right wing to claim straight edge: all you have to do is turn it into an ideology (rather than understanding it as a personal choice). Then you can claim that you are a "better," "more advanced," or "superior" person than others. That's the first step to fascism. Possibly, the second one is to tie these sentiments to a notion of "health." While straight edge can certainly contribute to personal health, a political notion of "health" is very dangerous and has been used by all fascist movements—you just have to study their language, fascists always speak of "disease," "plague," or "decay" when they refer to the people and communities they see as inferior. The third step—and this is where we come to today's explicitly fascist and neo-Nazi straight edge adaptations—is when you tie the notion of health to a "race" or a "nation" that you need to "defend" or "preserve" or whatever. Maybe we can speak of a three-step right-wing danger here: 1. self-righteousness ("I am better than you"); 2. social Darwinism ("I am healthier than you and will outlive you"); 3. outright nationalism/racism ("we are better than you and we must maintain our 'purity'"). I think what we have seen in recent years in Russia and Germany—and now apparently also in France, although I don't know much about this—is the third step being more and more clearly articulated. The first two, to be honest, have been haunting straight edge for a long time.

How can we resist these developments?

I think there is little point in arguing about what straight edge "really" means or in denouncing the right-wing adaptations as "distortions" of straight edge. Right-wing straight edge folks obviously have their own definitions and there is no higher authority to decide who is right and wrong. In the end, we would just exhaust ourselves by throwing definitions back and forth. I think what's more important is to make our ideas as present in the scene as possible and to make them compelling to the people who move in the scene. We will win kids by being welcoming, compassionate, and caring. These are strong values—all the other side got is hate.

Yes, but hate is also something very important. We hate oppression and exploitation. And, concerning the three points you talked about, we disagree with the first point. Because, yes, we do consider the vegan straight edge lifestyle as superior to other lifestyles.

Would you agree to say that, in your will not to make accurate definitions and in your promotion of spontaneity, you're in favor of an anarchist vision? And that for you, Veganism and Straight edge don't go necessarily together? Of course it is important to have strong feelings about the terrible consequences of oppression and exploitation. If you want to call that "hate," that's fine. But what you hate in this case is a system, and you hate it because you want people—*all* people, I suppose—to be happy. People on the extreme right, on the other hand, hate people and that is at the center of their ideology. To me that's a crucial difference, and that's what I meant.

As far as the superiority of vegan straight edge is concerned, I guess it depends on what you mean by that. If you think that it is the best way to contribute to as little cruelty as possible in your personal lives, I see no particular reason to argue with that—although I'd like to point out that being vegan straight edge in itself doesn't mean that you can't be an asshole. As I said before, if you want to set a really convincing example for a "cruelty-free" or a "compassionate" lifestyle, your vegan straight edge ethics have to be tied to broad political consciousness.

Related to this, the claim that vegan straight edge constitutes a superior lifestyle can become troubling if you really want to make this a universal norm. I mean, if we go to a fishing village in Senegal and tell people that their lifestyle is inferior to ours, our vegan straight edge ethics can easily become cynical and offensive. That's why I don't like to speak of vegan straight edge as anything "superior." I think that vegan straight edge as a political practice makes a lot of sense in certain contexts and under certain circumstances— but we must never forget that billions of people don't share our contexts and circumstances, and hence other things will make more sense to them. Life is diverse, complex, and complicated, and not only is it important to be aware of that, it also makes life exciting. And it is certainly one of the reasons why I don't like to argue about definitions. Definitions help us to negotiate the complexity of life—they are tools, but they hold no truth. That's why I think it's usually pointless to argue about them. You don't win over people's hearts

"Stagedive." Art by Phoenix X Eeyore.

by defining things—you win them over by setting examples of a more joyful life. Does this belief make me an anarchist? Maybe—if it fits your definition of anarchism . . .

Regarding the relation of veganism and straight edge, maybe this helps to illustrate my point about definitions being tools: to me, the two are not necessarily connected, because I define straight edge as abstinence from drugs/intoxicants, and people can abstain from drugs/intoxicants without being vegans. Hence, according to the definition of straight edge I use, there is no necessary connection. If you have a different definition, your conclusion might be a different one too. It can be a lot of fun to discuss these things, but we'll never get to the point where one of us is proven right or wrong— and I don't think that matters either.

WEAPONIZING SOBRIETY: FERAL ANARCHY AGAINST INTOXICATION CULTURE

Blitz Molotov

Blitz Molotov is a vegan, straight edge anarchist writer, illegalist, and zine distributor who runs Warzone Distro. "Weaponizing Sobriety" was written for this book and prereleased as a pamphlet.

"It is not a new idea that we who live in mass technological society suffer psychological addiction to specific machines like cars, telephones, and computers, and even to technology itself. But the picture is bigger and more complex..."

Weaponizing Sobriety: *Feral Anarchy Against Intoxication Culture*
By Blitz Molotov

"What I am describing is a human-constructed, technology-centered social system built on principles of standardization, efficiency, linearity, and fragmentation, like an assembly line that fulfills production quotas but cares nothing for the people who operate it. Within this system, technology influences

society. The automotive industry completely reorganized American society in the twentieth century. Likewise, nuclear weapons define global politics. At the same time, society reflects the technological ethos. The social organization of workplaces, as well as their architecture, reflects the mechanistic principles of standardization, efficiency, and production quotas."
—both quotes from *Technological Addiction* by Chellis Glendinning

Intoxication culture provides a normalized social environment for toxic escape. This specific form of escapism centers substance abuse and inebriation as preferred methods of emotional stress relief. As the misery of wage slavery and the monotony of industrial society create a desire for temporary escape, addiction is exploited for capital gain. This profit motive manufactures a landscape of encouragement (whether through corporate advertising or social tradition) which reinforces intoxication culture as a societal norm.

I have seen how intoxication culture expands its sphere of influence with the help of peer pressure and the propagation of intoxication as a pleasurable social activity. The realities of addiction and death are often concealed behind the facade of glorification or dismissed as mere "extreme cases." Besides, the interconnected network of drug overdose, nicotine addiction, and alcoholism make bad selling points. For those who profit most from products that yield higher addiction rates, intoxication culture is a grocery store of profit with a variety of items and brand names. Its membership is both proliferated by a desire to escape and encouraged as a form of positive social activity. And because intoxication culture exists in society as a socially dominating force, social isolation becomes a penalty for many who remain sober. Evidence of this can be seen with how common intoxication culture is, and how very few sober support networks exist, within the anarchist milieu. This makes socializing more difficult for anarchists who are personally fighting addiction, who then relapse due to inadequate sober support from friends and the social environment. Those attempting to overcome addiction often find themselves choosing between a socialized relapse or an isolated recovery.

As an anarchist, I recognize the relationship between capitalism, intoxication culture, and the state—which merely exists as an agency seeking regulation and domination rather than elimination. The "War on Drugs" proves nothing more than an excuse to racially target individuals for incarceration. Intoxication culture often becomes a primary weapon for dismantling movements while systemically serving as a form of social control and distraction. Capitalism requires total subjugation of mass society, beginning with the individual. On an individual level this includes—but is not limited to—internalized inferiority, self-destruction, and disempowerment.

It is for these reasons that I remain sober as an individual form of negation to the social order of intoxication. As an anarchist, I view straight edge as a weapon against the state's attempt to ensnare me in a trap of distraction and toxic self-destruction. My sobriety is anti-capitalist: a molotov thrown at a passing police car, a fire that engulfs a business district, a riot beyond measure.

My straight edge is anarchistic at the individual level of reclaiming and weaponizing my mind and body. This includes my ability to communicate without the mediation of inebriation or altered states. I want to explore social interactions which flower and defy the obstacles of social anxiety without the politician-like mediator of intoxication. In sobriety the fear that holds raw emotion hostage is a fear socially conditioned by social disconnection and civilized alienation. For many different reasons contextual to each individual, most people are shy when first meeting or interacting. But this allows for a process of trust-building and bonding—both of which are shortened or eliminated when mind-altering substances are present. Intoxication then becomes the mediator of social interactions, often misrepresenting the (sober) interests of individuals, and in many cases becoming a tool for manipulation.

Social lubricants like alcohol or other mind-altering substances provide a temporary release of tension and feelings from the captivity of emotional repression. A distorted sense of freedom follows this release; freedom is conceived through one's choice to consume mind-altering substances in addition to one's freedom to purchase them. Under capitalism, access to alcohol for example is determined by age. Age becomes a numeric identifier of privilege; a distinguisher between those who have the freedom to purchase and consume it and those who legally do not. This materializes a hierarchy which privileges those legally recognized as "adults" with the right to purchase and consume alcohol. Those who do not meet the age requirement are burdened with the social mockery of being "too young" and therefore viewed as lesser in a capitalist society dominated by the social construction of "adulthood." This hierarchy provides the social and psychological encouragement necessary for maintaining business with future buyers; in theory, the same youth who eventually enter adulthood.

My straight edge anarchy is positioned against the assumed legitimacy of intoxication culture as a marker of age-based social value. In youth there is anarchy in the courageous act of becoming an individual undefined by intoxication culture. For the youth who refuse to assimilate under peer pressure, there is anarchy in the fire set to the hierarchy of social values determined by intoxication culture. Anarchy begins with the individual; the individualist choice to conform to or defy a culture. Straight edge is the individualist negation of intoxication culture, positioning itself against a society of peer pressure which aids capitalism in its quest to profit from addiction and substance use. From this perspective, my straight edge is a youth-based refusal to assimilate into an adulthood defined by the legal right to consume intoxicants. From an anarchist point of view, straight edge is individualist rebellion ungoverned by intoxication culture.

Like the plastic and technological devices that captivate us with high-tech addiction, intoxication culture infuses addiction with death. The numbing effects of artificial reality distracting us with illuminated screens resemble the drugs that produce temporary artificial realities and perceptions to which we lose ourselves. The ecological destruction caused by the extraction of raw materials to uphold the techno-industrial society parallels the depletion of soil nutrients and chemical use of pesticides, fertilizers and growth regulators for tobacco agriculture. The death of ecosystems is the result of accommodating a popular demand motivated by addiction—whether through deforestation, mining, extracting, refining, and purifying metals or oil for technological devices, or through heavy energy/water consumption, solid/water waste pollution, by-products, and toxic emissions for brewing alcohol.

The surrendering of individuality to the homogeny of mass technological consumerism shares another commonality with intoxication culture: peer pressure. For example, in order to remain in communication within a general populated social circle, certain technological devices must be purchased and utilized. Without them, individuals are burdened with social isolation. Capitalists require mass participation in order to profit from the products sold—whether that be products related to intoxication culture or products related to technology. The technological-industrial society which conditions our fixation on plastics and high-tech devices interconnects with the totality of a capitalist quest for marketing addiction. From this perspective, straight edge anarchy for me is a wildness hostile to the pacifying qualities of technological addiction, intoxication, and substance abuse. My anarchy is a feral rejection of a deadening capitalist society in which life is converted to a culture of spectacles and high-def imagery commodified for consumption. I refuse to be subdued by the appeal of new gadgets and intoxication—both which socially engineer the hierarchies of class status and popularity. Rather than finding raw life in mere temporary moments of escape, I prefer raw life found in permanent rebellion—the destruction of the material capitalist world of misery that creates the desire for toxic and technological escapism.

As an anarchist, I refuse to tranquilize the chaos of my jouissance with inebriation. I exalt life vehemently against the pacifying qualities of marijuana, the cancerous addiction of tobacco, and the "correctional" anesthesia of psychiatric medications. The intoxication-based realities of poverty, addiction, and death motivate my personal desire to remain sober and supportive of those struggling. As long as I exist, my sobriety remains a weapon against capitalism, a weapon which cannot be confiscated by the social conformity essential to intoxication culture. Towards individualist revolt and a straight edge anarchist praxis, straight edge means attack.

"We were induced to drink, I among the rest, and when the holidays were over we all staggered up from our filth and wallowing, took a long breath, and went away to our various fields of work, feeling, upon the whole, rather glad to go from that which our masters had artfully deceived us into the belief was freedom, back again to the arms of slavery. It was not what we had taken it to be, nor what it would have been, had it not been abused by us. It was about as well to be a slave to master, as to be a slave to whisky and rum. When the slave was drunk the slaveholder had no fear that he would plan an insurrection, or that he would escape to the North. It was the sober, thoughtful slave who was dangerous and needed the vigilance of his master to keep him a slave."

—Frederick Douglass

QUEER EDGE MANIFESTO

SAFT—Sober Anarchist Feminist Trans Crew

This manifesto was originally written in Swedish in 2011. SAFT stands for "Sober Anarchist Feminist Trans." The Swedish acronym translates as "squash" or "cordial."

We queers kill ourselves with the help of alcohol and other drugs. We are lost in the dark after each desperate attempt to escape reality—the violence of heterosexism—and thereby we also lose our chance to confront and smash it. But it is time to wake up, to sober up, and to take back the streets. Whether society's poison is the nuclear family, heteronormativity, or booze—it is time for us to rise before we drown in it. They want to pacify us, to assimilate us into their nightmare of a meaningless existence, consumption, and eight hours of work a day.

We are Queer Edge. By distancing ourselves from and putting a spin on the term "straight edge," we hope to give Queer Edge the political substance it deserves. The only thing that is "straight" about us is the fist we wave right into the face of the dominant patriarchal macho brotherhood of white cis-men who, for the most part, make up the straight edge community. A fist right against the widespread heterosexism in which ideas of intersectionality are as absent as "en stor stark" is present. No one is free before everyone is free. We have not conquered a space until everyone has access to it. We have to create new spaces—spaces of solidarity—not new norms and exclusion.

The "Queer Edge Manifesto" handed out at the 2012 Stockholm Anarchist Bookfair.

Supposedly, we belong to a movement that questions norms, but there is still a devastatingly big part that maintains one of the strongest norms we have: the consumption of alcohol. It is a fact that not everyone can or wants to be in a space where alcohol is consumed. It is not mentioned often, but we know that there are many among us who fight their asses off every day to survive alcohol. Some live day by day and can never take sobriety for granted. And there are those who love to go out and dance but who can never do it since all social spaces involve alcohol. The same spaces exclude those considered too young.

We are not just queers fighting against gender and sexuality norms. We are also—to varying degrees—subjected to class oppression. We belong to the capitalist system. Alcohol soothes aching bodies and becomes a simple escape from the alienation of work and the hate of the world around us. But it doesn't create revolutions. A pacified working class doesn't rise. A pacified working class doesn't make revolution.

To really escape the system that oppresses us through alcohol is nothing but an illusion. Alcohol helps maintain the system. The system hands us a bottle and wants us to be lonely, quiet, and weak. Nothing is as profitable for heterosexist capital as queers who are drunk and high, developing an addiction rather than building barricades.

There is nothing strange about us falling into patterns of self-destruction, to direct our frustration toward ourselves rather than to confront our true enemies: social injustices, oppressive norms, and a desire constructed by capital. We need to stop tranquilizing the only self-explanatory weapon we have: ourselves, our unity, and our bodies.

The driving force in our lives should not be to reward ourselves with drinking. The driving force should be the victories we celebrate when we resist those who want to stop us from living our lives to the fullest. Our reward will be to see everyone being included and dancing soberly to our own revolution.

We wave an X-ed up fist in the face of the system, burn down liquor stores, take their booze, and replace it with our own version of it: the Molotov cocktail!

RECOVERY

A SOBER QUEER COMMUNITY TO HEAL AND PROGRESS

Sober Coven

This piece was originally written in Swedish by the Sober Coven collective. Sober Coven has published zines by the same name and is involved in organizing the annual Etown Queer Fest in their hometown of Eskilstuna, Sweden. (See also "Not for Me" by Elina, page 181.)

In 2015, we started the fanzine collective Sober Coven. We felt a need to write about our experiences of being sober for political reasons in a world where alcohol consumption is the norm. We are three friends and did two fanzines together on sobriety: one that we wrote and drew ourselves, and one that contained both our own material and that of others who wanted to share their thoughts and ideas. We all have different experiences of earlier use, and nonuse, of drugs and alcohol. We also all have experiences of codependency. We developed our sober ideals within the hardcore community, where we moved in the same straight edge circles. The straight edge movement has given us plenty: the belief in a sober life, in a collective power to change things, and in the ability to overcome passivity. But we also felt that the movement perpetuated "toughness" and masculinity, and that there was no place for us in the "brotherhood." The principle of solidarity was often enough forgotten.

Some years have passed since then. Today, we are less active in the hardcore community. We have taken our sober values to new places. We saw,

Etown Queer Fest poster, 2018.

for example, a great need for drug-free spaces in the LGBTQIA community to which we also belong. It is very important that a belief in drug-free living as a means to liberation and sustainable political activism takes hold in this community—perhaps more so than in any other.

Queer spaces have historically often revolved around drugs and alcohol. We have met in bars and nightclubs, the only places where we could be ourselves. Clubbing remains an important part of the culture. The Pride Festival, a very important event for the LGBTQIA movement, has turned from rebellion against the police to boozy carnival.

Yes, we sometimes need to escape reality: many of us suffer greatly from a world of oppression, in which isolation, internalized homo- and transphobia, and gender dysphoria take the lives of many. Numerous of our queer comrades have experiences of self-medicating with drugs. Also of addiction. Even the spaces we have created for ourselves are not always open to everyone. An age limit at queer events excludes all people under the age of eighteen, and alcohol renders an otherwise pleasant event off limits for people who try to stay sober or who suffer from trauma related to other people's use of alcohol or other drugs. We need alternatives to destructive patterns. We need a sober queer movement where people can come together to heal. We must not let people disappear, waiting in line for institutional help, or remaining in the closet with a spliff and a bottle as the only means of survival.

Since the queer front in our home town of Eskilstuna seemed rather dead, we decided—together with friends—to organize an annual sober LGBTQIA festival. The Etown Queer Fest has now been running for four years. The intention was to create a meeting place without alcohol tying everything— and everyone—together. Rather, we wanted to form unity through discussion, art, shared emotion, and joy. We wanted to create something *together*, instead of falling into the trap of isolated passivity, which happens all too easily. Since it is crucial for young LGBTQIA people to find peers they can identify with, it has also been very important not to have an age limit.

It can be difficult to pay fees and travel costs for speakers and artists when asking only for donations and not selling alcohol. But in our case it has worked very well, since our drug-free policy made it possible to seek money from foundations, educational institutions, and the city council.

Alcohol culture is strong, and many people are used to starting the evening with a few drinks before hitting the club. It is a challenge to get them to try an all-sober night out. But in our experience, the absence of drugs has allowed for closer relationships and awareness, for meaningful conversation, and a sense of belonging that we don't experience when alcohol is served. Besides, it is very nice not having to consider hangovers when scheduling early-morning activities! The responses we have received have been very positive, also from people who usually drink. It makes us very happy that people from our community want to be involved and create a sober festival with us!

We have experienced the straight edge movement's more masculine ideals, and the queer and feminist movement's more feminine ideals in different ways. As a woman or a nonbinary person, it can be difficult to really be taken seriously in the hardcore scene. At the same time, we can miss a sense of political sobriety in queer spaces. Alcohol might even be used there to challenge society's norms, for example when you think that downing a glass of beer undermines expectations of how nonmen should behave.

Outside of straight edge, sobriety often has low status. It is assumed that you will leave it behind in your teenage years. Many people feel insecure about going to events where they can't get drunk. If they end up at one, they might leave after some time to go drinking, which seems most important.

Straight edge creates unity around sobriety. This is something we want to see in the queer movement as well—but without the macho stuff! We don't believe in competing over who is the "most true," or in looking down on so-called "dropouts." We want to create an environment where people who fight addiction have a place and find support; where drugs can be replaced with a feeling of (true) belonging, communication, shared experience, and solidarity. We want to expand the straight edge ideology and apply it to the LGBTQIA movement—for ourselves and for others—in order to make a sustainable sober life possible.

How can we do this? How do we expand and change a movement that has its own norms and expectations? As always, there are no simple answers. There are many possible solutions, and everyone works, thinks, writes, and feels differently. We suggest starting with meeting one another and attempting to create new connections in order to build a way forward based on sobriety. Let us come together with the intention to create spaces where personal exchange is not inhibited by intoxication and drunken haziness. Anyone willing to try this with us is welcome!

CHANGE THE THINGS YOU CAN'T ACCEPT: A PRIMER TO RADICAL SOBRIETY MONTREAL

J.

J. is a cofounder of Radical Sobriety Montreal, "organized by and for radical addicts/alcoholics in recovery" as "a grassroots response to the reality of widespread addiction in our communities and our lives."

What do you do when you have a problem? You do your best to fix it. Who should be in charge of this solution? The people who are affected by it. How do you accomplish your goals? Direct action, without relying on the market or the state. As a punk and an anarchist, this is always how I've thought about things.

But for years, I had a problem I couldn't fix. Every day, I got drunk and high, and I couldn't stop. In AA, sometimes people chairing meetings will do a thing called "qualifying," where they'll speak briefly about what their addiction was like, so that others attending the meeting will understand that the chair is one of them, not just some busybody or outside social worker. I'll do a similar thing now. I know this book is primarily written within a straight edge context; the following will also serve to explain to those who are not drug users or addicts what it felt like, for me, to be in addiction.

You eat every day. If you need to work and don't have time to eat, you can do it, but you might feel a little sick or irritable. If you are particularly ill or distracted, you might go a day without eating, but when you finally feel back in your body again, you will notice that you are ravenous and you will certainly eat. When you are very hungry, you might eat something you normally would not enjoy. If you are suffering from extreme caloric deficiency, you might do things to obtain food that you don't want to do. You might do something dangerous like commit a robbery or eat something rotten. Getting food becomes a task that you pursue with single-minded devotion. Throughout history, people confronted with true starvation have resorted to eating grass, leaves, dirt, and of course other people. The point is that hunger is something that you can easily deal with for a few hours, but the longer it goes on the worse it becomes, and the less reasonable it is to expect to be able to overcome the urge to eat with willpower alone.

For me, the urge to drink became a need, which began to function the way hunger does for most people.[1] I had to drink every day; the alternative felt intolerable. If I absolutely needed to, I could make it a few days, but it was agonizing. If I worked all day without a drink, by the time I got out of work I was ready to do whatever it took to find one. I drank beers with cigarette butts in them, stole drinks off the tables at bars, walked into strangers' parties to steal liquor, stole money from my girlfriend or tips from my coworkers, drank the dregs of empty cans found in alleys, whatever. My thirst for alcohol was a need. It no longer really had anything to do with recreation.

This need differed from hunger in some key ways though. Unlike with a typical person's sense of hunger this need also gradually intensified; it was as though as you got older, your baseline level of hunger increased, while food began to feel less and less filling. What would you do in such a situation? Maybe you would show up to a meal with your friends at a restaurant having already eaten a huge bowl of rice, to make sure you'll feel full. Maybe you would bring food with you everywhere you went. Maybe you would be constantly dipping out to "run to the store." Maybe you would go to different grocery stores every day so no one cashier would know how much you bought. Maybe you would find casual backyard barbecues to be the most humiliating experiences imaginable, as everyone else ate a couple burgers in an unconcerned way while you seethed with jealousy, barely able to restrain your urge to eat everything on the premises and leave early to go sit alone and do what it takes to feel satiated. I did all of that, with alcohol.

My need differed from hunger too in that with each sip I consumed, it became exponentially harder to cut myself off. In practice it was impossible. I don't have any clear memories of drinking only one single beer, and I'm not sure that I ever actually did that in my life. Typically, once I started drinking, I drank until I passed out.

The final way that my drinking differed from hunger was in the obvious sense that alcohol is not sustenance but rather is a reasonably dangerous drug with mind-altering qualities and numerous long-term health consequences.

So, to qualify: I had a completely irresistible need to drink alcohol and use drugs, which increased in severity over time, and ended up with me blacking out on a daily basis. I prioritized drinking over my relationships, my health, my education, and my employment. I prioritized it over food and over sleep. I prioritized it over sex and over music. I prioritized it over my own happiness and, ultimately and to my great shame, over my politics. I was malnourished, lonely, exhausted, and had found myself in some sickened zone on the other side of depression. My gums were rotting away and increasingly I couldn't feel my feet for some reason. I couldn't remember much of what happened to me because I was walking around in a blackout so often. I was dangerously underweight and I had a near-permanent squint from trying to correct double vision. I stopped going to school even though I liked school. I reliably lost anything expensive, and routinely woke up in bizarre or dangerous situations. Most disturbingly, whole parts of my memory and personality had been walled off behind thick psychological barriers; this was my mind trying to protect itself from what was going on. Six years later, I am still very much in the process of gently taking down these barriers in my mind and learning about who I really am.

I didn't have the most dramatic drinking career. I was lucky enough to avoid prisons and institutions, and I got sober young enough that I wasn't yet affected by many of the long-term health consequences of active alcoholism such as liver damage. The point is not that I was the most tragic figure you could imagine, only that it was bad enough that I was desperately unhappy. Anyway, this piece is not actually about addiction, at least not directly. It's about fixing a problem. A problem I didn't know I could fix.

Being in (a certain heavy-drinking section of) the punk scene in Montreal, I was vaguely aware that people did get sober, but I was surrounded by people who drank just as much as me, and often more. I met people who would, without a trace of irony, give you a hard time for drinking water. Everybody drank and everybody I hung out with drank alcoholically, or so it seemed to me. When I found this scene, I felt like I had finally found my home. But when I thought, occasionally, about the possibility of quitting drinking, I had no idea how to even go about it. The few people I knew who didn't drink used other drugs heavily, and certainly didn't seem happier. Myself, I had tried to quit drinking for brief periods a few times and had found the experiences impossibly brutal and humiliating. Quitting did not seem at all like a realistic option. Other people, I had decided, could quit drinking. I could not. The idea of someone showing me how to kick alcohol and live a contented life was about as realistic as somebody descending from the clouds on angel wings to hand me the elixir of happiness. So, like many alcoholics, I spent a long, miserable time trying and failing to control my drinking.

Then one day someone descended on angel wings and handed me the elixir of happiness. This unexpected salvation came in the form of an old drinking friend who had disappeared for a while and then popped up again, sober and glowing. Asking what she had done to achieve this impossible state, I learned that she had gone to AA and liked it. My resistance to AA, which I thought of as basically an evangelical, prohibitionist cult, was in that moment totally overwhelmed with a wave of exhaustion and desperation, and I asked my friend to take me to a meeting.

I discovered that, against all expectations, I liked AA. As an anarchist, I was thoroughly impressed with the leaderless and democratic structure of the meetings. As a more-or-less atheist, I was happy to learn that AA did not really require me or anyone else to believe in God. I was astounded at the sincerity with which people, in particular men, talked about their feelings and supported one another emotionally at the meetings, and I was touched to see really profound friendships existing between people of totally different backgrounds, brought together by common cause. Though the literature was at times hokey and simplistic, I found the nuggets of wisdom in the "Big Book" to be legitimately life-changing.[2] And last but not least, I had to concede that AA meetings were both everywhere and free, satisfying the conditions set out in the phrase, "if it's not accessible to the poor, it's neither radical nor revolutionary." I kept going to meetings, and at this point I haven't had a drink in many years. In short, I went from sneering at the concept of a twelve-step meeting to being, with a few reservations, a satisfied customer of Alcoholics Anonymous.

The reservations I had were real though. Mainly, I had a problem with the individualism of AA. I have to make it clear here that I don't mean that people were selfish or only focused on themselves. In fact, AA literature and tradition make it very clear that the program only works when people do it together, help each other, serve their communities, and let go of self-absorbed, power-seeking behaviors. What I mean by "individualism" is a disinterest in changing broad structural conditions; the structural conditions for example that create and promote addiction on the one hand and punish and alienate addicts on the other. AA essentially has no opinion on these matters, and explicitly takes no position on political issues. It calls addiction a "spiritual malady," implying that addiction springs from an individual's spiritual pain, and the solution for that individual ultimately boils down to that person's spiritual practice.

Knowing the literature, and knowing what is meant by that phrase, I now basically agree that for a given value of "spiritual" and for a certain definition of "malady," that definition of addiction is broadly correct; but as a socialist (and a sociologist, now, as it happens), I don't think spiritual maladies come out of nowhere. Conditions allow or disallow certain illnesses to propagate. People with access to varied, healthy diets don't develop scurvy. Populations with access to clean drinking water are not ravaged by cholera. Vaccines protect some people from certain diseases while unsafe living conditions can expose some people to others. There is a socially determined aspect to health and well-being that even Western medicine's traditional hyper-focus on physiological determinants cannot ignore. This must apply to a condition like addiction as much as to any other. When I stopped drinking, I wanted to talk about these things; there was little in the AA literature about it, and people in the meetings often brushed over broader considerations of why addiction occurs, and what could be done about it on a social level, and how best a sober addict can relate to the fact of widespread addiction in the general population. When I would try to talk about these things at meetings, people were polite enough, but, understandably, were more interested in trying to keep their side of the street clean, first, rather than theorizing about huge social problems they didn't feel much qualified to comment on.

Actually, I have to note that today, I think I understand why AA as an organization takes no position on political issues. AA has been remarkably resistant to scandals or schisms. I believe that this is in large part because the organization, as laid out in its founding principles, refuses to accept money from outside sources, refuses to endorse or finance any enterprises, and refuses to express an opinion on what it calls "outside issues." This stance has enabled it to remain more or less united, avoid too much controversy, and serve its primary purpose of helping people stay sober. But my need to discuss social determinants for addiction was a major issue for me.

Another major issue I had with AA was, yes, "the whole God thing," as people often put it. It's an awkward fact for atheist members that even though AA has no mechanism for punishing, chastising, expelling, or coercing anyone who doesn't believe in God, the literature is written from what is pretty plainly a Protestant position dressed up in a (somewhat charmingly) vague spiritualism. The word God features in many of the twelve steps and throughout the literature (though in many places it is replaced with the more generic term "Higher Power"). As someone who doesn't believe in God, I found it at first ridiculous, then irritating, then unbearable, and then I made my peace with it and tried to figure out how to make the wisdom contained in the program work for me and my needs.

As an aside, my personal stance now is, first of all, that a real atheist needn't be much bothered by references to something that they don't even believe exists—that would make you more of an antitheist, really, which is still a type of theist—and secondly, that the word "God" can actually be seen as a very complicated kind of code word which can stand for all sorts of real things about the world. It's those things that I think of when I come across the word. If someone talks about God's love, I just think about the praxis of altruism and mutual aid. If I read about God's plan, I think about the undeniable fact that most things that occur are completely out of my control. If a philosophy suggests that I admit my wrongs to God, I understand that I am to reflect on my actions carefully, and with a sense of gratitude and safety if at all possible. When AA tells me that the organization has "but one ultimate authority, a loving God," I read the next line where it is explained that this ultimate authority expresses itself through the conscience of the group through democratic decision-making, and I am satisfied.

However, it took me many years to get to a place where I feel comfortable with "the whole God thing," and years ago when I joined the program I was dying to express myself about this issue, and to talk about addiction and sobriety through lenses that had nothing to do with spirituality. I wanted the clarity of analytical materialism. This, together with my uneasiness with AA's "nonpolitical" outlook, formed the kernel of my misgivings. Other issues included the gendered language used in AA; the outdated terminology; the lack of overt protections for more marginalized people; the overrepresentation of white people and of men; and related issues that mostly stemmed from the organization's background in the white American Protestant middle class of almost a century ago, and its current status as a group that admits practically anyone and expels practically no one—thus being a microcosm of all the different forms of unthinking bigotry ubiquitous in the population at large.

I say all these things about AA for two main reasons. First, because the group we eventually formed had an undeniable similarity to AA; and second, because just as undeniably it was formed in reaction to what we saw as flaws in AA.

A few months after my first AA meeting, and after speaking with friends I'd made in AA and with others in the community, a few of us organized an open event which we advertised as a meeting to discuss addiction in the community through an anarchist lens. This was held in my basement, and many people showed up out of interest, indicating a need for these types of conversations to take place. The group that eventually emerged from the meeting called itself Radical Sobriety Montreal. The name alluded to three main ideas: that it was possible for left-wing radicals and anarchists to be sober, that it was possible for sobriety to be a useful part of a radical praxis, and that it was possible to embody a sobriety that was more politically engaged than what we saw as the churchiness of AA or the supremacist attitude of straight edge. We were not affiliated with (or aware of) any other group using the same name.

In its original incarnation, Radical Sobriety was envisioned as working according to the following broadly anarchist principles, principles which bring us back to the opening paragraph of this piece. First, it would be a *by-and-for group*, that is, a group which serves the demographic it consists of: people who considered themselves to be addicts (or identified somehow with problematic substance use—the terminological debates around the term "addict" can be controversial) and were trying not to use. Second, it would be organized more or less as an *affinity group*, that is to say independent, grassroots, nonmarket, nonstate, and decentralized. Third, its goal would be to facilitate sobriety—left up to the individual to interpret, but basically meaning abstinence from the substance to which a person is addicted—as a *direct action* which addicts could choose to take.

We felt that it was important for Radical Sobriety to be a by-and-for group for several reasons. One major one, echoed by AA's policies, is that our experiences had shown us that in many ways the only people who really understand addiction are people who have been through it, and the people best placed to support addicts in recovery are other addicts in recovery. We also wished to be clear that we were not a group that existed to denigrate drinkers and drug users—we were a group *made up* of drinkers and drug users. We wanted our critiques of intoxicants and intoxication culture to come *only* from a place of first-hand experience, and *only* from a place of compassion for—and solidarity with—active users.

We also knew that new members would be far, far more likely to be able to put trust in us if we shared their experiences. Virtually all of us have done things which we would struggle to talk honestly about in "normie" company. For example, admitting that you used to walk around in a blackout screaming slurs at random passersby, or maybe that you had predatory sexual tenden-cies when you were drinking, or maybe that you were abusive to your ex when you were using, or that you routinely stole from your friends, is some-thing that is likely to result in your becoming isolated from leftist scenes unless you have a community that is particularly invested in restorative justice processes. This may occur for good reasons, but the fact remains that people in a lot of pain frequently hurt others, and they require a way to process their pain and move through it in order to stop doing so. They also require a way to be honest about what they have done, reflect on it, and be accountable to someone about it—even if the person or people they may have hurt want nothing to do with them. Having a group of people to talk to who have the same experiences as you and want to help you and process with you without denouncing you, can be crucially important. Not only does it mean that you have supportive people to talk to; it means that victims, survivors, or just people who are completely exhausted with you are not forced to do that emotional work.

Not that all we did was run around hurting people. For one thing, we were also often running around being hurt by others, as well as being broken down by our addictions, the legal system, and various kinds of cruelty, unfairness, exploitation, and oppression. Connecting with people who understand the specific kinds of trauma often experienced by people with addictions has been very important for many of our members. Further, maintaining as much as possible a left-wing, feminist, queer, and antiracist perspective means that the group has been a place for people to talk about traumatic experiences in ways they may not feel comfortable doing at an AA meeting.

Membership therefore, from very early on, was restricted to addicts in recovery, and/or anybody who basically identified in some way with the gist of that description. Membership also from very early on was mostly grown through word of mouth. We have done a couple of limited callouts asking people to contact an email address if they wanted to get in touch, and sometimes get strangers contacting us who have heard of the group and want to join, but mostly we have de facto been requiring new members to be vouched for in some way. Unlike with a traditional affinity group, this is not because we are worried about police infiltration—it is too easy to identify a fake addict, and anyways we don't really do anything illegal—but more to preserve our group's good track record as a safer space for people with mar-ginalized identities. I don't believe this was ever an explicitly decided-upon policy, but more of an unofficial tradition which has served us well.

As a type of affinity group based on anarchist principles, we have kept things nonprofessional. We have no leadership, no secretariat, no bureaucracy, and no dues. Any member may call a meeting at any time. Our meeting structure is loose and based on tradition rather than prescription. The only real rule we have is that people who have been using that day are not generally welcome to attend, but even this rule is flexible so as to accommodate members who are experiencing a relapse and need support.

Over the years, the group has become less focused on discussing the political roots and implications of addiction—though this is still an important element of what we do—and has evolved toward more of a focus on interpersonal support and mutual aid, both of which are foundational principles of Radical Sobriety. Abstinence as a direct action—a self-liberation from the tyranny of addiction—is all well and good, but it is very very difficult to achieve and even more difficult to maintain. Addicts and alcoholics in recovery almost always find themselves in the position of realizing that their addictive behaviors, while very much real and very serious, were symptoms of much broader issues, often trauma-based, which can take a very, very long time to come to terms with. Therefore abstinence itself can often be only a first step in a person's recovery process. Further, the experience of addiction is *itself* traumatic, and many people require extensive work on *that* too. For these reasons, we think it is absolutely crucial that addicts and alcoholics in recovery have access to very strong, very solid support networks while they do this work, and they should not be expected to go through these experiences on their own. And since many addicts and alcoholics in recovery have lost access to whatever support networks they had—if any, since many people in general are extremely isolated under capitalism—Radical Sobriety has attempted to provide members with such strong, solid support networks. We have helped members secure housing, access health care, deal with bureaucracies, end relapses, survive hospital stays, and so on.

We will continue to do this care work, independently of the market and the state, and independent of the nuclear family or the romantic couple, deeming this work to be a deeply radical act with measurably positive outcomes, which all of us are capable of doing. We hope to one day have a more active public presence, and maybe write articles, zines, flyers, and that kind of thing. We've even talked about organizing a conference, and we've put on a couple of workshops and written one zine already.[3] We have also spoken about expanding our organization, starting chapters in other cities, maybe even more chapters in Montreal—we encourage anyone and everyone to operate similar groups and we consider the model to be easily exported.

But for now, our primary consideration is the performing of care work for our members, in order to help them to grow into their full human potential, more able to love themselves and others, more able to survive under capitalism without too much undue suffering, and more able to dedicate themselves to the struggle for a better world.

NOTES

1   I am using hunger as an example because extremely uncomfortable hunger is probably the sensation most similar to cravings that has been experienced by virtually everyone. I recognize that I am therefore talking about hunger in a fairly normative way. There are people with histories of disordered or nonnormative eating who may experience hunger in quite different ways from those that I am describing as "typical."

2   The "Big Book" is the main collection of AA literature. The program of AA is in the first 164 pages, explaining how it works and how to do the steps. The second half of the book is given over to the life histories of various early members of AA, written in the first person and intended to provide a variety of experiences with which a new member could identify.

3   A review of the zine, titled *RS I*, can be found on dystopiaradio.wordpress.com. It includes links to PDF files for both online viewing and printing. —G.K.

DREAMING NEW MEANINGS FOR SOBRIETY

Clementine Morrigan

Clementine Morrigan is a writer, poet, rebel scholar, teacher, working witch, and member of Radical Sobriety Montreal (see page 262). For more information see clementinemorrigan.com.

For nine years, I was drunk or high most of the time. I spent my time drinking in alleyways, sitting in snow banks, getting kicked out of bars, and getting my ass kicked. I spent my time having sex in blackouts with dudes who treated me like shit and puking my guts out into toilets for hours on end. My life was pain and desperate attempts to escape pain, followed by still more pain. No matter how bad the consequences of my drinking, I couldn't stop.

I'm an incest survivor and I was drinking away a pain I couldn't name. In my blackouts, I would scream about it. I stacked trauma on top of trauma as I experienced more and more violence. I couldn't stop. Alcohol and drugs were my only escape, the only thing I could depend on, and even though they made my life chaos and pain, they were also what I needed and depended on. Caught up in the paradox of not being able to live with or without the booze, I drank and drank and drank.

There were things I wanted to believe in. I wanted to believe in freedom, in caring about other people, in caring about the world. I knew that I was queer. I knew that what happened to me as a kid was wrong. I knew that a lot of things in the world were wrong. I wanted to be able to act on my beliefs. I wanted to be able to live a life that was in alignment with these beliefs. But I was completely unable to. I was like a tornado of pain blasting through the life of anyone who came near me. I hurt people and I drank away the shame of hurting people, of being unable to live a life in alignment with the things I believed.

I was lucky enough to be told that I should attend twelve-step meetings from someone I could actually hear that from, someone like me who had a life and ideas that I could recognize myself in. She was queer and a sex worker, like me. She had the same political beliefs that I held, which were important to me even though I couldn't live up to them. She wasn't straight or living a straight life, and so I listened to her when she said I should try twelve steps. She said it worked for her. I knew that I probably needed to stop drinking. I knew for sure that I was an alcoholic. But I believed, based on the representations I had seen in the media, that twelve-step meetings were definitely not for me. I still wanted to be wild and free. I still wanted to be queer and to hold the beliefs that I held. I still wanted to be myself, even if I couldn't drink. She made that seem possible.

While twelve-step programs are often exclusively associated with Alcoholics Anonymous, who first introduced a twelve-step program for recovery in the 1930s, there are today numerous groups using variations of it.

When I went to my first meeting, I knew that I was in the right place. I listened to story after story of people describing the exact feelings I was feeling, the helplessness, the desperation, the shame, the inability to imagine a life with or without drinking. These people described the kinds of crazy fucked-up situations I knew so well, and because of that I trusted them. They talked about cops and ambulances, destroyed reputations and relationships, sex they couldn't remember, puking on the sidewalk in the middle of the day. And many of them, I could clearly see, were sober. Many of them had changed profoundly, had found a way to live without drinking. They made sobriety real for me. They showed me that someone who drank like I drank could stop drinking. I held on to the meetings for dear life.

I got sober in those meetings, and at six years sober I still go. Twelve-step programs saved my life and continue to inform my life in important ways. They showed me how to live with and how to transform the incredible pain that was driving me. They showed that I'm not alone and that there are ways to face and feel the things I was so afraid to look at. I honestly don't believe I would have stayed sober without the meetings and the steps. I still use a twelve-step framework to guide my actions today. It is still important for me to attend meetings, practice the steps, and work with other alcoholics. The twelve steps teach me how to live in a principled way. They show me how to align my actions with my integrity. By working the steps I was finally able to move from having beliefs that couldn't guide my actions to having principles that guide everything I do.

My life profoundly changed through staying sober and practicing the steps. Not only did I find a way to live with the things that had happened to me, but I found a drive to live and to build a beautiful life and to care about people and the world. I started to do work that was meaningful to me. I connected with my ethical and political beliefs. I continued to learn so that I could further align my actions with my principles. I built relationships and community and helped newcomers get sober. I started to do sober activism, advocating for more sober spaces in community and encouraging the creation of spaces and events not centered on drinking. I did a lot of writing and community organizing and facilitated workshops on intoxication culture. I started to think about the ways in which sober communities and harm reduction communities could work together, instead of being pitted against each other. Now all the violence I survived and the terrifying life I used to live are tools I use to try to make the world better and to help other people.

I also did a ton of work on myself. I went to therapy and worked to heal my trauma. I found out that I have complex posttraumatic stress disorder (PTSD) and I continue to do so much work to heal from that. I dove into my queerness and my gender and started to figure out who I was and who I wanted to be. For years, it was shocking to have the life I had built in sobriety. It was shocking to have friends and community and meaningful work and the chance to heal. I was so used to the bleakness, exhaustion, and terror of my previous life that it was hard to accept the gifts of this new life. Sobriety became the most important thing in my life, the foundation on which everything else rested, and sobriety remains the most important thing in my life today. But after a few years of sobriety I had to start looking deeply at what sobriety could mean for me. I had to start looking at the messages and meanings I had internalized about what a sober life should look like, and to decide if those were meanings that worked for me.

Within twelve-step culture, and also within dominant representations of addiction recovery, there is a particular narrative of what getting sober should look like. It's hard not to notice this narrative playing out in the stories you hear at meetings and also in media representations of addiction recovery. The idea is that you get sober, you get the job, you get the

From the *RS I* zine. Art by Charlotte Dora.

relationship, you get the family, you settle down, and you live a "normal" life. This is a narrative firmly rooted in heteronormativity and capitalism, and it's a narrative about becoming a good law-abiding citizen. It's a narrative that rewards complacency and complicity, that encourages competition and individualism. As a queer anarchist, it's not a narrative that speaks to me at all. It's not what I want and it's also not what living a principled life means to me. My sobriety is dependent on living a principled life, so it is very important that I am honest about my principles. Finding other possibilities for what being sober can look like is extremely important. Learning to interpret the twelve steps through a queer anarchist lens is essential for my recovery.

When I first joined twelve-step programs, I wanted to get sober but I also wanted to remain wild and free. In sobriety, I learned that I wasn't free at all when I was drinking. I was compelled to repeat a destructive pattern over and over and I had no way to stop. In sobriety, I finally had a chance at finding out what freedom meant to me but I got caught up in this narrative of what a sober life should look like. Since sobriety is the foundation of everything good in my life, since it is the foundation of my freedom, and since I got sober in twelve-step programs, I became very concerned with doing the right thing in the eyes of other people at the meetings. I confused their principles for mine. In fact, I made a lot of assumptions about what their principles must be, based on the stories I was hearing, without actually having conversations about it. I lost sight of my principles and either judged my fellow alcoholics or judged myself. I either tried to be like them or assumed that I wouldn't be accepted if I chose to be honest about who I am and what I believe.

I went through a period when I started drifting from twelve-step programs. I loved the community and support I found in those rooms, and I still believed deeply in the twelve steps. But without anyone coming right out and saying so, I felt judged and othered for wanting the life that I wanted. I assumed that I had to choose between my true desires and acceptance in a community that saved my life. As I grew in my sobriety, I came to a better understanding of who I am and what I want. My queerness flourished. I discovered that I'm polyamorous and slutty and that these things are deeply important to me as a trauma survivor who has always been shamed for my sexuality. I discovered my politics, my anarchism, my desire for a different world. While I saw anarchist principles at work in twelve-step programs, I also heard the heteronormative, capitalist narrative of what sobriety should look like, repeated over and over. I wanted to go to meetings and be honest about who I am, what I want, what I believe, and how the twelve steps actually made me queerer and more anarchist by teaching me to live in accordance with my principles. I wanted to, but I was afraid. I was afraid of being shunned or judged or dismissed by a community that meant so much to me. So, I started to distance myself and to seek out spaces where I felt free to be all of who I am.

It was around this time that I first got connected with Radical Sobriety in Montreal. Radical Sobriety is a support group for addicts and alcoholics, and while many of its members attend twelve-step programs, it is not affiliated with twelve-step programs. It's founded on the anarchist principle of mutual aid and it is committed to understanding addiction, recovery, and sobriety in relation to the systems of power that we navigate and resist. Radical Sobriety understands that addicts and alcoholics helping each other stay alive and live meaningful lives is intensely political and important work. We understand that addiction is related to trauma and to feeling overwhelmed by the fucked-up world we are living in. And we want to create visions of recovery that are in alignment with our principles and our dreams for different ways of living. We're a bunch of queers and punks and anarchists who give a shit about each other and the world. We care about each other and we show up for each other and we talk openly about how our recovery is connected to our desire for a new world. We don't want to get sober to be successful within the current systems. We want to use our sobriety to help tear that shit to the ground.

Radical Sobriety helps me to understand and articulate how my addiction is connected to my experience of trauma. Our meetings are often heavily trauma informed and we talk about addiction as a response to the harm we have been subjected to, both personally and collectively. Radical Sobriety shows me how my sobriety strengthens my resistance to systems of power and my commitment to building a different world. Being connected to a community of other addicts and alcoholics who are also critical of the mainstream narrative of recovery helps me to imagine new meanings for my sobriety. With the help of Radical Sobriety I have come to see my sobriety as a tool for being present in my life, being committed to my values and my principles, and working to create new ways of living and relating to each other. Radical Sobriety is what finally allowed me to really begin to embody my principles, completely and honestly. I finally discarded the shame of failing to conform to a narrative I never believed in to begin with. With the help of my Rad Sob friends I directed my energy toward the life and world that I want to create.

Radical Sobriety also helped me to return to twelve-step meetings with more courage, more honesty, and more integrity. I am no longer afraid to be all of who I am and to share my honest beliefs at twelve-step meetings. I have found that I wasn't judged or shunned in the ways I expected. When I am brave enough to be honest, I open up an invitation for others to know me, and also the opportunity for them to know themselves differently. Many people have opened up to me about queerness, sex work, a desire for polyamory and different styles of love and relationships, support for harm reduction and the autonomy of drug users, anticapitalism, anticolonialism, and other and shared political beliefs. In fact, I found many twelve steppers to be way more radical than I thought. Some people may have their opinions about what I share, but no one silences me and my voice offers other visions to the collective imagining of what sobriety can mean. Even though I am back at twelve-step meetings, I continue to regularly attend Radical Sobriety. There is something so important and meaningful to me about sharing space with people who not only share my experience of addiction and recovery but are also committed to creating new ways of being in the world.

It may not seem like much: just a bunch of punks and anarchists and queers talking about our feelings and our dreams and helping each other find ways to live and grow and heal, just a handful of people sitting in a circle on a living room floor or in a park, but the work we are doing here is planting seeds and watering them. We are creating the foundations for new ways of living, both personally and collectively. We are creating the conditions under which we can dream new worlds into being.

I STOPPED DRINKING AND I HATE YOU ALL

Laura Dinosaur

This is a reprint of a pamphlet published by Active Distribution in 2016. For this book, Laura wrote a short update in September 2018, which replaces the original chapter "So, what now for me then?" Laura lives with her partner and dogfriend in south London and is researching trauma, mental health, and addiction, and how they intersect with class and poverty.

Dear london,
I recently gave up drinking and its made me think twice about our relationship. I used to think you were fun and interesting. Now, I can barely stand to be around you. You've got boring and rude, and your politics just aren't as sound as I thought they were. I'm writing to you now to try and explain why I might be seeming distant lately, or why I might be snappy and judgemental. I'm sure

i stopped drinking

and i hate you all

that a lot of the problem is mine, probably most of it, but
I'm going to get it off my chest anyway and see if we can
clear the air and get back to working together. I hope this
letter doesn't upset you. I suppose its inevitable really, I've
been quite honest and blunt but try and bear in mind that
everything I say probably doesn't apply to all of london and
probably I don't mean all of the time . . .

WHY I GAVE UP SOMETHING I WAS SO GOOD AT

I'd been drinking since I could get booze, but I think that I've probably been
drinking most days since I was 21 which incidentally happens to be when
I started working full time (in central london at the now defunct virgin
megastore). I'd been partying hard before that and now made regular trips
to the after-work-pub with my work mates in an attempt to pretend we were
friends that hung out, rather than shiftworkers trying to forget we were
working in the belly of the beast for a bunch of dickheads and idiots who
may as well have been selling farts.

It was a long drinking career. I can remember the day that I realised
that two cans a night wasn't cutting it any more and that I should upgrade
to three for my casual evenings drinking. I can look back on that day with
a sense of foreboding for what was to come, but I also look back on it with
a patronising laugh at my own childlike naivety: two cans! How cute. Two
cans being enough to unwind and get to sleep . . . aw. It's like a baby's portion.

I could have drunk that for breakfast just before I stopped. Not that I
was drinking for breakfast. I've managed to remain pretty functional over
the years. I think we all have. It was just getting a bit silly, not to mention
expensive. Depending on the day obv, I was sitting around in the bookshop and drinking up to six, seven (?) cans, then I'd totter off home, cycling
like a pillock and wake up in the morning feeling grand. It was the lack of
hangovers that was scaring me the most just before I gave up. I've had some
pretty spectacular hangovers in my time which normally involve throwing up all day and not drinking again until at least the next day. I'd always
looked on the hangover as penance, just do your time feeling like shit and
wishing you had choked on vomit in the night, and then gradually everything returns to normal. The hangovers were getting longer last year, a two
day headache was starting to be a normal punishment, but this winter they
just seemed to disappear. That very much influenced "the stopping." There
were also the additional aches and pains that were reoccurring: the ache
over where I imagine my right kidney is; the shooting pains in my chest;

the tingling numbness in my feet; the vision never seeming to return quite back to normal. And the traditional ones: the money I was pissing away; the arguments with my friends and partner whilst drunk and hungover; the boredom.

It was all compounded in the week that two anti-fasc went to prison. Me and a friend were doing prisoner support and for me that turned into rushing to get as much work done in the morning and afternoon as I could and then, as soon as business hours were over, getting well and truly sloshed whilst talking about how shit it was and trying to drown the anger.

So yeah, I stopped. I'd been thinking about it for a while and then one day after a party I took the "never drink again" thing very seriously.

"THE STOPPING"

I don't really remember actively doing much to stop. It helped a lot that I was with someone who was also stopping (although it seemed to have wildly different effects on our moods). I just didn't drink any more. The day after I stopped I went to the Community Acupuncture Clinic at the Common House. When I told them I was trying to stop, they taped seeds to my ears. No, really. They put these tiny mustard seeds held by hypoallergenic tape over the points in the ears that help assuage the jittery urges. I kept going back and had those things there for most of a month. I pressed them whenever I wanted a drink and then didn't drink. The guys at the clinic were very, very supportive of the decision without being judgemental, just a kind of "okay, you're doing this thing, how can I help?" attitude, which I'm very grateful for.

The first couple of weeks I was pretty down. "Mildly and consistently numbed and depressed" is a direct quote from myself at that time. My friend who I was staying with (who had also just stopped) was getting up, putting the fire on, taking the dog out and getting to work, all before I'd managed to decide if it was worth getting up at all. I mostly decided that it was and just got on with it.

Some of you kept asking if I felt "fantastic." No. I don't. Fuck off. Stop asking such a ridiculous question. Am I meant to feel "fantastic"? Is "fantastic" a natural state of being? That's quite an expectation . . . Stop poisoning yourself and feel great . . . Take away your coping mechanism and feel fantastic . . . I think it might take a bit longer than this, and might need some doing rather than not-doing to reach the dizzy heights of fantastic.

Some of you were really supportive (and still are) which is lovely and has helped a lot. It's hard to know what to say to someone congratulating you for not doing something, but it made a big difference. Especially as to whether I was viewing the changes that came from it as a positive change or a negative one. And especially when set against those of you that took the piss. This didn't have as much of an impact on my resolve as it did on my idea of you. It's annoying to be criticised by grown-ups when it's so transparent that they're being defensive. I used to be someone that could be relied on to drink with, someone who understood the necessity of it and didn't seem to be worried about the effect it was having on me. Suddenly, I changed my mind, drawing attention to something you ignore and, you appear to think, judging you with my abstinence. Does it make you feel bad about your drinking? Because I don't care. This wasn't really about you. It's a shame, cause I'll never think of you the same again. You stopped when it became obvious that I wasn't going to start again just to stop your self scrutiny, but I've been taught that, for you, your self-image is more important than my freedom to do what I want, and that's the kind of lesson that's hard to forget.

WHY I HATE YOU ALL NOW

I avoided places for a while, worried that I would be tempted to drink in the contexts that were so connected with it: the bookshop, the basement, parties, pubs, friends houses, pretty much everywhere really. When I started dipping my toes in to the social again it was something else entirely that tempted me . . . the ringing in your ears that comes with being drunk. It's hard to sit in a room full of drunk people and not be able to hear you all when I'm sober. You get very loud when you're drunk cause of that ringing and start to speak slowly and deliberately as the booze catches up with you. When I'm sober I find it possible to listen to the person talking to me and to also catch most of what most of the rest of you drunk people are screeching self-importantly to your neighbour. This makes it hard to love you.

I was at a house party at the home of some "rad" activisty types recently and I heard some crackers: "sexual assault course"—what a phrase! It's how I'd describe your standard club night or a drink in central london. It's a great phrase and I wish I'd come up with it instead of the loud, beaming, self-confident man telling the room he'd declared the stairs a "sexual assault course" now. Gross. That's not why I come to my friends' houses. I come to avoid guys like you, who think that grabbing a handful of arse whilst someone's pushing past you in a tight space is funny-ha-ha, and not funny-uh-oh.

Or the guy that thought cause he chooses to wear a big beard and carry a big rucksack that its hilarious that people might think he's a suicide bomber. That's not funny mate. They're probably giving you dodgy looks cause you look like an obviously privileged white guy who has made a life choice to look like a dirty hippy. They're probably thinking "check out this guy, all he needs is a wash and a shave and he could go get a job being my fucking boss." I know I was. I'm sure its gratifying to align your self so strongly with the oppressed but no one thinks you're a suicide bomber. You are white. That's a particularly shitty part of racism that is an every-day reality for many, many brown people. You can't fucking own it like a keffiyeh.

I got asked at the most recent beach party "are you overwhelmed?", and it struck me that people seem to have a strange understanding of what its like to be me and sober whilst hanging around in london . . . its underwhelm-ing. I'm not awkward and quiet because I just can't let go without the drink, or I'm scared of talking. I just can't be bothered. When faced with something as lovely as a beach party: all that effort put in to getting the systems there; and the outdoors; and the water, and also faced with the people who are there to consume it . . . it's just a bit of a let down. How many of you are even going to remember it past a vague recollection of trying to dance on a slope and falling down into wet sand whilst having a pee. It just seems a shame, a waste. Add that to the shit you say and do when you are drunk, and it makes me sad I've been rolling around in the mindless decadence for ten years. It just seems a shame. And yes, a waste.

I know all of the excuses too, cause I've used them myself to explain shitty things I've said and done when I've been drunk and to justify the rave-induced oblivion. "We've got to let our hair down," "I'm just joking," "We're all friends here," "I'm just having a good time" . . . What kind of scene is it that resorts to bullshit to have fun? Getting sloshed and acting like bankers, saying shitty things that you wouldn't say sober cause a sober audi-ence would call you out on them, being a dick and not dealing with it cause you don't remember . . . Copying the shittiest bits of the outside world and playing them out in our homes, communities and friendships. Great. Some dead men said "in vino veritas." Well, if that's true, *you're all fucking dead inside.*

And I am being a judgemental prick. It makes me want to drink again so that I can stand to be around you all, but I'm bored of being a drunken fool, and scared of how much I will have to drink to forget quite how much of a fool I am, and was. I don't want to have to numb myself to be able to stand being around people who should want better in the first place and I don't want to spend my time with you biting my tongue.

LIVING WITHOUT THAT COPING MECHANISM

How do I feel now? Pretty up-and-down and all-over-the-place. Drinking did a lot for me. It helped me relax, and it helped me ignore the bullshit around me. Without it I feel like I'm noticing more and more shitty, shitty things and that I don't get the oblivion time to forget about them. I'm getting pretty bad headaches now when I get stressed, and I'm more likely to get stressed cause I don't have some regular down time. I've had some of the most intense mood swings that I've probably had since I was a teenager, going from despairing and hopeless to capable and enthusiastic in an afternoon.

I thought that I had manic patches before, but they nothing compared to the ones I've been getting recently. I've managed to book flights, and gig tickets, and cycle across east london barely remembering the journey cause I'm rushing on . . . something, I don't know. An intense energy that makes me feel out of control.

I'm spending more time alone which is nice, given that I'm developing a low tolerance life-style. And I think that has to do with the biggest plus of giving up drinking: bye-bye anxiety! Seriously, this is something that I'm so happy about, and had I realised how much stopping drinking would have helped, I would have done it ages ago. I've been struggling, and I mean struggling, with anxiety for a while now. It's been a pretty intense nervous energy that's taken hold of any worry that I've had and driven them through the roof. It made things pretty hard. And its just gone. Now if I start to worry about something, I can ask myself how likely it is that that might happen, and if the answer is "not very likely" then I can just stop thinking about it. Awesome. No more endless worrying about friends dying on their bikes, or the boat sinking whilst I'm out or unrelated-to-anything feelings of doom in the pit of my stomach. I guess that energy is going somewhere though, and then come the manic patches. We'll see where that ends up.

I've also got a lot sharper. I think that the downside to that is the noticing of things and the intolerance that I was writing about before, but the upside is a coherence in my thoughts. As an example: I used to think that I had forgotten how to write an essay. It's something that I did at school as a kid, and was all right at it. When I started back at school four years ago I figured that I couldn't do the written stuff as well as I remembered because I'd had such a long break from it, but even after two years of written work it wasn't getting any easier. I kind of thought that I just couldn't articulate things clearly any more, as I had trouble writing flyers and text for call outs etc. The idea of writing an article or a zine was nice, but something I was never going to do. Then after I stopped drinking, I just found it easier. The writing I've done at school in the past few months felt easy enough that I was pretty sure that I hadn't done well, but it turns out I had. It just feels easier now to read some things, come up with an opinion or an idea and then write that down so that other people might understand what I'm getting at.

SEPTEMBER 2018

It's been two years since I wrote "I Stopped Drinking and I Hate You All." I'm still not drinking, which I guess is the most important thing.

Since then I have been through the breakup of a long and important relationship. I had my dog put down. I left the organisation I had been involved in for nearly a decade and I dealt with the death of a loved friend all while struggling with my mental health and damn bastard poverty and I've done it all without alcohol and I'm very happy that I did. Waking up every day and reminding yourself that something has changed can be hard but it's much easier without a hangover.

Unfortunately my anxiety came back, with a vengeance. Without the fogginess of the alcohol and after a very scary time of realisation, I've realised that I have a form of PTSD from a raucous and shitty childhood. Something that alcohol did for me was to numb the memories of experiences I was passively ignoring. It let me get on with my life without dealing with my past, which is useful, but only up to a point. Now I'm trying to ignore the equal pressures of capitalism and organising to take a break and try and deal soberly with my past.

If I were to add any advice on giving up now it would be to find a meeting or a group. In london there are still quite a lot of resources despite the dismantling of the National Health Service and I am lucky enough to be able to go to a centre in Brixton where I meet with other people from all walks of life and we talk about addiction, the main thing we have in common. It's made me realise that lots of people self-medicate and that me and my problems aren't special or unique. I find that reassuring.

I'm happier now than I have been for a decade.

I'd still love to be able to drink one beer, and I still don't think I am able to.

I still hate drunk people, but now I just wonder if they are drinking cause they lack a better medicine.

I'm working on my next zine about how addiction and mental health interact with capitalism.

AND WHAT NOW FOR OUR RELATIONSHIP?

Now, if I was intending to write a text encouraging you to throw off your beery overlords and commit to a life of "Lucid Bacchanalianism" then I think that I might have not done so well. But I wasn't. I think that I was writing this for myself to get some understanding of where I've been, where I'm at and where I'm going. I also wrote it cause I don't have the energy or the inclination to pull people up on their shit all the time. Consider this me having-a-go at you, and let's have done with it. I'm hoping that getting it all over and done with in one ranting, highly hypocritical text might do me for a little while at least. That said I am going to give a little bit of dad-vice from someone who recently gave up to anyone who might be planning to.

THINGS THAT MIGHT HELP

- space away from people drinking that you can have whenever you want.
- if you're lucky enough to come to the decision at the same time as a friend, then do it together. Don't take it personally if they slip up, they can always pick it up again, and you might need them to be forgiving if you do.
- it sounds obvious but try writing a list of the reasons that you are giving up so you can look back at it when the beer monster is whispering in your ear.
- be prepared for a whirlwind of emotions. I wasn't, it seems obvious now, but it took me by surprise.
- try letting your significant others know that they might need to bear with you for a while.
- tonic water with lime in it tastes like a weak gin and tonic. Cocktail bitters in water taste weird enough that your brain is convinced that it must be alcoholic or why else would you be drinking it. Non-alcoholic beer and wine can get you through a party. Don't be afraid to cheat yourself. It's not booze, but it can help to pretend and you won't have a hangover. (Unfortunately it doesn't get you drunk either).
- don't expect to feel fantastic, and come up with a witty and cutting retort for when people ask you if you do.
- be prepared to cut some relationships out. There are people that you aren't friends with, that you are drinking buddies with and when you stop the drinking that buddiness disappears. It wasn't hard, it happened naturally and I don't miss them.

I hope that we can get over this, cause there are things about you that I still love. You are my only city and I hope that we can work out our differences and remember that ultimately we are on the same side,

Love and Rage, Laura

DIARY OF A STRAIGHT EDGE JUNKIE

Tom O'Brien

Tom O'Brien is a forty-one-year-old vegan straight edge dad of two from Liverpool. He has played just about anything from pop punk to D-beat in a myriad of bands.

I grew up in Liverpool, England. I have been incredibly lucky for the life I was born into. My mum and dad, two ex-hippies, brought me up with a very strong left-wing influence. I was always encouraged to think for myself, even if their position was fairly clear. I was brought up politically aware. Our house didn't look like a Crass gig, but they broke stuff down that was on the news, currently and historically. I remember writing to Thatcher to tell her to stop sanctions on South America and support for Apartheid. My parents were both teachers and it was just them, my little brother Joe, and me, so we lived very comfortably. I had a childhood surrounded by music, camping in France, Greek legends, museums, *Lord of the Rings*, and learning.

I don't remember a time in my childhood when there wasn't music around. Me and my dad put together my first mix tape when I was three. It was a mix of stuff I'd heard on the radio, like The Jam, Dexy's Midnight Runners, Madness, and stuff I'd heard around the house, such as Beefheart, Kraftwerk, and Holger Czukay. I was surrounded by an amazing array of sounds from The Beatles, Hendrix, and Stones to Miles Davis, Eberhard

Tom O'Brien, Liverpool, January 2019.

Weber, King Crimson to Motown and Stax stuff to Prince to a lot of Zappa/ Mothers of Invention and Incredible String Band to contemporary classical stuff like Berio and Stockhausen. Kraftwerk were huge to me—they really painted a whole world in my head.

To keep up to date with whatever was new in the world of weird and won- derful in the pre-internet days, there was one spot in Liverpool that had it all and was also the gathering place for all the weird and wonderful folk of Liverpool. That was Probe Records. I have a very clear memory of when I was about eight, being in town with my dad and walking towards Probe and this full-on UK82 punk with a mohawk and covered in studs tried to bum money from my dad. I was scared but totally fascinated by this collection of crazy and scary-looking people hanging around while walking into this dark dingy shop with crazy record covers on the wall (and I was used to the covers of *Weasels Ripped My Flesh* and *Trout Mask Replica*). I was sold.

Remember that this was the 1980s, and there wasn't the countercultural melting pot that there is now. There were your squares/trendies/scallies/ jocks, and then: everyone else. That divide was easy to pick up on, even as a young kid. I was about eleven when I started to start going out on my own musically and with the knowledge that there was a whole other world if you scratch under the surface. So, I got straight under there and started to have a look around.

I knew of straight edge long before I became straight edge. There was a little crew of straight edge kids in Liverpool focused around the band Withdrawn. Before I got into the hardcore scene specifically, I'd seen them around at some other shows, and I saw Withdrawn on the rare occasion they played in Liverpool. I always thought they were a bit standoffish or a bit too cool. (Later, I found out this was not the case at all, but the fact that me and my mates were a bunch or drunken morons at the time probably didn't help.) Yet I always looked on with intrigue and quiet admiration.

When I first learnt that straight edge was a thing and not just the name of a song, I was baffled as to why anyone would want to live drug-free. The idea seemed ridiculous to me. I know now that this was because the addic- tion element of my behaviour was already active.

By the time I was nineteen, I knew my drinking and drug abuse was getting bad. After going out with friends and consuming whatever, they would all go home, sleep it off, and wait until the next night out or session at someone's house. Meanwhile, I was carrying on by myself, day or night. I had a few groups of friends to drink/use with. With each group doing something once or twice a week, I could hook up with one of them most nights. I knew I had to make a change. A friend of mine had recently gone straight edge, which made the transition easier. I became straight edge when I turned twenty.

I also played in bands. I played bass for Unborn on the Unborn/Purification split, on a Statement cover of "Meat Means Murder" by Conflict, and on a few songs for the XVX powerhouse Forward to Eden. I sang for a youth crew band called xSafeguardx who recorded one super rough demo ("Survival of the Pack"). And I played guitar for a militant vegan blackened D-beat band called Eakra. To make the list complete, I also played bass in two sludge bands, Redrighthand and Charger, a pop punk band called Dropout, the D-beat band Cracked Cop Skulls, and the UK82 punk band Instant Agony; guitar in the power violence band Ocksen, a metalcore band called 12th Angel Calling, and the old-school band Area Effect; and I sang in the metalcore band Noyade.

Addiction happens to other people, not you. When you're drinking and taking the same substances as everyone else—especially if they are "accepted" substances: alcohol, powder cocaine, ecstasy/MDMA, and amphetamines—you can't be an addict. Addicts are those heroin smack head junkies. So even when it got to the point when I was clearly drinking too much, taking speed and pills and other stuff whenever it came around (most weeks), I knew it was an issue and I needed to do something about it—but I wasn't an "addict," again that's junkie stuff. It was only years later when I started taking heroin and got sick one day because I didn't have any, that I realized I was an addict. And only when I went for six months to a residential rehab did I learn that I had been an addict since those early days of substance use.

I fell into it all because I was mentally unwell. I was diagnosed with depression and anxiety at fifteen and put on medication. The meds did nothing, and I had no insight into my illness, so every time I went back to the doctors, they just upped the meds until I was on the full dose, then change to another medication, and on and on. This messed with my developing teenage mind, while not actually improving anything. It cut off all my high and low emotions. Not experiencing these ranges of emotions left me unable to learn from experiencing them. So if the doctor wasn't doing anything to help me live with my mental state, I would self-medicate to get me away from myself for at least a time; to rid myself of that anxiety and fear, if only temporarily.

I did that until it all became too much, then I went straight edge. It was the greatest thing to ever happen to me. I felt free. Unfortunately, my mental health issues didn't go away with my intoxication. When it seemed there was no escaping this illness, I had no knowledge of how to deal with it. No escaping what my head was telling me, no escaping the anxiety and the misery. Don't get me wrong: these things weren't bombarding me daily, but when they hit, they hit unfiltered. So, in short, eventually I had a breakdown. I became incredibly paranoid, believed I was born as part of a government plan. They would watch me, and others, throughout our lives. Every person we would meet and encounter would be a plant by the government, each with different approaches, so they could watch and record our responses. I believed this was a way to gauge people's reactions as a way to plan out larger social control and manipulate society.

I also developed a funny feeling, almost like I was living in a dream. I felt like I was sat in my head looking through my eyes watching my life, a total disconnect. I wouldn't find out until about fifteen years later that this was called depersonalization. So with my mental health really taking a dive, after being straight edge for about four years, I didn't know what was happening to me. Mental health services were no good. They said I could get a referral in two to three months, and then the waiting list was six months after referral. I felt totally lost, scared, and paranoid. I remember a period of about six months when I was really fighting the urge to do something to again escape myself. It was that constant hopeless feeling of wanting to be anywhere except in my skin and in my head. Straight edge was my whole identity; it was the catalyst that helped me escape this prison I'd ended up in with intoxication. I couldn't just actively put myself back there, but I couldn't carry on as I was, and eventually it just got to be too much.

I never thought I'd break edge, never. At the time I was playing in a band whose other members were keen substance users. I'd been with them for just over a year while straight edge, no problem, but when the walls really came closing in, I fell back into old habits. The band was dark and I immersed myself in that darkness with increasing alcohol and drug use, both feeding each other. This led to a destructive relationship that, after two years, led to a messy break-up. Not only was my mental health not good at this point, but my self-worth, which had never been that good, was worse than fucking awful.

So with the usual tried and tested methods not working, I had heard of a few lads I had known for years from round and about who had got into heroin. So as a fairly good idea of how bad my mental health was, I knowingly got in touch with them with the idea that heroin was probably the thing I needed in my life. I had lost my friends from the last relationship and friend-ships had broken down with old straight edge friends. Only partly because I broke edge; the most important reason was that I had closed myself off because of the guilt of breaking edge. This all contributed to heroin taking hold. It gave me a newfound calm and peace, shutting down all my emotions. It also gave me an instant new circle of friends. I was also working at the time (in a secure mental health unit, but that's stories for another time!) and always had some money, so I was a junkie's best friend.

To my twisted mind this was, initially, a friendly oasis. Things started going very wrong within the year. I realized that I had a habit the first time I got sick, but I fooled myself (as all addicts do) that I've just gotten in a bit too deep and would just go on until I got three or four days to sit out a withdrawal. Of course, those days never come. Without all the ins and outs, I was using for about eight years. Which isn't actually that long in heroin circles, but it was long enough to be in that 24-hour-a-day hell. You get little bursts of wanting to stop. The first few are squashed because you don't realize just how strong addiction is. Then there's family and friends who all start to find out, and they want and try to get you to stop, however you can't stop for anyone but yourself. Doing it for your family, kids, or whoever just doesn't work.

The more your habit grows, the more chaotic becomes your life, and then when you hit points where you want to stop, you're just not equipped to deal with everything. So after around two years of being off and on—a week here and there, maybe a month some other time—I eventually got myself to a six-month residential rehab that specialized in CBT (Cognitive Behavioral Therapy), and that was the thing that enabled me to stop and save my life. I'm not saying that you finish your time there and you're cured. As someone in there said: "Rehab is just the dressing room, the life afterwards is the actual match." But through the CBT program I learned why I sought solace in intoxication, where that stems from, and what the behaviours are that kept that cycle repeating itself. It all comes down to behaviours.

Six years ago today, I was in my second month of the six-month program at that residential rehab, and six years down the line things are amazing. It's been a very hard struggle, though. You come out of the rehab and you're alone again. There are recovery communities but aside from the practical help they offered I found little interest in what they were doing. So I reached back out to the hardcore scene. In rehab, I realized that one of the reasons my substance abuse and self-destruction started increasing and carried on was because I had taken myself away from the DIY hardcore punk scene. It was so much of who I am, and I had struggled to live solely in the regular world without the connection to those people and the ideas that we all hold so dear. Don't get me wrong: I'm not saying I stopped going to shows so became a junkie, there's obviously a lot more at play, but I did know that reengaging with the scene would give me back me, give me not only a place of belonging but somewhere I felt I truly belonged, and somewhere, and something, I believed in. So I deal with my history very openly. I'm maybe sometimes too quick to tell people, but I feel I'd like it to be me to tell them rather than them hearing it from others. I don't have anywhere near as many cravings or triggers as I used to, in fact it's extremely rare. Initially, I was very mindful to never be in a potentially risky situation. Over the years, fewer and fewer situations could be seen as risky, and the life I've built around me just doesn't include those situations.

An idea you learn about at some point can't change the things that have already happened in your life and stop a ball that's already started rolling. The human brain is so complex and amazing that just as it can achieve all these amazing things, it can also dig into the depths of your soul and just ruin it. That's not to discredit straight edge by any means. It keeps millions of people clean and sober and helps people overcome addiction or stop them before they end up there, but it can only help as one part of various tools. Once things get too dark, no amount of Youth of Today records can help you.

I didn't get much support from the straight edge scene, but that's not entirely the scene's fault. As soon as I broke edge, I cut myself off. I felt so ashamed. I got rid of all my straight edge shirts. (I had even bought the Mouthpiece Straight Edge varsity jacket from Tim McMahon, and that went.)

I felt a stinging guilt just looking at that stuff. How could I have done this to something I believed so much in? How could I now be the subject of all those songs? So, I disappeared. Also this was in the early 2000s. There wasn't as much public knowledge around addiction as there is now. We were also all kids. I don't hold any blame towards anyone at all. I had seen people break edge who I hung out with, and they just became the latest people to break edge. In most cases, you just didn't see them again. Now, it was just my turn, I guess. With regards to my close straight edge friends, I honestly couldn't tell if they reached out, because I just shut myself away, and I ruined some of those friendships forever.

I suppose my environment could have reacted better, but couldn't you say that for pretty much any situation? I wasn't talking about my feelings or what was going on with me. I was by no means that "stone wall, no feelings male," but I just wasn't being honest about my mental health. I gained the nickname Tommy P, short for Tommy Positive, that's how good my mask was. So how were they to know what was going on with me? Also you have to look at how the scene was then. We were still fairly fresh out of the '90s XVX warrior era. While I still think that 90 percent of that stuff is important, the absolutes around straight edge were damaging.

Once I got over the guilt thing, and once I believed that my own life was important and that I deserved to not only be alive but deserved a happy life and it was okay for me to be happy, I had to focus on what does and would make me happy. Straight edge was definitely in that list and quite high up. Then I got over the concern of people telling me I couldn't reclaim. Basically, they were saying that because of a song someone wrote in 1980 about how they felt about intoxication, I was no longer allowed to label myself with two words that would really help me stay clean and live. Well, to quote Ian MacKaye's response to a kid whose friend had said that caffeine wasn't straight edge: "Tell your friend: Fuck you!" I see straight edge as a progressive thing. But how can we progress if we cut off people from our community because of bad mental health? For me all those records and those songs that so many people label as cheesy, with messages that are apparently played out, helped me dig deep and gave me definite strength. They still do.

One of the most beautiful and the most frustrating things about straight edge is that there is so much variety and elements open to interpretation. But the philosophy behind it all is so simple you can't deny it: stay sober, think for yourself, and don't follow the herd. That can never get old.

Where are we at today as a counterculture/movement/community? As anyone who was around in any counterculture pre-internet will know, the internet changed everything. I'm not one of these older dudes that complains that things where so much better way back when, because it's just not true, but things are of course different. With the internet giving everyone access to everything, people often just focus on their own preferred subgenre. We have lots of pockets.

I think straight edge is the same. However, the rise of vegan anarchist straight edge stuff has been brilliant for the culture, I think. Personally, for me the crusty side of straight edge is a dream come true, well musically anyhow, but my edge will always be in runners, sports shorts, and a side part with a fade. Regarding straight edge being a viable political stance, I was always firmly in the Birthright camp.

I don't think it's my place to comment on the strengths and weaknesses of straight edge currently as a whole. Look at what you think your own strengths and weaknesses are! And use your strengths to benefit others. In doing so, you'll learn how to improve your weaknesses.

"Through this veil of shadows, the light of truth is my only guide. A knight unyielding . . ."

ALCOHOLICS AUTONOMOUS: ADDICTION AND SOBRIETY BEYOND RECOVERY

Jack Fontanill

Jack Fontanill is an aspiring nonhuman based in Chicago and sometimes high in the Sierras or wherever his vehicle happens to be parked. He has many achievements which include but are not limited to receiving a mug from the Catholic Church at seventeen for exemplary leadership and winning the D.A.R.E. essay contest at age ten. His interests include destroying the world and building a force capable of withstanding the destruction of the world. "Alcoholics Autonomous" was written for this book and prereleased as a pamphlet.

This is the second time I have attempted to write this essay. The first time I thought it was about me. This time I know, I feel, it is deeply about us or some sort of we which may not yet be formed or may be in its very formation today. What's important yet is that this is always about something bigger than you or me—but it is exactly only as big as you or me could ever imagine it to be.

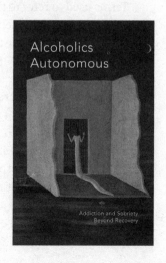

AGAINST ADDICTION

There are many terms used for the phenomenon of consuming substances to a degree deemed by society to be dangerous or destructive. "Substance abuse" and "addiction" are probably the most common ones. "Substance abuse," according to Google Dictionary, is defined as "overindulgence in or dependence on an addictive substance, especially alcohol or drugs." The obvious problem with this definition is that most societies accept a degree of substance use as normal and the line where this becomes "overindulgence" and therefore "substance abuse" is inconsistent and culturally defined. Daily consumption of coffee, for instance, is accepted in most cultures. Where this is not the case, however, drinking coffee every day might be considered substance abuse. Likewise, weed is acceptable in many cultures to try a few times, and sometimes is considered substance abuse if used more than a few times, and sometimes is okay to use every day, depending on who you ask.

"Addiction," perhaps, provides a slightly more accurate description. According to Merriam-Webster, "addiction" is defined broadly as "persistent compulsive use of a substance known by the user to be harmful." Google Dictionary provides an alternative definition: "the fact or condition of being addicted to a particular substance, thing, or activity." Based on these definitions, it must be concluded that our society, and every individual, is full of addictions. Using technology, working a job, eating most things you find at the store, powerlifting, and shooting heroin are all addictions. This is an essay against addictions. It is written with the recognition that our lives are not, and maybe never could be, free from them. It is a recognition that the struggle against addiction is also a struggle against empire and the categories it forces upon us. This is not a neutral essay. This is not the 12 steps.

Terms used to refer to the process of no longer being addicted to a substance are also mostly unhelpful. Some common ones are "recovery," "clean," or "sober." I will not use the term "recovery," for it seems to point to a former self, a "non-addicted self," that one might return to. There is no other self to return to and we are never anything more or less or different than what we are right now. I have never recovered and I shall never recover. I have simply embraced the things which make up this other thing I call a self and agreed to continue to build myself up or knock myself down depending on how I feel in every moment. I will also not use the word "clean" for the obvious reasons that this implies that people who are addicted are "dirty," which further implies all sorts of racism, classism, and bourgeoisie middle-class values.

In this essay, I will use the term "sober" because it appears to be the least problematic. "Sober," according to Merriam-Webster, is defined simply as "not drunk" or "not addicted to intoxicating drink." I will use this term, "sober," to also refer to the lack of use of other mind-altering substances, such as drugs. One might argue that most things are drugs and most of us are not sober and one might be right. If something comes to mind that you think might be a drug and wonder if maybe this essay might be about this thing, it is probably about this thing and most other things that people use to escape their bodies or alter their bodies' perception of this thing we call the world. I will use the terms "joy," "freedom," and "autonomy." I may even use the term "love." I will use these terms and I will mean them. I will not mean some abstraction of them. This will be an act of communication. It will not be a demonstration of anything called facts.

In an attempt to chronicle my full list of credentials, I will mention the following. I spent years, starting from the age of 12, using things called drugs and this other thing called alcohol which is also a drug but filed as if it was something else for whatever reason. My drug of choice was opiates for the years that I spent using drugs heavily but I was also known to use a great number of amphetamines, weed, cigarettes, Wendy's junior bacon cheeseburgers, cocaine, and whipped cream cans in which I would suck out the Nitrous Oxide and throw the can out the window. My drugs of choice to be addicted to now that I am no longer an addict are coffee, various forms of crime, and abstract ideas that I can't understand well but like to pretend that I understand well. If you ask me today why I used drugs I will have many extravagant and well-reasoned arguments about why I used drugs because of society or empire or capital. If you asked me when I was seventeen why I used drugs I would have said, "because I feel like it, fuck you." When I write about my experiences using drugs I am writing through the lens of a person who is defined as the same person but is now 25 and filters those experiences through the lens of this 25-year-old.

When I was 16 I crashed my car into a tree because I was on a mixture of Vicodin, Adderall, caffeine, and marijuana, and my body did not like this combination on this particular day, and so I had a seizure. As a result of this experience I was arrested and got a DUI and almost killed a friend and almost killed myself. When I was 16 I lost my license because of this. When I was 16 I said that I would never use "hard drugs." When I was 17 I started using heroin and this was the drug that I enjoyed more than any other drug. I also tried smoking crack but mostly did not like it. I never tried crystal meth and therefore am happy I can say I stayed true to my pledge at 16 to never use "hard drugs." My progression of drug use happened quick and my progression to no longer being addicted to these particular substances happened slow. I was in outpatient rehab at least three times and was suspended from school also at least three times. I was arrested more than three times but I couldn't say how many times. I went to inpatient rehab one time for 40 days and 40 nights and I have been sober since that first day, August 18, 2010. Today is August 19, 2018, and I have just begun to pretend to understand what all of this means and write about it.

DISCOURSE ON ADDICTION

There are many things that are said in the media and at family parties about addiction and people who are called addicts because the substances they are addicted to are deemed unacceptable by society. One thing that people like to say about those who are addicted to substances in a way that is not socially acceptable is that they have had bad childhoods or exceptionally traumatic experiences. Some people who become addicted to substances have in fact had very traumatic experiences but we have also all had very traumatic experiences and this world we live in is filled with trauma and most experiences in it are terrifying. I would not say that I have ever experienced any sort of trauma which I would describe as exceptional, though I know many people, namely women or non-men, who have experienced trauma which to me appears exceptional but is also, unfortunately, not exceptional and is, in fact, the state of normal in this world.

Some of these people use drugs and some of these people do not. Sometimes getting sober requires addressing these underlying traumas and sometimes it requires an understanding that there is no escaping trauma unless there is an escape from this world. When I say "this world," I mean the world that has been placed upon us. I do not mean the earth, but a certain perception of the earth and the creatures and power structures on it. I mean something like "society," but I do not mean "society" because I do not quite believe that something like "society" exists, though I have and will continue to use the word to mean a group of people with a certain perception of the earth and the things on it. This world is something most of us inhabit in a certain way but it is also something which we can break from or live in the cracks of. A world is also something we can build and there are multiple worlds in this place called earth. The world I mean when I say society is only one, though it may be the most powerful, for now.

Healing from trauma is often marketed as an individual process and sometimes it is, but the individual is never a separate thing from the spaces they inhabit and healing is also always a communal or social process as well. If it is true that addressing addiction requires addressing trauma, then it is true that addressing addiction requires addressing this world and the necessary break from it that we must make if we wish to take addiction seriously. It requires addressing colonialism, racism, misogyny, and all sorts of other mindsets we have been taught. We are all very traumatized and we are all very in need of a new sort of culture or world. We do not need more doctors to tell us we are traumatized; we need more spaces to talk about these things collectively and unlearn all we have been told. We need new ways of relating to one another. Any hope for truly addressing trauma will not be an individual one but a cultural one. It will not be given to us, it will be built, *by us*.

Another thing that people in hospitals or in college lecture halls like to say is that addiction is a disease. I am looking on a website about addiction that tells me that "modern science says addiction is a disease, not a choice." Modern science also brought the atomic bomb, nuclear power plants, unspeakable forms of torture, and GMO corn. I do not take cues from this creature called modern science. Merriam-Webster tells me that a disease is a "disorder of structure or function in a human, animal, or plant, especially one that produces specific signs or symptoms or that affects a specific location and is not simply a direct result of physical injury." I write in my notebook that modern civilization is a disease and am left more confused about what a disease really is. I read the second definition, "a particular quality, habit, or disposition regarded as adversely affecting a person or group of people," and become even more convinced that modern civilization is a disease and begin to make plans to destroy it. I also become sure that addiction is a disease like most things, but it is also like most things.

Rather than continue to ponder whether addiction is a disease I begin to wonder why capital might want to define it that way. What does having a disease imply about the thing that you have? For one, it implies that maybe there is some sort of cure or course of action that can eradicate it (or that maybe there one day could be) and that most likely this cure or course of action is available for purchase somewhere at a drug store or at a special residential facility that doesn't accept most insurance (despite their website saying they accept most insurance). It also implies that it is not the fault of the person using and that they are simply sick. This makes me feel better because most people feel bad for those who are sick but I have no argument for or against it since I still do not know what this thing called a disease really is and people should feel bad when they see their friends suffering even when they do not have diseases. I know I never made a choice to get addicted but also recognize that I made most of the choices I made while addicted of my own accord. On the other hand, I also feel I may have been possessed by some sort of demon and can take no responsibility for the things I did when I was high or stealing from my friends or family to get high (I'm sorry).

Ultimately, "disease" is just a word like any other word that is used to describe a group of things which certain humans find to be similar. What matters is what the implications of calling it one thing vs. another are. The implications of calling addiction a disease are better than the common implications of not calling it a disease which are that all people who are addicted are weak (I am weak) or self-centered (I am self-centered). It would be preferable to find a third way of speaking about addiction which recognizes that it may or may not be a disease and people who use may or may not be self-centered, but also that we should support friends who wish to live a life that is different than the one they are living now, and sometimes even encourage them to live a life that is different than the one they are living now when we see the one they are living now bringing them to an untimely death, unfulfilling life, or a life full of causing harm to other people. One could argue here that life is not necessarily preferable to death or maybe even that the pursuit of death is also a noble pursuit, and it would be hard to prove otherwise, but this is an essay about life and for those who want to live a life, for I do not know how to speak about death as I have not experienced it—or, if I have, I do not recall it.

One could also ask whether a sober life is inherently a preferable way of life. While I could say that it has certainly been preferable for me, I do not wish to make a philosophical and certainly not a moral argument for sobriety. This is not a persuasive essay. This is not about convincing anyone to be sober. This is an essay for those who wish to be sober and are looking for something other than what has been offered to them. This is also an essay for those who wish to use drugs and are looking for something other than what has been offered to them. This is about recognizing the complexities of this phenomenon we call addiction and building something new to address it, together.

WE ADMITTED

If you ever attend a rehab clinic or a psychology course or read a magazine about addiction, you will hear many things said about the way in which one must become sober and the proper steps to take to maintain this sobriety. Most of these things will be stated as fact and they are facts in so far as all opinions are facts, but there are also other facts that may not have been presented to you which should be considered.

The most common prescription for the disease of addiction is the "12 step program." There are many 12 step programs today but the most common ones are Alcoholics Anonymous (AA) and Narcotics Anonymous (NA). These 12 step programs are presented as clear and concise ways to go from being an addict to being an upstanding sober person in 12 steps. I do not wish to discredit these programs as I have seen them work for many people and even myself for a period of time. Instead, I would like to point out that the thing that makes programs like AA or NA work is not the steps themselves or the organization but something else.

The first step in the 12 steps of Alcoholics Anonymous states, "We admitted we were powerless over alcohol—that our lives had become unmanageable." This first step is simply a recognition that alcohol, or "our addictions," as in the case of NA, are a problem. While this admitting may be an important part in the process of getting sober, it is not the most important part of this step. Instead, the important thing here is the *we*. *We* admitted *we* were powerless over alcohol—that *our* lives had become unmanageable. From the very beginning of the program, one is made to identify with a *we*. Rather than see oneself as an individual with an addiction that needs to be dealt with individually, we begin to identify with a certain common experience among the people in the room of a meeting. The *I* begins to become less important and we begin to see ourselves as a part of a certain collectivity. It is this collectivity that presents the real potential for the success of a program like AA or NA, but it is not only AA or NA which can offer this. This bond can also be found elsewhere.

In addiction there is often no recognition of any common bond beyond the self and a certain practice. In this sense, addiction *is* a certain form of self-centeredness. Addiction sucks us into the trap of the ego. It cements the self. It is a process of isolation and also many times a product of isolation. This is not to say that there are never bonds formed around non-sobriety, but that addiction exists outside of these bonds and consumes one's life beyond what is held in common. This is not true of all substance use but it *is* true of addiction. Addiction is all-encompassing, it consumes the body and the mind, it is a way of living, a way of living for the self. When we begin to feel we are not just an individual self but part of a common trajectory, we begin to find a reason to live beyond our addictions.

When I left rehab I felt alone. The only thing I had in common with all of my friends, save a few, was that we all liked to get high. I now no longer had this activity in common and as such no longer had any friends or any sense of a *we* that I was a part of. This *we* is what is desperately needed if one wishes to remain sober, but the bond that makes up the *we* cannot revolve around using drugs. I found this *we* in many places over the course of the past eight years. As I began to feel more alienated from most of my peers, I looked for an outlet, a place where I felt a certain bond or common life. I knew that I did not want to drink or do drugs and I also knew that I was not like most people so I looked for others who seemed to not be like most people and who also did not want to drink or use drugs. This is where I found straight edge. Straight edge presented for me a certain sense of identity and community that I desperately needed. It also presented a certain set of *practices*. It presented a certain way of *being* in the world. There were readymade images, activities, and groups to identify with. I no longer was an individual struggling to remain sober, I was straight edge, and that meant something more than my individual choice to remain sober. I was something beyond myself.

This is just one example, and the thing which I have identified as the *we* that I am a part of has shifted and changed over time, but that is the point. There is nothing inherently better in the *we* of the NA program or straight edge than there is in the *we* that can be found in many other groups or movements. I still call myself straight edge despite the moralisms and contradictions of it. I still call myself an anarchist despite my suspicion of ideological labels. I still wear my one-year NA keytag despite my disillusion with the NA program. I still don't eat meat despite my disdain for the liberalism of veganism. These things have kept me alive throughout my years of sobriety by providing a sense of camaraderie. They have connected me to something larger than this thing I call my self.

ON PURPOSE

When one first stops using the substances that they are addicted to there is often a certain feeling of senselessness, meaninglessness, and loneliness which can most accurately be described as despair. "Despair," according to Wikipedia, is a "loss of hope in reaction to a breakdown in one or more of the defining qualities of one's self or identity." The very thing you have spent years doing is no longer a part of yourself—and in most cases this was in fact the defining part of you, as it consumed your whole life. While despair cannot be avoided, the void of having no purpose to your life is often too much to bare and turns many back to their addictions very quickly. This is also what turns so many to religion in the form of Christianity or Buddhism or Science.

As we search for a new sense of meaning and a reason to live, we inevitably find religions as they are the best advertisers. They have the most widely accepted and talked-about answers to the problems of existence. They offer a clear vision of a world and the individual's place within it. They can even be very successful in helping people who were addicted to certain substances to no longer be. They offer both a purpose and a sense of community around that purpose. The problem, however, is that they do not seek to address the structures that most often cause addictions. On an individual level, these institutions may work to keep one sober by appeasing the void through offering answers about existence and promises about universal meaning. When they attempt to work against addictions, however, they are merely acting as Band-Aids. They are sometimes effective but they do not seek to fix the roots of the problem.

In order to feel a sense of purpose one need not recognize a certain meaning inherent to life for there probably is no such meaning. Or, if there is, we should probably never know it, though sometimes I feel as if other animals may know it and could tell us if only we were better communicators. The beauty or maybe the sheer ugliness of this nonexistence of meaning is that whatever one chooses to do in every moment is in fact the very meaning of their own life. One's purpose can be created, destroyed, and recreated new in every moment. What we should seek is to create the conditions that allow for the full enactment of this purpose. Eventually we will recognize that us actualizing our meaning in the world will inevitably run into the same limits that others will hit in their own pursuit of meaning. This is where we begin to find something in common. Our search for individual joy inevitably comes into contact with this thing we call society, or this world, and we will either fall back into despair over our inability to be free, or we will undertake a certain struggle against this world. This is where the individual pursuit of joy becomes a collective one. We begin to act against despair. Not out of hope, but out of necessity. To fight addiction it is necessary that we find lives worth living.

It is important to note here that there are some forms of community that do not offer purpose and there are some forms of purpose that do not offer community. Community based around the neighborhood in which you live, for instance, does not offer purpose. The only common bond shared is one around the space which you inhabit. There is no common perception of the world or how one wishes to live in it. It offers no purpose, no *trajectory*. In fact, it is arguable whether this is any form of community at all. One could also develop a very individual purpose that only focuses on the self and one's own trajectory in the world. What we will soon find, however, is that we will be left feeling isolated and in despair once again. We fail to identify with something outside of ourselves and as such are still slaves to our own ego. We may pick up our addictions again or we may resign ourselves to a life of despair. We *should* seek out individual meaning and purpose in the world but once we do it is necessary to find others who share this purpose, who bring this purpose beyond an individual pursuit.

ON JOY

What we seek, then, is the reconciliation of one's sense of purpose and the *we* in which one sees themselves. It is this reconciliation, in the case of my own addiction, which has kept me sober. Initially, I aligned with a certain discourse around addiction tossed around at rehab clinics and worship services and felt my purpose was to help others who were suffering from this thing called addiction. I also aligned with a certain community at AA or NA meetings in a trailer somewhere behind a church or in basement that shared this purpose along with an addiction to coffee and cigarettes. As I became bored with the NA program, I began to find this purpose in different basements centered around straight edge and hardcore. There was a set of practices I engaged in with others who shared a similar view of the world and I felt a sense of meaning in my actions. Over time, I became disillusioned with hardcore bros who only wanted to slam in the pit claiming to be a movement, and with punks competing for social capital claiming to be political, and so I began to look elsewhere. I became more involved with radical politics and began to identify with people who came together around different bonds and practices outside of music. I found people who shared my perception of the world and wanted to act in the world to make a different reality.

I find this line on a page of my notebook: "Insurgency = making thoughts a practical gesture. Acts of rebellion are acts of truth." It has no quotes around it. I do not remember writing it. I search for this quote on Google and find nothing. I begin to wonder if maybe I wrote this sentence but come to no conclusions. Nevertheless this sentiment is important for those struggling with addictions. When we become newly sober, what we need desperately is a truth, any truth. We find this truth inside ourselves for there is no truth to be found elsewhere or if there is, I could not tell you how to find it. We let this truth sink in deeply and become a part of our selves. The self and this truth become inseparable. However, we do not stop there. We recognize this truth, our truth, and we wish to make it reality. We seek a practical gesture. We seek enactment of our truth. In doing so, we find others with a common truth, a common view of the world, a common definition of joy and misery. As we find others in joy, our truth expands. The joyous moments we experience are the ones that exist in the cracks, the exceptions to the monotony surrounding us. We become a force in the world. We are not the only force and we are not the strongest force but we are determined. We begin to act, together.

ON NEUTRALITY

One might say here that a collectivity and a sense of purpose can come from anywhere, and that your local police force or a white supremacist group or becoming a member of the flat earth society can provide these things and one would be right. However, this is not a neutral essay and I have no investment in the sobriety of those I would otherwise find detestable. While it is doubtful this essay will reach anyone on the cusp of deciding whether the community they wish to be part of is a white separatist group or the police force or the Democratic Party, allow me to say a few things about why these are unfit choices.

As has been stated, a certain new form of life is required to address addiction in any serious way. Serving empire, in the form of the military or the police or the Catholic Church or working for Tesla is not a purpose, it is a lack thereof, it is a default. It is seeking a further entrenchment in the confines of the world that has been placed upon us. It is a nonexistence. To truly exist is to position yourself against certain ideas of this world so as to make yourself real against them. Failure to stand outside of the roles placed upon us by this world makes us nothing other than *things*. We are chess pieces, moved around daily in the pursuit of a purpose that was never our own. Might diving into a life as a police officer keep you sober? Possibly, probably not, but possibly. But what will you have done? You will have ceased to exist. You will have foregone an opportunity to identify something in yourself worth living for. You will instead receive a false opportunity to uphold a reality that is not of your making and which only presents false promises about your well-being. You will be sober but you will have lost the battle against addiction. You do not exist.

A life devoted to service of empire, then, is not a life at all. Further, empire has created this world that is full of addictions. Trace an addiction back far enough and one will almost always find this to be true. Allow me to suggest, then, a life devoted to fighting the conditions that cause so many addictions. This could mean a life devoted to workplace sabotage, teaching others how to garden, the fight against boredom, helping others deal with interpersonal conflict, destroying a bank or banks or all currency, fighting white supremacy or misogyny. All of these are meaningful pursuits that fight against the conditions that perpetuate addiction.

ON LIFE

I search on the internet for "how to recover from addiction." The first website tells me, "You don't recover from an addiction by stopping using. You recover by creating a new life where it is easier not to use." I agree with this sentiment emphatically and read on to see what their theory for the overthrow of capital is and am sorely disappointed. It is true that a completely new way of living is needed if you wish to stay sober. It is true that you will probably need new friends and new places and new ways of seeing things. It is also true that anyone who takes addiction seriously will recognize the necessity of negating this world we live in. We must create the conditions for lives worth living. Going to work at a job you hate for forty hours a week is not compatible with this sentiment. Being a black person in this place called America is not compatible with this sentiment. Being a woman in this world is not compatible with this sentiment. Prisons, factory farms, logging sites, shopping malls, and the existence of the police are not compatible with this sentiment. These do not allow for the conditions of joyful lives.

Let us understand, then, that the war against addiction is also a war against this world. On its surface this may appear a deeply political proposal but this is not about politics this is about life and for those who want to live life, and especially for those who do not. The expectations that this world puts on us are often too much to handle. The policing is too much to bear. The acceptable forms of expression are never enough. The lack of true bonds among creatures is heartbreaking. Everywhere we turn, our eyes see devastation. It is no surprise that so many of us need drugs or alcohol to survive, the alternative is often debilitating. We push on nonetheless. We commit ourselves to a struggle against this world and the ways it forces addictions on us. We begin to build something new.

We reject the label of addict as just another identity category that empire wants to place on us in order to further subjugate us. If we are understood as a category we become easy to exploit. We have addictions but we are not addicts. Likewise, we reject the use of this label as some sort of handicap or disability in need of pity or consideration as a defect. Addiction is a part of everyone's lives. We make no claim for safe spaces for those struggling with addiction, there is nowhere safe in this world, just as there is nowhere free from addiction. What bonds us is a commitment to fight the power

structures that exacerbate and cause so many addictions. We share no identity category—we share only a common struggle.

A VISION

A network of spaces formed around the goal of creating a new world and
making a break from this one. Simultaneously, a commitment to promoting sobriety within these spaces and supporting those who are fighting
addictions. Sober spaces, but not formed with the purpose of sobriety.
Sobriety is not our goal. Because we take addiction seriously, our goal is a
new world. Promoting sobriety is simply a vehicle to reach and encourage
people who are in need of meaning and purpose. We have a purpose. Our
purpose takes seriously the war on addiction in a way that AA or NA does
not. We should offer it to those who see the same things we do. We should
make ourselves visible. Leaving flyers outside of rehab clinics, building
friendships with those new to sobriety, having sober meetups at a space in
town, building our own spaces for people who wish to become sober and
need somewhere to start. As much as possible, building alternatives to the
ones offered us by this world. We want autonomy in our health as much as
any other aspect of our lives. This means autonomy from the hospitals that
don't take us seriously, the police who only want to throw us in jail, and the
rehab clinics that just want our money. This means collecting naloxone in
case of overdose, learning how to mediate fights among friends and how
to deal with mental health issues, and creating spaces where people can
go to be sober. It also means collecting and distributing clean syringes for
those who do not want to be sober. We do not have a moral position on
sobriety. We want joy and freedom for the addicted person just as much
as the sober person.

We must also recognize that addiction will not be eradicated. Even
among those considered sober we see lives full of addictions. Addictions to
God, coffee, cigarettes, television; addictions to money, power, intelligence,
and beauty. We are still addicted. We will still have friends who are addicted.
We will still have friends who we cannot help despite our deepest love for
them and our deepest wishes for their well-being. This is simply a part of this
world, and it will most likely be a part of the next. We seek to rid our lives of
the systems that push so many into addiction, but this does not mean that
addiction will go away. We should do our best to help those who are addicted
and to take seriously the factors that push people into addiction, but this
does not come from a place of charity. We cannot help everyone, we are just
as helpless. But we are also just as powerful. We seek a shift in culture, not

any sort of evangelical conversion. Our pasts are places to build from, but they are not the thing that unites us. What unites us is the vision of the world we want to live in. The dream which we want to see as reality. The dream is the only meaning. We are looking for those who want to find us.

ALL NIGHTER

Kent McClard

Kent McClard edited the zines *No Answers* (1984–1991) and *HeartattaCk* (1994–2006). In 1990, he founded Ebullition Records. He is one of the most influential and respected figures in US hardcore punk and has been straight edge for over thirty years. The 1995 Ebullition Records compilation *XXX: some ideas are poisonous* is one of the most precious straight edge collections of all time. This text is taken from *HeartattaCk* no. 23, August 1999.

It is 7 AM and I have just come off an all nighter playing a computer game called EverQuest. I started playing at 5 PM last night. I told myself I would go to bed at midnight, and then 1 AM, and so on and so on. I couldn't stop until I was just too tired and fucked up that I had no choice. As soon as I broke the binge I purged the game from my system and canceled my account. The best time to get out is always at the low points. I am supposed to be at work soon, but I am tired and my wrist is aching from repetitive use syndrome. So I thought I would write something for *HeartattaCk*, which isn't helping my wrist much but whatever . . .

    I know a lot about addiction and compulsive behavior. At many times in my life I have been engulfed by addiction. At an early age I realized my capacity for self-consumption and I did what I had to do to keep myself alive. I don't drink and I don't use chemicals for entertainment because of my personality. I won't even eat foods with alcohol in them. I am simply too afraid of what I am capable of to even take the smallest chances with such substances. I can truly say that if I used drugs or drank alcohol I would either be a drunk or an addict or more likely dead. I simply can't control myself. My passions always take control of me and I burn myself until there is nothing left to bum. And then I walk away to my next obsession.

My latest fling with addiction was with the on-line game EverQuest. I would play for hours on end. I even did 64 hours straight with no sleep. I would sacrifice sleep and whatever needed to be sacrificed to play. I was out of control. When I couldn't play I was constantly thinking about the game, and I would dream about it at night. At times I would become completely dysfunctional when I couldn't play; not capable of getting anything done at work or at home. Recently, on a vacation that I took I had just come off a long stint with EverQuest and I was going through severe withdrawals during my vacation. I couldn't sleep, and I had a hard time concentrating on real world things. It was like I was in some sort of fucked-up daze.

Before that I was totally obsessed with an on-line game called Ultima On-Line, and before that Legends Of Kesmai, and before that Dragon Realms. I have been obsessed with computer games since I got my hands on a computer in the late '70s. I love them and sometimes I hate them. It can be hard to juggle the needs of life when all you really want to do is get lost in some alternate world via the computer terminal.

I have had problems with other addictions of course. For a long time I was obsessed with Magic: The Gathering. I spent literally thousands of dollars on cards, and still own thousands of cards. I played it constantly and thought about it when I wasn't playing. I played in a lot of tournaments and even placed in the California Regional Championships and then played in the Nationals in Columbus, Ohio. I also flew out to Dallas, Texas to play in a $40,000 tournament. I played, and played, and played, and then one day I quit. I had become obsessed with something else and moved on.

I was once obsessed with salt water aquariums. I mean really obsessed. Addiction is like an avalanche; it starts small but builds quickly into something very intense. One day my roommate came home with a very small goldfish bowl and a goldfish. I started to take an interest in the goldfish. The next weekend I got a much larger tank and a few more fish. The following month I bought a 100 gallon tank. I then started reading about salt water fish. I bought a 150 gallon salt water tank. I then bought a 200 gallon tank. I had thousands of dollars worth of fish and corals. I built a huge system at one point in the Ebullition office. It consisted of a 200 gallon tank and five smaller tanks that were all hooked together in a series. I then decided that I wanted to build a 5,000 gallon tank. I bought a bunch of books written by this fellow that ran the aquariums at the Smithsonian Museum in Washington, DC. The tank there was 5,000 gallons and it was what I wanted.

I started to build the tank. It was eight feet long, four feet deep, and four feet wide. It was made out of 3/4" plywood, fiberglass, and it would be reinforced with metal banding and it would have 1" glass. I never finished the tank. For a long time I had known that I was out of my fucking mind. Crazy with obsession. I speculate that I may have been the only vegan that could claim to control so much life. I constantly felt guilty about having the fish and corals, but I just couldn't resist. My interest was all consuming. I had tried to sell my tanks several times, but every time I fixed them up to sell them I became interested once again.

Finally, I decided that I had to get out. I was moving Ebullition from one office space to another space and this was it. I sold everything I owned to a local store for $200. It was the best deal that he ever made. Hell, if he had known the nature of my problem he could have made me pay him to take the stuff. I would have done it. I had to get out on that day or risk not getting out at all. I still keep the unfinished tank today. It is a testament to the limitless nature of my insanity.

For the last seventeen years I have been obsessed with hardcore. I move in and out of interest as I dabble with other obsessions, but I always come back to hardcore. I have been lucky, I think. I could have easily put all my energy and passions into drugs and alcohol. I got lucky. I discovered hardcore at an early age and gave it my everything. Straight edge has kept me alive. It isn't something that I can ever forget. I will be straight edge until the day I die simply because I realize that I have no other choice. I don't trust myself. I don't want to end up flushing my life down a toilet. I mean sure I have wasted countless hours and countless dollars on all kinds of asinine hobbies, but no matter how bad those addictions get they can't kill me. I might lose my job (I have seriously considered closing Ebullition before so I could play computer games full time) or fuck up my inter-personal relationships because I can't stop playing some computer game, but it isn't going to kill me. I will survive.

I can't say that is true with regards to substance abuse. I have broken out of addictions many times, but they were always addictions that were solely psychological. I have never had to deal with a physical addiction that was compounded by the psychological. I don't think I could get out if I had to deal with a physical addiction on top of my naturally addictive personality.

Straight edge for me is about survival. I don't consider myself to be anything more than a statistic waiting to happen. When I see a homeless man drunk and passed out on the street or when I hear about the latest hardcore/punk icon to OD on some hard drugs I breathe a sigh of relief that it didn't happen to me. The only difference between those people and myself is the fact that I never got started. I have no delusions that I am somehow a stronger person or more capable of dealing with substances. I know what a demon is, I have lived with demons and fought with them. A demon can eat out your insides and spit you out like a piece of trash. I live with fear. I understand what can happen. It doesn't take much effort to go from being in control to being under-control. It happens in an instant. One moment I am having a good time playing a game, or spending time with some interesting hobby, and the next thing I know I can't think of anything else, I can't do anything else, and I am at the mercy of my interests.

Life is what you make of it. I do what I want and I expect everyone else to do the same. You try to figure out what works for you and do the best you can to live your life. I know that is the way it is for all of us. For me I need the straight edge. I need it to live. That is all it is to me. Nothing more, and nothing less. I really don't care what other people do, as long as they don't get in my space. And I try to do the same for others. Straight edge for me has never been about other people, or about belonging to a group, or about feeling better than other people. It has always and always will be about self-protection. I use it to guard myself against forces that I don't feel capable of dealing with. A simple matter of self-preservation.

. . . So now I have to go home and find something to do; find something to take my mind off of EverQuest. It is going to be a tough week for me. My hope is that working on *HeartattaCk* will keep me busy. If I want to get through this then I have to stay occupied. Down time is real bad when you're trying not to get sucked back into something that has been occupying every spare moment of your existence. What am I supposed to do with my time when I have been spending 60+ hours a week on one activity? It is like this huge void in my life that has to be filled up or patched up or repaired.

HITTING THE STREETS

Reeves Hankins

Reeves Hankins is a self-described extroverted introvert who prefers to be in nature with his dog. He was born in Richmond and now resides in Northern Virginia, a place he affectionately refers to as purgatory. Reeves has been in the cycling industry for most of his life and works for one of the largest bicycle companies in the world. "Sobriety has been an integral part of my life from early on. Straight Edge has shaped my view of the world. Vegan because I can afford to care."

I grew up in a family of recovering drug addicts, though I was lucky enough to not have witnessed their drug abuse firsthand. Some of my earliest childhood memories took place in the rooms of Narcotics Anonymous meetings. As many people know, NA is a nonprofit organization which helps those with a substance use disorder seek a sense of community and hope.

I've identified as Straight Edge for the last fifteen years of my life. At thirty years old, it's not something I hear many of my peers say, even those that repped the X as teens. I was raised in a community of recovery and many of the individuals within the NA program were extremely influential on who I am today. Growing up, I spent several nights a week in a circle of people who poured their hearts out, seeking support from one another. My youth was shaped by their stories of struggle, addiction, and pain. I listened to people talk about their addiction, life after incarceration, and disease transmitted through drug use. You better believe it scared the fuck out of me.

Fast forward to my early, awkward teenage years while I was living with my father in rural Virginia. I attended school with kids who had nothing to do but party on the weekends. Every Monday, we'd get the scoop on what kind of alcohol showed up at a party, how many bong hits so and so took, and who fucked who in an intoxicated slumber. I couldn't identify with this in the slightest because I knew all too well where that path would lead me. Not fitting in, I was actively looking for friends and camaraderie elsewhere. I was into music, which is what really held me together through my youth. I hung out with a handful of older guys and would occasionally go to their band practice. Despite them drinking and smoking while I was around, I never had any interest. These guys used to call me "the Straight Edge" and I had no clue what they were talking about. Until one day, I got asked to go to a show with them. I told my dad I was going to stay with a friend, hopped in a crowded car, and we made our way to the city. We showed up at this venue that was known as Nancy Raygun at the time, where a few bands were to play, including some Straight Edge bands. I overheard someone saying that the people with black X's marked on their hands didn't drink or smoke. Instantly, I had this feeling of acceptance and I remember that like it was yesterday.

A few years later, I graduated high school and started traveling. I landed on the west coast of Canada and met some of my closest friends. The Pacific Northwest scene is pretty unique and really opened my eyes to what this movement could be. Not just the hardcore scene but people in general are much more progressive there than what I had become accustomed to back in Virginia. The individuals I met enabled me to better understand and become more empathetic towards people who struggled with addiction.

During this time, I was introduced to radical politics and got involved with an anarchist collective. Faced with the realities of racial, social, and economic injustices around the world, I began to see drugs as tools of oppression. I could no longer stand on my self-proclaimed pedestal, with the realization that I was no better than the next just because I chose to abstain from drugs. A lot of things were put into perspective over the course of my twenties. Through my travels, I witnessed firsthand the struggle of people globally. I found myself in a position to help, as opposed to judging and condemning based on social conditioning, environmental factors, or mental illness. How can I judge someone in need of escape? How can I judge someone who doesn't know another way? I've come to look down on no one unless I'm picking them up.

My purpose through my Straight Edge identity has changed and matured over the years. I believe that a sober mind is a powerful tool that has the ability to better the world. What keeps me going is the active rebellion we live every day. Walking this path for me is a lonely one. But I know why I don't and cannot succumb to drug use or addiction. For me, I abstain from the pitfalls of drug culture that society doesn't teach us. I'm Straight Edge because I believe in liberation of all. I'm Straight Edge because my government imports drugs into poor communities and then locks up the individuals who buy them. I'm Straight Edge because it stands in the face of the wrongdoings of our world and those who seek to destroy it. I have found a path within the culture surrounding the Edge that enables me to view the world from a place of compassion.

I'm currently writing this after receiving news of a family member who is being kept in a medically induced coma from a drug overdose. The rawness of this situation has forced me to take a closer look at what it means for me to be Straight Edge. It not only reaffirms my beliefs but it encourages me to ask myself what I can do for those around me. How can I proactively prevent shit like this from happening? I can't put myself in the shoes of someone facing addiction but I can acknowledge the illness and its crippling effects. I can also take notes from someone like my father, a recovering addict, who I credit for my sobriety. This guy is a "recovery carrier" and has been uplifting countless numbers of people for over thirty years. I've watched him dedicate the majority of his free time to attending meetings, creating and hosting meetings in prisons, and welcoming those in need with open arms. He's been in Narcotics Anonymous for over three decades and is still passionate about his sobriety and helping others.

I've recently attended some NA meetings and have found them to be incredibly isolating to certain minority groups. The NA program claims to be nonreligious, yet one must "admit to God that they are powerless over their addiction." I know I'm not the only one who cringes at this declaration. Other than the dated NA program amidst others, where do those struggling go for help? What's to be done for those that fall through the cracks or don't fit the mold?

My hope is that this gets you thinking how we as members of a sober community can help. There are people who are destined for the hellholes of our prison system or forgotten by our failing health-care system. Those imprisoned are disproportionately people of color or are affected by mental illness and drug addiction. We talk amongst ourselves about social justice but not how to achieve such justice. There are many steps to take in overcoming

injustice and inequality but the first step I can take is creating change in my direct community. Younger demographics care about these issues more than ever. How do we focus, influence others, and commit to a change bigger than ourselves? First of all, that's not going to happen by attending music shows and simply sharing ideas back and forth with each other. As much as this has been an incremental part of my upbringing, if we're being real, that's a lot of hot air. There's no way we can change the world within the confines of a music venue. We could start by establishing or working with safe places which focus on inclusivity, understanding, and acceptance, with the realization that to be alive in this time is fucking hell.

We will all have battles to face, which nobody but ourselves can understand, but we can support one another through solidarity. We can work with currently established organizations that assist recently released inmates assimilate back into society. We can give these people some vision of hope and provide the inspiration needed to dig out of the pits of our justice system. We can step in where many organizations are failing those struggling to obtain sobriety. Many of my Straight Edge friends have developed their own trades and are passionate about things that could have a tremendous impact on someone's life. What if we all dedicated a day every month to our communities using our skills to help uplift those affected by poverty and drug addiction? By teaching how to develop urban gardens, giving haircuts, providing reading and writing lessons, and helping sign people up for health care, we can lay foundations for a healthier future.

The point is, the majority of us have skills and passions that enable us to have purpose and promote ourselves within our individual social network. However, not many of us are using these skills to actively promote the ideology of sober living to people who need it the most. Organizing events that focus on uplifting the community is something that hardcore kids are capable of. I see these show promoters busting their asses to put on shows at secret venues with huge turnouts. Individuals like Ace Stallings, who is a prominent figure within the Richmond hardcore scene, are capable of connecting thousands of people through their passion and love of hardcore and Straight Edge. Imagine an organized mobilization and message of sobriety hitting the streets which manifested the ideas we spoke of so valiantly behind closed doors. Something like this could build as other organizations choose to support and get involved. This idea could be scaled "street by street, block by block, taking it all back."

ABOUT THE AUTHOR

Gabriel Kuhn lives as an independent author and translator in Stockholm, Sweden. He is the editor of *Sober Living for the Revolution: Hardcore Punk, Straight Edge, and Radical Politics* (2010); *Antifascism, Sports, Sobriety: Forging a Militant Working-Class Culture* (2017); and several other PM Press books. He has been straight edge for thirty years.

ABOUT PM PRESS

PM Press was founded at the end of 2007 by a small
collection of folks with decades of publishing, media, and
organizing experience. PM Press co-conspirators have
published and distributed hundreds of books, pamphlets,
CDs, and DVDs. Members of PM have founded enduring
book fairs, spearheaded victorious tenant organizing campaigns, and worked
closely with bookstores, academic conferences, and even rock bands to deliver
political and challenging ideas to all walks of life. We're old enough to know what
we're doing and young enough to know what's at stake.

We seek to create radical and stimulating fiction and nonfiction books, pamphlets,
T-shirts, visual and audio materials to entertain, educate, and inspire you. We
aim to distribute these through every available channel with every available
technology—whether that means you are seeing anarchist classics at our bookfair
stalls, reading our latest vegan cookbook at the café, downloading geeky fiction
e-books, or digging new music and timely videos from our website.

PM Press is always on the lookout for talented and skilled volunteers, artists,
activists, and writers to work with. If you have a great idea for a project or can
contribute in some way, please get in touch.

PM Press
PO Box 23912
Oakland, CA 94623
www.pmpress.org

PM Press in Europe
europe@pmpress.org
www.pmpress.org.uk

FRIENDS OF PM PRESS

These are indisputably momentous times—the financial system is melting down globally and the Empire is stumbling. Now more than ever there is a vital need for radical ideas.

In the years since its founding—and on a mere shoestring— PM Press has risen to the formidable challenge of publishing and distributing knowledge and entertainment for the struggles ahead. With over 300 releases to date, we have published an impressive and stimulating array of literature, art, music, politics, and culture. Using every available medium, we've succeeded in connecting those hungry for ideas and information to those putting them into practice.

Friends of PM allows you to directly help impact, amplify, and revitalize the discourse and actions of radical writers, filmmakers, and artists. It provides us with a stable foundation from which we can build upon our early successes and provides a much-needed subsidy for the materials that can't necessarily pay their own way. You can help make that happen—and receive every new title automatically delivered to your door once a month—by joining as a Friend of PM Press. And, we'll throw in a free T-shirt when you sign up.

Here are your options:

- **$30 a month** Get all books and pamphlets plus 50% discount on all webstore purchases

- **$40 a month** Get all PM Press releases (including CDs and DVDs) plus 50% discount on all webstore purchases

- **$100 a month** Superstar—Everything plus PM merchandise, free downloads, and 50% discount on all webstore purchases

For those who can't afford $30 or more a month, we have **Sustainer Rates** at $15, $10 and $5. Sustainers get a free PM Press T-shirt and a 50% discount on all purchases from our website.

Your Visa or Mastercard will be billed once a month, until you tell us to stop. Or until our efforts succeed in bringing the revolution around. Or the financial meltdown of Capital makes plastic redundant. Whichever comes first.

Sober Living for the Revolution: Hardcore Punk, Straight Edge, and Radical Politics

Edited by Gabriel Kuhn

ISBN: 978-1-60486-051-1
$22.95   304 pages

Straight edge has persisted as a drug-free, hardcore punk subculture for 25 years. Its political legacy, however, remains ambiguous – often associated with self-righteous macho posturing and conservative puritanism. While certain elements of straight edge culture feed into such perceptions, the movement's political history is far more complex.

Since straight edge's origins in Washington, D.C., in the early 1980s, it has been linked to radical thought and action by countless individuals, bands, and entire scenes worldwide. *Sober Living for the Revolution* traces this history.

It includes contributions – in the form of in-depth interviews, essays, and manifestos – by numerous artists and activists connected to straight edge, from Ian MacKaye (Minor Threat/Fugazi) and Mark Andersen (*Dance of Days*/Positive Force DC) to Dennis Lyxzén (Refused/The (International) Noise Conspiracy) and Andy Hurley (Racetraitor/Fall Out Boy), from bands such as ManLiftingBanner and Point of No Return to feminist and queer initiatives, from radical collectives like CrimethInc. and Alpine Anarchist Productions to the Emancypunx project and many others dedicated as much to sober living as to the fight for a better world.

"Perhaps the greatest reason I am still committed to sXe is an unfailing belief that sXe is more than music, that it can be a force of change. I believe in the power of sXe as a bridge to social change, as an opportunity to create a more just and sustainable world."
—Ross Haenfler, professor of sociology at the University of Mississippi, author of *Straight Edge: Clean-Living Youth, Hardcore Punk, and Social Change*

"An 'ecstatic sobriety' which combats the dreariness of one and the bleariness of the other—false pleasure and false discretion alike—is analogous to the anarchism that confronts both the false freedom offered by capitalism and the false community offered by communism."
—CrimethInc. Ex-Workers' Collective

Antifascism, Sports, Sobriety: Forging a Militant Working-Class Culture

Julius Deutsch
Edited and translated by Gabriel Kuhn

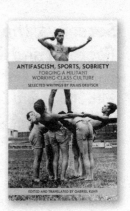

ISBN: 978-1-62963-154-7
$14.95   128 pages

The Austromarxist era of the 1920s was a unique chapter in socialist history. Trying to carve out a road between reformism and Bolshevism, the Austromarxists embarked on an ambitious journey towards a socialist oasis in the midst of capitalism. Their showpiece, the legendary "Red Vienna," has worked as a model for socialist urban planning ever since.

At the heart of the Austromarxist experiment was the conviction that a socialist revolution had to entail a cultural one. Numerous workers' institutions and organizations were founded, from education centers to theaters to hiking associations. With the Fascist threat increasing, the physical aspects of the cultural revolution became ever more central as they were considered mandatory for effective defense. At no other time in socialist history did armed struggle, sports, and sobriety become as intertwined in a proletarian attempt to protect socialist achievements as they did in Austria in the early 1930s. Despite the final defeat of the workers' militias in the Austrian Civil War of 1934 and subsequent Fascist rule, the Austromarxist struggle holds important lessons for socialist theory and practice.

Antifascism, Sports, Sobriety contains an introductory essay by Gabriel Kuhn and selected writings by Julius Deutsch, leader of the workers' militias, president of the Socialist Workers' Sport International, and a prominent spokesperson for the Austrian workers' temperance movement. Deutsch represented the physical defense of the working class against its enemies like few others. His texts in this book are being made available in English for the first time.

"An almost completely forgotten episode in labor history."
—Murray Bookchin, author of *Anarchism, Marxism and the Future of the Left*

"A foretaste of the socialist utopia of the future in the present."
—Helmut Gruber, author of *Red Vienna: Experiment in Working-Class Culture, 1919-1934*

"The insurrection of February 1934 . . . left behind the glorious memory of resistance to fascism by arms and not merely by speeches."
—E.J. Hobsbawm, author of *The Age of Extremes: The Short Twentieth Century, 1914-1991*

Soccer vs. the State: Tackling Football and Radical Politics

Gabriel Kuhn
with a Foreword by Boff Whalley

ISBN: 978-1-62963-572-9
$20.00   352 pages

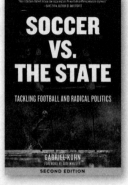

Soccer has turned into a multi-billion-dollar industry. Professionalism and commercialization dominate its global image. Yet the game retains a rebellious side, maybe more so than any other sport co-opted by moneymakers and corrupt politicians. From its roots in working-class England to political protests by players and fans, and a current radical soccer underground, the notion of football as the "people's game" has been kept alive by numerous individuals, teams, and communities.

This book not only traces this history but also reflects on common criticisms—that soccer ferments nationalism, serves right-wing powers, and fosters competitiveness—exploring alternative perspectives and practical examples of egalitarian DIY soccer. *Soccer vs. the State* serves both as an orientation for the politically conscious football supporter and as an inspiration for those who try to pursue the love of the game away from televisions and big stadiums, bringing it to back alleys and muddy pastures.

This second edition has been expanded to cover events of recent years, including the involvement of soccer fans in the Middle Eastern uprisings of 2011–2013, the FIFA scandal of 2015, and the 2017 strike by the Danish women's team.

"Gabriel Kuhn's Soccer vs. the State *is a wondrous reminder of all the times and ways and places where football has slipped its chains and offers what it always promised: new solidarities and identities, a site of resistance, a celebration of spontaneity and play."*
—David Goldblatt, author of *The Ball Is Round* and *The Game of Our Lives*

"There is no sport that reflects the place where sports and politics collide quite like soccer. Athlete-activist Gabriel Kuhn has captured that by going to a place where other sports writers fear to tread. Here is the book that will tell you how soccer explains the world while offering means to improve it."
—Dave Zirin, author of *Game Over* and *Brazil's Dance with the Devil*

"Gabriel Kuhn has written the programme notes for the most important match of all, The People's Game vs. Modern Football."
—Mark Perryman, cofounder of Philosophy Football

Playing as if the World Mattered: An Illustrated History of Activism in Sports

Gabriel Kuhn

ISBN: 978-1-62963-097-7
$14.95   160 pages

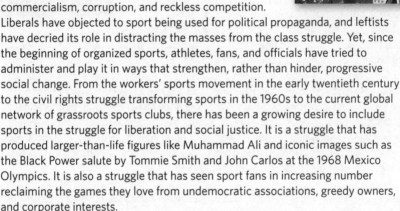

The world of sports is often associated with commercialism, corruption, and reckless competition. Liberals have objected to sport being used for political propaganda, and leftists have decried its role in distracting the masses from the class struggle. Yet, since the beginning of organized sports, athletes, fans, and officials have tried to administer and play it in ways that strengthen, rather than hinder, progressive social change. From the workers' sports movement in the early twentieth century to the civil rights struggle transforming sports in the 1960s to the current global network of grassroots sports clubs, there has been a growing desire to include sports in the struggle for liberation and social justice. It is a struggle that has produced larger-than-life figures like Muhammad Ali and iconic images such as the Black Power salute by Tommie Smith and John Carlos at the 1968 Mexico Olympics. It is also a struggle that has seen sport fans in increasing number reclaiming the games they love from undemocratic associations, greedy owners, and corporate interests.

With the help of over a hundred full-color illustrations—from posters and leaflets to paintings and photographs—*Playing as if the World Mattered makes this history tangible. Extensive lists of resources, including publications, films, and websites, will allow the reader to explore areas of interest further.*

Being the first illustrated history of its kind, *Playing as if the World Mattered* introduces an understanding of sports beyond chauvinistic jingoism, corporate media chat rooms, and multi-billion-dollar business deals.

"Gabriel Kuhn dismantles the myth that sports and politics do not belong together."
—Mats Runvall, *Yelah*

"Creativity and solidarity are as indispensable in sport as they are in social struggle. If you have any doubt, read this book."
—Wally Rosell, editor of *Éloge de la passe: changer le sport pour changer le monde*

Life Under the Jolly Roger: Reflections on Golden Age Piracy

Gabriel Kuhn

ISBN: 978-1-62963-793-8
$20.00   320 pages

Over the last couple of decades, an ideological battle has raged over the political legacy and cultural symbolism of the "golden age" pirates who roamed the seas between the Caribbean Islands and the Indian Ocean from 1690 to 1725. They are depicted as romanticized villains on the one hand and as genuine social rebels on the other. *Life Under the Jolly Roger* examines the political and cultural significance of these nomadic outlaws by relating historical accounts to a wide range of theoretical concepts—reaching from Marshall Sahlins and Pierre Clastres to Mao Zedong and Eric J. Hobsbawm via Friedrich Nietzsche and Michel Foucault. With daring theoretical speculation and passionate, respectful inquiry, Gabriel Kuhn skillfully contextualizes and analyzes the meanings of race, gender, sexuality, and disability in golden age pirate communities, while also surveying the breathtaking array of pirates' forms of organization, economy, and ethics.

Life Under the Jolly Roger also provides an extensive catalog of scholarly references for the academic reader. Yet this delightful and engaging study is written in language that is wholly accessible for a wide audience.

This expanded second edition includes an appendix with interviews about contemporary piracy, the ongoing fascination with pirate imagery, and the thorny issue of colonial implications in the romanticization of pirates.

"In addition to history Gabriel Kuhn's radical piratology brings philosophy, ethnography, and cultural studies to the stark question of the time: which were the criminals— bankers and brokers or sailors and slaves? By so doing he supplies us with another case where the history isn't dead, it's not even past!"
—Peter Linebaugh, author of *The London Hanged* and coauthor of *The Many-Headed Hydra*

"Gabriel Kuhn does a masterful job of, piece by piece, dismantling all the popular myths about Golden Age piracy. And then, more masterfully still, he picks up the pieces and weaves together an understanding of why, knowing what we know, we still love us some goddamn pirates."
—Margaret Killjoy, author of *The Lamb Will Slaughter the Lion* and *The Barrow Will Send What It May*